COOKING WITH HERB SCENTS

The Western Reserve Herb Society
Cleveland, Ohio
A Unit of The Herb Society of America

Edited by
Donna Agan

Illustrated by
Eleanor Donley, Margaret Hutchison, Jane Jones

1991

Library of Congress Catalog Card Number: 91-65882

ISBN 1-880022-00-1

CONTENTS

ACKNOWLEDGMENTS to Western Reserve Herb Society members and friends who helped in the production of this book:

Eleanor Donley, for her guidance as art director and graphics designer. Her sketches of the Western Reserve Herb Society Garden appear throughout the book, with larger views highlighting the divider pages of each section.

Jane Jones, for her watercolor paintings of the Western Reserve Herb Society Garden on the front and back covers of the cookbook. Jane also assisted in the layout of the cookbook and its graphic design.

Margaret Hutchinson, for her illustrations of favorite herbs in the Herb Scents section.

Viola Saunders, for her research in compiling information about each herb discussed in the Herb Scents section.

Irene Manni, Nancy and Hank Samson, for all of their computer work which made manuscript editing an easier task.

Blanche Harvey, Lucile McCullagh, Betty Neavill, Virginia Rady, Faith Swanson, and Joy Walworth for editorial support.

The Recipe Testing Committee: Roxanne Bell, Mary Bemer, Kay Benko, Audrey Bergren, Jolie Bishop, Arline Blankenberg, Pat Goodman, Elsie Kres, Alma Leavitt, Louise Littlepage, Aina Lustig, Kathy Mahovlic, Lois Mills, Bonnie Porterfield, Beatty Raymond, Donna Schenk, Elizabeth Scher, Ann Shafer, Lynda Simmons, Thea Steinmetz, April Walton, June Winzeler, and Catherine Wright.

INTRODUCTION

COOKING WITH HERB SCENTS is the fifth in a series of cookbooks published by the Western Reserve Herb Society, a Unit of The Herb Society of America. When our first cookbook, SAVORY SEASONING, appeared in 1957, its mission was to promote the growth of culinary herbs in our gardens, and their use in the foods we prepared in our kitchens. Since that time, herbs have become so popular that we are currently enjoying an herbal renaissance. To celebrate this renaissance, we have created a new cookbook containing further information on how herbs can help good cooking become even better.

As in previous cookbooks, we include a Sweets and Sours section which contains new recipes for sauces, vinegars, chutneys, and confections, including detailed instructions for crystallizing violets and other edible decorations.

The Beverage section features a list of herbs and blossoms which may be used in herbal teas, along with instructions for their harvesting, drying, and preparation.

A new section, called Herb Scents, contains recipes for popular seasoning blends and flavored butters. Most of these recipes are created with readily available dried herbs and spices, though some call for fresh herbs to give them their distinctive flavor. The Herb Scents section is followed by an illustrated list of our favorite herbs, along with a notation where many of them can be seen when you visit our public Herb Garden, adjacent to the Garden Center of Greater Cleveland.

A symbol appears next to the title of certain recipes. Our charter members, who formed the Western Reserve Herb Society in 1942, were not only devoted gardeners, but many were fine cooks as well. To mark these heritage recipes, we chose rosemary for our symbol, in remembrance of those members who enjoyed sharing recipes as much as they delighted in sharing herbs from their gardens.

It is a pleasure to continue this tradition of sharing. We hope you find COOKING WITH HERB SCENTS an interesting and useful book.

Donna Agan
Editor

GARDEN PLAN

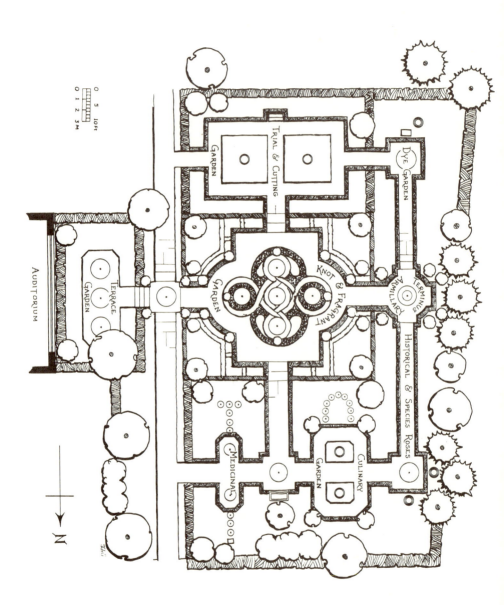

Reproduced from HERB GARDEN DESIGN by Virginia B. Rady and Faith H. Swanson and used by permission of the University Press of New England.

6

DEDICATION

This cookbook, fifth in a series produced by the Western Reserve Herb Society, is dedicated to our beloved Herb Garden and to our member Elsetta Gilchrist Barnes, A.S.L.A., who created its beautiful plan.

Appetizers

The long walk edged with spring bulbs passes between the knot garden and the terrace.
It then continues on to the Garden Center.

THYMELY SALUT

When you find that perfect brand of Port Salut cheese you will be serving this easy appetizer often. They will also complement soups and salads.

1 loaf French bread, 12-14 inches long, slice 1 inch thick
½ pound Port Salut cheese
¼ cup olive oil
2 tablespoons crushed thyme

Place bread slices on a cookie sheet. Lightly toast under broiler unit. Remove from oven and brush each piece with olive oil. Top with a generous slice of Port Salut, sprinkle with crushed thyme. Return to oven and broil until cheese melts and bubbles.

NOTE: You may want to add a pinch of garlic powder to the olive oil.

GAZPACHO SHRIMP

yield 4 - 6 servings

1 pound shrimp, cooked, cleaned and chilled

GAZPACHO SAUCE:
½ chopped green or red bell pepper
½ cup diced cucumber
½ cup chopped ripe tomatoes
2 tablespoons minced onion
1 tablespoon lemon juice
3 tablespoons chili sauce
1½ tablespoons ketchup
1 tablespoon olive oil
1 clove garlic, finely minced
2 tablespoons prepared horseradish
1 teaspoon cider vinegar
¼ teaspoon Worcestershire sauce

In a small bowl combine sauce ingredients. Cover and chill for at least 2 hours.

When ready to serve arrange shrimp on a platter and place sauce in a serving bowl.

Gazpacho sauce makes a fine dressing for salad greens. To make a quick cool soup, add a cup or two of chilled tomato juice.

BOURSIN-FILLED MUSHROOMS

yield 6 - 8 servings

Mushroom caps may be filled ahead and refrigerated. Broil just before serving.

16-18 large mushrooms
½ cup Boursin, softened (see note)
¼ cup crabmeat
2 tablespoons finely grated Parmesan cheese
2 tablespoons sherry
¼ cup fine bread crumbs

Clean mushrooms, remove stems and save for another use. In a small bowl combine Boursin, crabmeat, Parmesan and sherry. Mix thoroughly. Fill each mushroom cap with about 1½ teaspoons of mixture. Sprinkle with bread crumbs. Place in shallow broiler-proof baking dish. Cover and refrigerate until ready to serve.

Just before serving, place filled mushrooms under preheated broiler until tops are golden brown. About 5 to 8 minutes. Serve hot.

NOTE: Use purchased, or for a homemade Boursin, see Page 269.

OCTAVIA'S STUFFED CELERY

yield 8 - 10 servings

A member's mother recorded this recipe in 1935.

5 large celery ribs

FILLING:

1 (8-ounce) package cream cheese, softened
1 teaspoon Worcestershire sauce
1½ tablespoons mayonnaise
½ cup chopped walnuts or pecans, toasted
1 teaspoon grated onions

Garnish: paprika (optional)

Clean celery and soak in ice water to crisp. Drain and wipe dry. Cut into 2-inch lengths.

In a mixing bowl, combine filling ingredients. Stir until well blended. Fill each piece of celery with a generous amount of the mixture. Sprinkle with a dash of paprika, if desired. Arrange on a serving plate, cover and chill until ready to serve.

The cheese filling also makes a good spread for crackers or little finger sandwiches.

HERBAL CHEESECAKE

Plan to make this herb-filled cheesecake two days ahead of serving for flavors to mellow.

PREPARE CRUST:

1 tablespoon butter or margarine, softened
⅓ cup seasoned bread crumbs
½ cup grated Parmesan cheese

FILLING INGREDIENTS:

⅓ cup melted butter or margarine
3 (8-ounce) packages cream cheese, softened
2 cloves garlic, finely minced
2 tablespoons dried parsley flakes
1 teaspoon crushed oregano
1 teaspoon crushed thyme
½ teaspoon freshly ground black pepper
1 teaspoon Worcestershire sauce
4 large eggs, at room temperature

Preheat oven to 350°F. Grease bottom and half way up the side of 9-inch springform pan, using 1 tablespoon softened butter.

In a small bowl combine bread crumbs and grated Parmesan. Press crumbs in bottom of pan and around greased sides. Set pan on a baking sheet and bake crumb coating for 10 minutes. Remove pan from oven and set aside.

Place cream cheese in a large mixing bowl and beat until fluffy. Beat in melted butter and seasonings. Add eggs, one at a time, and beat thoroughly after each addition.

Pour filling into prepared pan. Place in oven and bake for 1 hour. Turn off heat and let cheesecake *remain in oven for 30 minutes,* with door ajar. Remove to rack and let cool to room temperature.

Cover with plastic wrap and refrigerate for 24 hours before serving. For a special party dessert place the Herbal Cheesecake on a serving platter and surround with a variety of herb sprigs and edible flowers such as nasturtiums, pansies, violets and calendulas.

ANTIPASTO VEGETABLE PLATTER

yield 8 - 10 servings

3 large sweet peppers: red, green and yellow
3 large carrots

MARINADE:
⅔ cup olive oil
¼ cup cider vinegar
2 tablespoons tarragon or basil vinegar
¼ cup lemon juice
1 (3.53-ounce) tin oil-packed anchovies, do not drain
1 teaspoon sugar
1 teaspoon Dijon-style mustard
¼ cup crumbled Roquefort cheese (or shredded Parmesan)

Garnish: 1 cup black olives, fresh parsley sprigs

Cut pepper in half and remove seeds. Cut in quarters. Scrape carrots and cut into ¼-inch slices. Cook vegetables separately until just tender-crisp. Cool before marinating.

Prepare marinade: Place ingredients, except cheese, in food blender and beat until anchovies are pureed. Stir in cheese by hand. It should remain crumbly.

Place vegetables in a large glass bowl, add marinade, cover, and refrigerate overnight.

Just before serving remove vegetables from marinade with slotted spoon and arrange on serving platter. Garnish with black olives and parsley sprigs.

Leftover marinade makes a wonderful dressing for salad greens.

CHEDDAR-NUT SPREAD

yield about 2 cups

4 cups shredded, sharp cheddar (about 1 pound)
1¼ cups mayonnaise
2 green onions finely chopped
1 (2-ounce) jar pimientos, drained and chopped
1 cup chopped toasted pecans or walnuts

Place all ingredients in a large bowl and mix until thoroughly blended. Cover and chill until ready to use. Let stand at room temperature for 20 minutes before serving. Serve with crackers or party bread rounds.

HERB-FILLED BRIE

yield 8 - 10 servings

1 (3-ounce) package cream cheese, softened
½ teaspoon crushed basil*
½ teaspoon crushed oregano
¼ teaspoon garlic powder
1 (14-ounce) round Brie cheese

In a small bowl combine cream cheese with crushed herbs and blend thoroughly.

Divide Brie round in half by cutting crosswise. Spread cream cheese mixture on one half of Brie round, top with other half and gently press together. Wrap in plastic wrap and chill. Serve with crackers.

Other herb combinations may be used. Try rosemary and sweet marjoram. Pulverize rosemary to a fine powder before mixing with cream cheese.

DRUMETTE FLING

30 chicken drumettes (about 2½ pounds), washed and patted dry

MARINADE:
¼ cup packed brown sugar
¼ cup apricot nectar
¼ cup Tamari sauce (or light soy sauce)
1 tablespoon cider vinegar
2 tablespoons lemon juice
2 tablespoons sugar
1 teaspoon ground black pepper
½ teaspoon hot pepper sauce
1 clove garlic, minced

Combine marinade ingredients in a small bowl and whisk until well blended. Place cleaned drumettes in a gallon-size plastic food storage bag and place in a large bowl. Pour marinade over drumettes. Make sure all pieces are coated with marinade.

Secure bag with wire twist and regrigerate for 2 hours or overnight. Move drumettes around in plastic bag several times to distribute marinade.

Before serving, preheat oven to 350°F. Line a jelly roll pan or cookie sheet with foil. Spray with vegetable oil. Remove drumettes from marinade with a slotted spoon. Place on baking sheet and bake in oven for 30 to 45 minutes, until tender and golden brown. Serve warm.

SWEET AND SPICY WINGS

1 pound chicken wings
¼ cup margarine (½ stick)
2 tablespoons honey
2 tablespoons light corn syrup
2 tablespoons coarse-grained spicy mustard
½ cup finely ground bread crumbs
½ cup finely chopped pecans
½ teaspoon onion powder
⅛ teaspoon cayenne pepper
1 teaspoon finely crushed lemon thyme

Preheat oven to 375°F. Line cookie sheet with foil. Spray with vegetable oil.

Wash and dry chicken wings. Cut off wing tip section and discard.

In a small saucepan, melt margarine over medium heat. Stir in honey, corn syrup and mustard. Simmer for about 5 minutes, stirring occasionally. Remove from heat and let cool for 10 minutes.

In a pie pan, combine bread crumbs, nuts and seasonings. Be sure lemon thyme is crushed to a fine powder.

With tongs, dip each wing part in honey-mustard sauce, then coat with crumb mixture. Shake off excess. Place on prepared baking sheet. Reserve honey-mustard sauce.

Bake for 30 minutes. Remove pan from oven and drizzle remaining honey-mustard sauce over each wing. Return to oven and bake 15 minutes more or until well browned. Serve warm.

CRABMEAT IN ARTICHOKE CUPS

2 tablespoons butter or margarine
8 medium mushrooms, coarsely chopped
4 green onions (part tops), finely sliced
½ pound crabmeat
¼ cup minced fresh parsley
2 teaspoons lemon juice
2 tablespoon sherry
⅓ cup grated Gruyere or Swiss cheese
¼ cup pine nuts
2 (7¾-ounce) cans artichoke bottoms, drained

Preheat oven to 350°F. Lightly butter a 10-inch Pyrex pie dish or shallow casserole.

Melt butter in a frying pan. Add mushrooms and onion, cook over medium high heat about 4 minutes. Stir in crabmeat, parsley, lemon juice and sherry. Reduce heat and cook 2 minutes more.

Fill each artichoke bottom with a spoonful of the crabmeat mixture. Sprinkle with grated cheese and pine nuts. Place in prepared baking dish.

Bake for 15 minutes or until cheese is melted and pine nuts are lightly toasted. (May be prepared early in the day and refrigerated until ready to bake.)

GRUYERE SQUARES

2 cloves garlic, finely minced
3 tablespoons olive oil
4 slices firm-textured white bread
½ pound Gruyere cheese

In a small bowl combine garlic and olive oil. Set aside.

Preheat oven to 425°F. Use a large cookie sheet.

Remove crusts from bread slices, cut into quarters. Place on cookie sheet and bake for 5 minutes. Remove from oven. Brush top of each square with garlic-oil.

Cut cheese into thin slices to fit bread, place a slice on each square. Return to oven and bake until cheese is bubbly, about 5 minutes. Serve warm.

These toasty squares are good with salads and soups, especially with French onion soup. Place a Gruyere Square in the bottom of each soup bowl and ladle over with the hot soup.

BLUE DANISH SPREAD

yield about 2 cups

½ pound Saga Blue Cheese
1 (3-ounce) package of cream cheese, softened
¼ cup minced fresh parsley
1 tablespoon minced fresh dill or (½ teaspoon crushed, dried)
2 tablespoons lemon juice
½ cup finely chopped walnuts, toasted

In a small bowl combine all ingredients. Stir until thoroughly blended. Pack in serving container and chill. Bring to room temperature before serving.

HAM CHUTNEY SPREAD

yield about 2 cups

½ pound baked ham, rind removed
1 small onion, quartered
¼ cup margarine, softened
2 tablespoons spicy-brown mustard
¼ teaspoon ground coriander
¼ teaspoon ground allspice
1 tablespoon chutney (such as Major Grey's)
2 teaspoons honey
2 tablespoons mayonnaise, to moisten, if necessary

Cut ham into small chunks. Place ham and onion in work bowl of food processor. Pulse to coarsely chop. Add remaining ingredients, except mayonnaise. Continue to process until mixture has good spreading texture.

Moisten with a little mayonnaise, if necessary. Pack in serving container and chill.

These spreads may be used for tea sandwiches, to serve with crackers, or as a filling for stuffed celery.

MUSHROOMS MARINATA

yield 6 - 8 servings

This is an easy appetizer with a zesty herb flavor.

½ pound fresh mushrooms, approximately

MARINADE:

1 teaspoon grated onion (or dried minced onion)
1 tablespoon sherry wine
4 tablespoons soy sauce
2 tablespoons tarragon vinegar
1 teaspoon sugar
½ teaspoon garlic powder
1 tablespoon fresh chopped parsley
1 teaspoon each: fresh minced dillweed, basil and oregano
  (or use ¼ teaspoon each of the dried herb)

Combine marinade ingredients in a glass measure and whisk to combine. Set aside.

An hour before serving, wipe mushrooms clean, cut into quarters or halves, depending on size, and place in a glass serving bowl. Restir marinade and pour over mushrooms. Marinate for an hour at room temperature. Stir occasionally. Serve with picks for spearing the mushroom pieces.

Mushrooms absorb flavors quickly but will lose texture if allowed to marinate much more than an hour. Mushrooms Marinata also makes a tasty addition to a tossed salad.

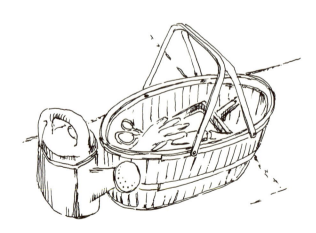

ARTICHOKE APPETIZER

yield 4 - 6 servings

1 (15-ounce) can artichoke hearts, drained
1 cup mayonnaise (not salad dressing)
1 cup grated Parmesan cheese
1 teaspoon lemon juice
½ teaspoon Worcestershire sauce
2-3 drops hot pepper sauce
1 tablespoon capers, drained and chopped
½ cup chopped pecans or walnuts, toasted

Preheat oven to 350°F. Lightly grease a 1½-quart casserole.

Cut artichoke hearts into small pieces and place in a mixing bowl, mash slightly. Blend in remaining ingredients, except nuts.

Spoon mixture into prepared baking dish (mixture should be only about 1-inch deep), sprinkle with chopped nuts. Bake in oven for 20 minutes or until bubbly and lightly browned on top. Serve warm with crackers.

CHEESE TRIANGLES

yield about 48 pieces

This appetizer must be frozen before baking and can be prepared up to a month ahead of serving.

1 (16-ounce) carton of Old English Cheese
2 sticks margarine, softened
1 teaspoon onion powder
¼ teaspoon garlic powder
¼ teaspoon Worcestershire sauce
8 drops hot pepper sauce

2 loaves thin-sliced white sandwich bread, crusts removed

Cut cheese into chunks, place in mixing bowl or food processor, and let soften. Add seasonings and blend until smooth. Set aside.

Remove crusts from bread. Spread bread slices with cheese mixture; stack three slices together. Cut in triangles, 4 to a stack. Then spread cheese mixture on sides, tops and bottoms of each triangle.

Place on cookie sheet and put in freezer for 2 hours or until firmly frozen. Then place in plastic freezer bags and keep frozen until ready to use.

NOTE: *Do not thaw before baking.*

Just before serving, preheat oven to 350°F. Lightly grease a cookie sheet. Place frozen cheese triangles on cookie sheet and bake for 20 minutes or until golden brown.

NOTE: Cheese triangles are tasty treats to serve with soups or salads.

MOLDED SHRIMP SPREAD

yield 6 - 8 servings

An old favorite. This molded party spread should be prepared a day ahead. Use this same recipe for a special salad treat.

1 envelope unflavored gelatin
½ cup cold water
1 (8-ounce) package cream cheese, softened
1 (10¾-ounce) can cream of shrimp soup
1 (4½-ounce) can tiny shrimp
1½ cups finely chopped celery
1 small onion, finely minced
¼ cup finely minced green or red sweet pepper
½ cup mayonnaise
½ teaspoon curry powder

Soften gelatin in ½ cup cold water, set aside.

In a small saucepan combine soup and cream cheese. Cook over medium low heat and stir until smoothly blended. Add gelatin, stirring until dissolved.

Drain shrimp and rinse in cold water. Redrain and stir into soup mixture along with remaining ingredients. Taste to adjust seasoning. You may want to add more curry powder.

Pour into a lightly oiled 4-cup mold and chill until firm. Serve with crackers or party rye.

To serve as a salad, pour mixture into a shallow 11 x 7-inch dish, or use 8 individual salad molds. Chill until firm.

PITA BITS

yield about 4 cups

1 package of 6 regular pita bread rounds
¼ cup olive oil, approximately
3 tablespoons finely grated Parmesan cheese
2 teaspoons powdered Italian herb blend (see Page 258, or use prepared low-salt seasoning such as Vegit)

With kitchen scissors, cut pita rounds into 1-inch pieces. Place in large mixing bowl. Gradually pour on olive oil and stir until pita bits are well coated. Sprinkle with Parmesan cheese and seasoning, stir to coat. Let stand 15 minutes.

Preheat oven to 325°F. Use 2 shallow baking pans.

Spread pita bits in a single layer in baking pans and bake for 15 minutes. Remove from oven and turn pieces over. Bake for another 10 minutes or until lightly browned. Cool completely before storing in airtight container.

SANTA MARIAS

yield 6 - 8 servings

Dieters will appreciate this appetizer. This recipe may also be used for a molded salad.

2 envelopes unflavored gelatin
3½ cups Bloody Mary mix (or zesty tomato juice)
2 tablespoons each: finely chopped celery, cucumber, onion, and green pepper
1 tablespoon fresh snipped dillweed

Garnish: cucumber, zucchini slices or crackers; small shrimp (cooked and cleaned), or black olive slices

In a 1-quart saucepan soften the gelatin in Bloody Mary mix. Turn heat to low and stir until gelatin is dissolved. Remove from heat and add chopped vegetables and dill.

Pour into a 9 x 9-inch pan. Chill until firm.

To serve cut in squares and place on slices of cucumber or zucchini, or plain round crackers. If desired, garnish with a small cooked shrimp or a slice of black olive.

TOASTED TORTILLAS

yield 32 quarters

1 package flour tortillas (usually 8 to a package)
¼ cup olive oil, approximately

Garnish (optional): ⅓ cup grated Monterey Jack cheese and chili powder

Preheat oven to 300°F. Use cookie sheets.

Brush each tortilla lightly with olive oil. Cut into quarters with kitchen scissors and place in single layer on cookie sheets. Bake until crisp, about 20 minutes. Serve plain or add garnish. Place a few shreds of cheese on each piece, sprinkle with chili powder and return to oven until cheese melts.

Toasted Tortillas (without cheese garnish) may be stored in airtight containers.

SUGARY BACON CURLS

yield 6 - 8 servings

These popular appetizers are too fussy to make just before a party. Plan to prepare a day in advance.

½ pound lean bacon
½ cup packed brown sugar
2 tablespoons Dijon-style mustard

Preheat oven to 325°F. Line broiler pan with foil. Poke holes in foil to allow fat to drain.

Cut bacon slices in half. In a small bowl combine brown sugar and mustard. Press sugar mixture onto both sides of each bacon slice. Place in single layer on broiler pan. Bake for about 25 minutes. Do not let bacon overcook or burn. Watch carefully.

Let bacon slices cool to touch. Then roll each piece into a curl and secure with a toothpick. Cover and keep refrigerated until ready to reheat in a 300°F. oven.

VARIATION: Wrap sugared bacon around a whole water chestnut. To prepare, drain chestnuts. Place in a small bowl and sprinkle with soy sauce. Let stand for 20 minutes. After bacon is cooked and cool to touch wrap each water chestnut with a slice of bacon. Secure with toothpick. Refrigerate until ready to reheat.

POTATO SKINS

yield 24 quarters, 12 halves

It is more convenient to prepare these popular snacks ahead of time; then crisp in oven just before serving.

6 large baking potatoes
½ cup melted butter or margarine
2 teaspoons Cajun style seasoning (or favorite herb blend)
salt and pepper, optional
1 cup grated cheddar cheese

Garnish: cooked bacon bits, salsa, sour cream, chopped chive or parsley.

In oven, or microwave, bake potatoes until tender. When cool to touch, cut each potato in half (or quarters); scoop out insides, leaving about ¼-inch of potato shell. Reserve scooped-out potato for other uses.

Preheat oven to 425°F. Use large cookie sheet or jelly roll pan.

Place potato skins on baking sheet, brush with melted butter, sprinkle with seasoning. Bake until skins are crisp, about 15 to 20 minutes. Remove from oven and sprinkle with grated cheese. Return to oven until cheese is bubbly.

Add choice of garnish, if desired, and serve hot.

CHEDDAR OVER ENGLISH MUFFINS

yield 12 halves, 48 quarters

6 English muffins

CHEESE TOPPING:

1 cup mayonnaise (not salad dressing)
1½ cups grated sharp Cheddar cheese
2 tablespoons capers, drained and chopped
½ cup finely minced onion

In a small bowl combine cheese topping ingredients. Stir until well blended. (May be prepared ahead and chilled. Will keep in refrigerator for a week.)

When ready to serve, split muffins and spread generously with cheese topping. Place on broiler pan and broil until cheese is bubbly and turns golden brown. May also bake for 15 minutes in preheated 400°F. oven.

Cut into quarters and serve hot.

VARIATION: Add 1 (7-ounce) can crab meat, drained, to cheese mixture. Use this combination the same day.

EDYTHE'S SNAPPY MEATBALLS

yield about 90 small meatballs

The spicy-sweet sauce is thickened with gingersnaps. Let the flavors mellow by preparing a day ahead of serving.

3 eggs
¾ cup milk
2 cups fresh bread crumbs
1 teaspoon Dijon-style mustard
1½ teaspoons salt
¾ teaspoon ground pepper
1 large onion, finely minced
3 pounds of lean ground beef

In a large mixer bowl, beat eggs and milk. Add bread crumbs, mustard, salt and pepper and blend. Let stand for 5 minutes. Add minced onion and ground beef. Beat on medium speed until thoroughly combined.

Preheat oven to 350°F. Lightly grease a large shallow baking pan.

Shape meat mixture into tiny balls, about the size of a walnut, and place in baking pan. Bake for 20 minutes. (Meatballs may also be microwaved. Follow instructions for your model.)

SAUCE:

¾ cup minced onion
15 gingersnaps
1¼ cup seedless raisins
¾ teaspoon salt
1 teaspoon ground pepper
½ cup granulated sugar
4 cups water
¾ cup ketchup
juice of 1 lemon

Combine ingredients in large saucepan. Bring to boil. Reduce heat to a simmer and cook until sauce is thickened, stirring frequently. Add cooked meatballs to sauce and simmer 15 minutes.

Meatballs and sauce may be made ahead and refrigerated. Reheat just before serving. If sauce is too thick, add a small amount of water. To serve, place in chafing dish to keep ingredients warm while on buffet table.

Beans, Grains, Pastas

The entrance into the knot garden is flanked by boxwoods. A bronze plaque on the stone wall dedicates the Herb Garden to the people of Cleveland.

BEANS, GRAINS, PASTAS —
COOKING TIMES AND PROPORTIONS

1 cup dry measure	Water	Cooking time** (approximate)	yield
Black beans	4 cups	1½ hours	2 cups
Black-eyed peas	3 cups	1 hour	2 cups
Great Northern beans	3½ cups	2 hours	2 cups
Kidney beans	3 cups	1½ hours	2 cups
Lentils & split peas (no soaking needed)	3 cups	1 hour	2½ cups
Limas (baby)	2 cups	1½ hours	1¾ cups
Pinto beans	3 cups	2½ hours	2 cups
Small white beans (such as navy)	3 cups	2½ hours	2 cups
Barley (pearl) can be presoaked overnight	3 cups	40 minutes	3½ cups
Brown rice (long or short-grain)	2½ cups	45 minutes	3 cups
Rice (long-grain, white)	2 cups	20 minutes	3 cups
Rice (aromatics)	1¾ cups	20 minutes	3 cups
Rice (Italian arborio)	2½-3 cups simmering liquid	25 minutes	2½-3 cups
Buckwheat (kasha)	2 cups	15 minutes	2½ cups
Bulgur wheat	2 cups	20 minutes	2½ cups
Wild rice	3 cups	35-60 minutes	3½-4 cups
Whole wheat berries (soak overnight, do not drain water to cook)	3 cups	1 hour	2 cups
Elbow macaroni	2 quarts	10 minutes	2 cups
Pasta (sea shells, medium size)	2 quarts	10 minutes	1½ cups
Pasta (rotini)	2 quarts	10-12 minutes	2 cups

Dry pastas are difficult to measure due to the various shapes. The amounts listed are guides. Weighing pasta will give a better measure. As a rule allow 4 ounces of dry pasta for each serving.

**QUICK COOKING METHOD FOR DRIED BEANS

Place beans in saucepan and cover with cold water. Bring to a rapid boil and boil for 2 minutes. Remove pan from heat, cover and let stand 1 hour. Drain water. Then add fresh water or broth according to recipe.

APPLE BEAN BAKE

yield 4 - 6 servings

This dish may be prepared ahead for reheating just before serving.

2 cups dry Great Northern beans, rinsed and picked over
4 tablespoons butter or margarine
4 tart apples, peeled and cubed
1 medium onion, diced
1 clove garlic, minced
½ cup ketchup
¼ cup packed brown sugar
1 tablespoon Dijon-style mustard
½ teaspoon ground cinnamon
¼ teaspoon ground nutmeg
⅛ teaspoon ground cloves

Garnish: 4 slices bacon, fried crisp and crumbled.

Soak beans overnight in water to cover. (Or use the quick-cooking method explained on first page of this section.)

Drain beans and recover with fresh water, bring to a boil, reduce heat and simmer until beans are tender. Drain and set aside.

Preheat oven to 350°F. Lightly grease 2-quart casserole.

In a large frying pan melt butter over medium-high heat. Add apples, onion, and garlic. Saute until tender.

Stir in ketchup, brown sugar, mustard, spices and cooked beans.

Transfer mixture to prepared casserole. Bake until bubbly, about 30-40 minutes.

Garnish with crumbled bacon just before serving.

SWEET AND SOUR BAKED LIMAS

yield 4 - 6 servings

1½ cups dried baby limas, rinse and pick over; soak overnight in water to cover. (or use quick-cook method)
¼ pound lean bacon, diced
½ cup chopped celery
½ cup chopped onion
½ cup diced carrots
¼ cup packed brown sugar
1 tablespoon cider vinegar

To cook, drain water from beans. Place beans in 4-quart saucepan, cover with fresh water, about 3½ cups. Bring to a boil; reduce heat to simmer, cover and cook until beans are tender, about 1 hour.

In a frying pan cook diced bacon until crisp. Remove pieces with slotted spoon, drain on paper towel.

Pour off all but 1 tablespoon fat from frying pan. Add celery, onions and carrots to pan. Cook over medium heat until tender-crisp.

Preheat oven to 350°F. Lightly grease a deep 2-quart baking dish.

When beans are tender, drain off excess water, leaving about ¾ cup of liquid in saucepan. Add cooked bacon and vegetables.

Place brown sugar and vinegar in frying pan and over low heat stir until sugar is melted. Add to beans and vegetables. Taste for seasoning.

Place bean mixture in prepared baking dish and bake for 2 hours. May be prepared ahead and reheated.

CHILI BIANCO

yield 6 - 8 servings

A tasty chili without tomatoes.

2 cups dried Great Northern beans
   (or use 2 (15½-ounce) cans cooked white beans)
5¼ cups chicken broth
1 clove garlic, minced
1 large onion, diced
¼ teaspoon ground cumin
1 sweet yellow pepper, seeded and diced
1 teaspoon crushed oregano
1 teaspoon chili powder
¼ teaspoon ground coriander
¼ teaspoon white ground pepper
¼ teaspoon ground cumin (additional)
2 cups diced cooked chicken white meat

Garnish: 1½ cups grated white cheddar or Monterey Jack cheese, taco chips, and Avocado Cream

Rinse and pick over dried beans. Soak overnight in water to cover. Or use quick-cook method described on first page of this section.

Drain beans and place in 4-quart saucepan. Add chicken broth, garlic, onion and ¼ teaspoon ground cumin. Bring to a boil, then reduce heat to a simmer. Cover pan and cook until beans are tender, about 1½ hours.

Add diced yellow pepper, oregano, chili powder, coriander, white pepper, additional cumin and diced cooked chicken. Stir to combine and simmer for another 30 minutes. Taste to adjust seasoning.

Serve hot in bowls garnished with grated cheese, taco chips and Avocado Cream.

AVOCADO CREAM
1 cup dairy sour cream
1 ripe avocado, peeled and seed removed
1 tablespoon lime juice

Combine ingredients in small bowl. Mix until smoothly blended.

BLACK BEAN AND YAM STEW

1 cup dry black beans
1 tablespoon margarine
2 medium onions, chopped
2 cloves garlic, minced
2 cups stewed tomatoes (or 4 ripe tomatoes, peeled and chopped)
1 cup beef broth
¼ teaspoon ground cumin
1 tablespoon red wine vinegar
1 large yam, peeled and cubed
1 cup chopped cooked ham
¼ cup dry sherry
1 tablespoon lime juice (or lemon)

Garnishes: sliced green onions and unflavored yogurt or sour cream.

Wash and pick over beans. Soak overnight in cold water.

To cook, drain beans, place in large saucepan, cover with fresh water. Bring to a boil, reduce heat to simmer and cook until beans are soft, but not split open. Drain beans before adding to stew mixture.

In a 4-quart Dutch oven melt margarine over medium-high heat. Add onion and garlic, cook until soft. Add stewed tomatoes, broth, cumin, and vinegar. Reduce heat to simmer and cook for 10 minutes. Add beans, yam cubes and chopped ham. Simmer about 30 minutes, or until yams are tender. Stir in sherry and lime juice.

Serve in bowls with a dollop of yogurt and a sprinkle of green onion slices. Hot corn bread is good with this stew.

BLACK BEAN CHILI

¾ cup dry black beans
1 tablespoon margarine or olive oil
1 clove garlic, minced
1 small onion, diced
1 small green pepper, seeded and chopped
1 pound lean ground beef
1 (28-ounce) can whole tomatoes (do not drain)
1 (12-ounce) can crushed or stewed tomatoes (do not drain)
2 teaspoons chili powder
¼ teaspoon ground cinnamon
¼ teaspoon cayenne pepper (or to taste)
2-3 drops hot pepper sauce

Garnishes: dairy sour cream, chopped onion, diced green pepper, and shredded cheddar cheese.

Wash and pick over beans. Cover with cold water and soak overnight.

To cook, drain beans, place in a large saucepan and cover with fresh water. Bring to a boil; reduce heat to simmer. Cook beans until soft but not split open.

While beans are cooking, melt margarine in large frying pan over medium-high heat. Add garlic, onions and green pepper. Cook until soft. Add ground beef and fry until brown, stirring to break up pieces. Spoon off any excess fat.

Add this mixture to cooked beans along with tomatoes and seasonings. Simmer for an hour for flavors to blend.

Serve in bowls with a selection of garnishes.

REUBEN'S BAKED BEANS WITH SHORT RIBS yield 6 - 8 servings

*Slow-baking in an old-fashioned bean pot adds great flavor to this hearty dish.
Plan to serve Quick Boston Brown Bread (see Page 81) for a traditional touch.*

2 cups navy beans
6 cups water
1½ pounds meaty beef short ribs
¼ cup molasses
1½ teaspoons dry English mustard
¼ teaspoon ground ginger
2 tablespoons brown sugar
1 teaspoon salt
¼ teaspoon black pepper
1 medium onion, peeled

Rinse and pick over beans. In a 4-quart sauce pan soak beans overnight in 6 cups water.

To cook drain off water and replace with 6 cups of fresh water. Bring to a gentle boil and cook for 20 minutes. Remove from heat and drain, reserving liquid.

Preheat oven to 250°F. Use a 2-quart bean pot.

Trim excess fat from short ribs and place in bottom of bean pot.

In small bowl combine ½ cup of reserved liquid with molasses, mustard, ginger, sugar, salt and pepper.

Add beans to pot. Stir in molasses mixture. Place whole onion in center. Use reserved cooking liquid to just cover beans. Place lid on bean pot and bake in slow oven for 6-8 hours. Check several times during baking to make sure beans are covered with liquid. Add a little hot water if necessary.

Remove lid from bean pot for last 30 minutes of baking.

VARIATION: Pork and Beans. Instead of beef short ribs use 1½ pounds boneless pork loin. Cut into small cubes. Trim off excess fat. Melt 2 tablespoons oil in frying pan over medium-high heat. Add pork cubes and brown on all sides before placing in bean pot with other ingredients to bake.

SPICY HOPPIN' JOHN

yield 6 servings

Hot corn bread is good to serve with this hearty dish.

1 cup dried black-eyed peas
1 cup dried red kidney beans
1 tablespoon butter or margarine
1 medium onion, chopped
1 stalk celery (with some leaves), finely diced
1 small garlic clove, minced
¼ teaspoon ground cumin
⅛ teaspoon *each:* cinnamon, nutmeg, cloves
2 quarts water, approximately
1 cup diced cooked ham
½ cup long-grain rice

2 teaspoons chicken soup base or bouillon cube
¼ teaspoon hot pepper sauce, or to taste

Rinse and pick over peas and beans. Place in a large saucepan. Cover with cold water and soak overnight. (Or use quick-cooking method.) Drain peas and beans and set aside.

In a 5-quart saucepan melt butter over medium-high heat. Add onion, celery and garlic. Cook until just tender. Add drained peas and beans and water to cover, about 2 quarts. Bring to a boil; then lower heat to a good simmer. Add seasonings and ham. Simmer until beans are tender (but not overcooked), about 1 hour.

Add rice, soup base, and hot pepper sauce. Simmer until rice is tender, about 20 minutes. The mixture should remain moist. If necessary, add a little more water. Taste to adjust seasoning. Serve hot in soup bowls.

ESAU'S LENTILS

yield 4 - 6 servings

A high-protein dish that is little changed since ancient times.

1 cup brown lentils, rinsed and picked over
1½ cups water
2 tablespoons oil (or bacon drippings)
1 medium onion, chopped
2 tablespoons purple basil vinegar (or red wine vinegar)
1 tablespoon brown sugar
salt and pepper, to taste

Place lentils in a 2-quart saucepan. Add water and bring to a boil. Reduce heat to a simmer. Cover pan and cook until lentils are *just tender,* about 30 minutes.

While lentils are cooking, heat oil or bacon drippings in a small frying pan. Add onions and cook until soft. Stir in vinegar and brown sugar. Simmer for 3 minutes.

When lentils are tender, stir in onion mixture. Let stand about 5 minutes. Taste for seasoning. Add salt and pepper. Serve hot.

NOTE: Herbs such as thyme, rosemary or parsley may be added.

PASTA WITH TOMATO-LENTIL SAUCE

yield 2-4 servings

Lentils supply the protein in this basic tomato sauce.

½ pound thin spaghetti, cooked and drained
1 tablespoon olive oil
1 medium onion, chopped
1 clove garlic, minced
½ cup chopped fresh, ripe tomatoes
1 (15-ounce) can tomato sauce
1 (6-ounce) can tomato paste (optional)
2 teaspoons sugar (optional)
1 cup water
⅓ cup dry lentils, rinsed and picked over
½ teaspoon *each:* crushed oregano, basil and thyme
salt and pepper, to taste

Heat oil in large sauce pan over medium-high heat. Saute onion and garlic until tender.

Stir in remaining ingredients. Reduce heat to simmer and cook until lentils are tender, about 60 minutes. Taste for seasoning. Serve over hot pasta.

NOTE: Red lentils would be a good choice for they cook quickly and blend into the sauce.

STIR FRIED VEGETABLES AND TOFU

yield 4 - 6 servings

A vegetarian entree.

1 cup long-grain natural rice
3 tablespoons olive oil
1 clove garlic, finely minced
1 teaspoon minced fresh ginger root (optional)
½ cup sliced green onions
½ cup water
2-4 tablespoons soy sauce
3-4 drops hot pepper sauce
½ teaspoon *each:* sweet marjoram and thyme
1 tablespoon minced fresh parsley
6-ounces tofu, drained and cut into small cubes
1½ quarts vegetables: Choose several favorites from the following to cut into
   bite-sized pieces or thin slices:

broccoli	carrots	cauliflower
bok choy	pea pods	red or green pepper
green beans	celery	zucchini

Cook rice according to package directions; set aside and keep warm.

Prepare vegetables. Keep each vegetable separate.

In a large frying pan heat oil. Add garlic, ginger and onion. Cook until transparent but not brown.

Stir in carrots and other vegetables requiring a longer cooking time. When almost tender stir in other vegetable choices in turn. Continue to stir and lift until each vegetable is tender. Do not overcook.

Stir in tofu. Add water, soy sauce, hot sauce and herbs. Cook to blend flavors, about 2 minutes. Taste and adjust seasonings. Serve immediately over hot rice.

VARIATIONS: Sliced fresh mushrooms, water chestnuts and fresh bean sprouts may be added.

SPICE AND RICE

An interesting side dish to serve with grilled chicken, pork or lamb.

3 cups cooked rice (prepared according to package directions)
½ cup raisins (after rice is cooked, add raisins to plump in the hot rice)
1 tablespoon butter or margarine
1 medium onion, chopped
1 rib celery (with leaves), diced
1 tablespoon honey
1 tablespoon lemon juice
½ teaspoon salt
¼ teaspoon *each:* ground cinnamon, ground nutmeg and ground cardamom
3 tablespoons pine nuts, toasted

In a large saucepan melt butter over medium heat. Saute onion and celery until tender. Stir in remaining ingredients, except nuts; reduce heat and simmer for about 5 minutes.

Gently stir in rice and raisins. Cover and let stand for about 5 minutes before serving.

NOTE: Pine nuts may be quickly toasted in a small frying pan over medium heat. Stir several times for even browning. Add to rice mixture just before serving.

CITRUS ONION RICE

This seasoned rice will complement a chicken stir-fry, grilled lamb or veal.

2 cups water
1 cup long-grained rice
½ cup finely minced fresh parsley
¼ cup finely slivered green onions
1 tablespoon minced fresh mint leaves
Grated peel from 1 lime
1 teaspoon Tamari sauce
½ teaspoon Oriental sesame oil

Bring water to a boil in heavy saucepan. Stir in rice, reduce heat to simmer. Cover and cook rice until water is absorbed, about 20 minutes.

Remove from heat, add remaining ingredients. Stir to combine. Cover pan and let mixture stand for 10 minutes before serving.

RISOTTO MILANESE
WITH SHRIMP AND VEGETABLES

yield 4 servings

A tossed salad and crusty bread are all that's needed to accompany this rich-tasting dish. Have all ingredients assembled before starting to cook Risotto, because it requires constant attention until completed.

2 tablespoons butter
2 tablespoons olive oil
½ cup chopped onion
2 cups Arborio Rice*
⅓ cup dry white wine
4 to 5 cups *hot* chicken broth (may not need full amount)
¼ teaspoon saffron threads (optional, but adds traditional flavor)
6 asparagus spears, cleaned and sliced
½ cup sliced fresh mushrooms
½ pound fresh-cooked shrimp, shelled and deveined, cut in pieces

½ cup grated Parmesan cheese
2 tablespoons cream
salt and pepper, to taste

In a large frying pan melt butter with olive oil over medium-high heat. Add onion, cook until transparent. Add rice, stir until rice has absorbed the butter and oil, about 3 minutes.

Add wine, ½ cup of the hot broth, and saffron. Stir until liquid has been absorbed. Adjust heat so rice absorbs broth but does not become dry. Continue adding small amounts of broth and stir continuously until rice absorbs each addition and becomes tender, about 20 minutes.

When rice is tender, add asparagus and mushrooms and more broth if necessary. Cook until vegetables are tender, 2-3 minutes. Stir in shrimp and cook until just heated through. Stir in Parmesan cheese and cream, add salt and pepper to taste. Serve immediately.

*Other types of rice will not produce quite the same results as the short-grained Italian rice.

MOLDED RICE SALAD

yield 6 - 8 servings

1 cup long-grain natural rice
½ cup aromatic rice
⅔ cup minced onion
2 tablespoons rice wine vinegar
¾ teaspoon curry powder
1½ tablespoons chopped capers
½ cup finely shredded carrot
¾ cup frozen green peas, thawed
¾ cup chopped celery
½ cup chopped pecans, toasted
¾ cup mayonnaise (approximately)

Cook rice according to package directions. Should have about 3½ cups of cooked rice.

While rice is still hot, place in large mixing bowl. Add onion, vinegar, curry and capers. Stir to combine.

Cool slightly; then add carrots, peas, celery and pecans. Mix with enough mayonnaise to moisten.

Pack in 6-cup ring mold or 2 loaf pans, (9 x 5-inch). Chill for 4 hours, or overnight.

To serve, turn out onto plate lined with lettuce leaves. Garnish with tomato wedges.

PLUM TOMATOES STUFFED WITH RICE AND CHEESE

yield 4 - 6 servings

½ cup long-grain rice
1¼ cups chicken broth
1 cup grated sharp cheddar or gruyere cheese
2 tablespoons minced fresh parsley or chives

8-12 firm-ripe fresh plum tomatoes
salt and pepper

Cook the rice in broth until tender. Let cool slightly; then mix with half the grated cheese. Add parsley or chives.

Slice tomatoes in half lengthwise, scoop out seeds. Season with salt and pepper. Place in shallow, broiler-proof casserole. Fill each tomato half with a scoop of cheese-rice mixture. Divide remaining cheese evenly over the tops. Place under broiler until cheese is melted and bubbly.

FOUR HERBS AND RICES

⅓ cup *each:* wild rice, brown rice, long-grain rice and aromatic rice
1 tablespoon olive oil
1 tablespoon butter
6 green onions, finely sliced (use some green tops)
1 clove garlic, minced
1 carrot, scraped and finely chopped
1 rib celery (with leaves), chopped
2 cups chicken or beef broth
3 cups boiling water
1 teaspoon crushed marjoram
¼ teaspoon crushed thyme
¼ teaspoon crushed rosemary
¼ cup fresh parsley, chopped
salt and pepper, to taste
⅓ cup toasted almond slivers

Rinse and drain wild rice and natural brown rice, if indicated on package directions.

In a 4-quart saucepan heat olive oil and butter over medium-high heat. Add onions and garlic. Cook until tender.

Add carrots, celery, the broth, hot water and herbs. Bring to a boil. Stir in rice. Reduce heat to simmer. Cover and let cook until rice is tender and moisture absorbed, about 1 hour.

Taste for seasoning. Add salt and pepper. Add slivered almonds the last 20 minutes of cooking time.

This dish may be made ahead and reheated just before serving.

BROWN RICE AND BULGUR PILAF

yield 6 - 8 servings

2 tablespoons cooking oil
1 clove garlic, minced
¼ cup chopped onion
1 rib celery with leaves, diced
1 carrot, scraped and shredded
½ cup brown rice
1 cup bulgur
2 cups chicken (or beef) broth
1 cup boiling water
½ teaspoon curry powder
½ teaspoon crushed marjoram
1 tablespoon chopped fresh mint
  (½ teaspoon crushed dried mint)
¼ teaspoon ground cumin
⅛ teaspoon ground allspice
¼ cup pine nuts, or slivered almonds, toasted

In 4-quart Dutch oven heat oil over medium-high heat. Add garlic, onion, celery and carrot. Cook until just tender, about 5 minutes.

Add brown rice and bulgur. Cook about 3 minutes. Stir to keep rice and bulgur from sticking to pan.

Add broth and hot water, herbs and spices. Bring to a boil, then reduce heat to a simmer. Cover pan and cook until rice and bulgur are tender and liquid is absorbed, about 30 minutes.

Add pine nuts to mixture during last 10 minutes of cooking.

If mixture becomes too dry before rice and bulgur are tender, add a little more broth.

CLUTTERED RICE

yield 6 - 8 servings

This dish may be seasoned spicy-hot or mildly spiced, according to taste.

1 (6-ounce) package long-grain white and wild rice mix (without packaged seasonings), cook according to package directions.
1 pound bulk sausage (hot or sweet Italian)
2 tablespoons cooking oil
2 tablespoons butter or margarine
½ cup sliced fresh mushrooms
3 ribs celery, chopped
4 green onions, finely sliced (or 1 medium onion, chopped)
1 cup chopped green bell pepper
¼ cup chopped green chilies (optional)
¼ cup chopped fresh parsley
1 teaspoon chili powder (or more to taste)
¼ teaspoon ground cumin
¼ teaspoon hot pepper sauce (to taste)
½ teaspoon crushed oregano
½ teaspoon crushed sage
1 cup medium-thick white sauce (see Index)
1 cup shredded Monterey Jack or sharp cheddar cheese

While rice is cooking, fry sausage in large frying pan until brown. Stir to break up pieces. Remove with slotted spoon to bowl lined with paper towels to remove excess fat.

Pour fat from frying pan. Wipe with paper towels.

Preheat oven to 350°F. Lightly grease a 12 x 8-inch shallow casserole.

Heat oil and butter in frying pan. Add mushrooms, celery, onions and peppers. Cook until tender. Stir in parsley and remaining seasonings. Cook for 1 minute.

Add cooked rice and sausage to pan. Stir in white sauce to combine.

Spoon into prepared baking dish. Arrange cheese evenly on top. May be covered and refrigerated until ready to bake. Or bake immediately, for 30 minutes, or until cheese topping bubbles and turns golden brown.

WHEAT AND BARLEY PILAF

yield 4 servings

3 tablespoons butter or margarine
4 green onions, finely sliced
1 rib celery with leaves, chopped
1 cup grated carrot (2 small)
1 cup pearl barley
¼ cup cracked wheat
½ teaspoon crushed marjoram
¼ teaspoon crushed summer savory
¼ teaspoon ground cumin
¼ teaspoon ground pepper
1¾ cup beef stock

Garnish: 2 tablespoons each of chopped fresh parsley and chives

Melt butter in heavy saucepan over medium heat. Add onion, celery and carrot. Cook until soft.

Add barley, cracked wheat and herbs. Stir and cook about 3 minutes, or until barley becomes just slightly browned. Stir to keep from sticking.

Add beef stock. Reduce heat to simmer and cook until barley is tender and has absorbed the liquid, about 35 minutes. If needed, add more liquid.

Stir in fresh parsley and chives just before serving.

MINTED COUSCOUS PILAF

yield 4 - 6 servings

This complements chicken or lamb dishes.

2 tablespoons olive oil
¼ cup finely sliced green onions

½ cup finely chopped celery
1½ cups couscous (precooked)
2 cups chicken broth
¼ teaspoon ground allspice
3 tablespoons chopped fresh mint leaves
3 tablespoons pine nuts, toasted
2 tablespoons butter

In a large frying pan heat olive oil over medium-high heat. Add onion and celery. Cook until tender, about 2 minutes. Add broth and bring to a boil. Stir in couscous, allspice, and mint. Remove from heat and add pine nuts. Cover pan and let stand for about 5 minutes, or until liquid has been absorbed.

Just before serving stir in butter. Transfer to serving dish and serve immediately. May be made ahead and reheated just before serving. Add a little more broth if mixture seems too dry.

PASTA IN SALSA CRUDA

yield 4 servings

The flavor of fresh herbs is necessary for this uncooked sauce.

⅓ cup olive oil
1 cup tomato juice
½ cup sliced black olives
½ cup shredded Gruyere cheese
4 ounces mozzarella cheese, diced
3 large fresh basil leaves, chopped
2 teaspoon marjoram leaves, minced
2 tablespoons minced chive
1 tablespoon chopped parsley
salt and pepper, to taste
1 pound fettuccini, cooked and drained
¼ cup cream

Combine first 9 ingredients in a bowl. Season with salt and pepper. Let stand at room temperature for 30 minutes.

Just before serving, cook and drain fettuccini. Place in a serving bowl, add sauce and toss to coat. Add cream and mix again. Serve immediately.

WILTED GREENS OVER PASTA

3 cups dry Penne (tubular pasta)
1 pound Swiss chard or spinach

5 slices bacon
1 clove garlic, minced
½ cup chopped onion
½ teaspoon hot pepper flakes, crushed
2 teaspoons Dijon-style mustard
2 tablespoons white wine vinegar
1 teaspoon sugar (optional)
1 cup grated Romano or Parmesan cheese
½ cup coarsely-chopped pecans, toasted

Garnish: reserved crumbled bacon and toasted pecans

Cook pasta according to package directions. Drain and keep warm. Wash greens and trim off tough stems. Drain excess water and slice into thin strips.

In large frying pan cook bacon until crisp. Drain on paper towels. Crumble and reserve for garnish.

Drain all but 2 tablespoons fat from pan. Add garlic, onion and hot pepper flakes. Stir over medium-high heat until onions are tender, about 3 minutes.

Add sliced greens and stir until just wilted, about 3 minutes.

In large serving bowl combine mustard, vinegar and sugar. Add cooked pasta. Toss to combine. Stir in cooked greens and cheese. Serve immediately with garnishes.

HERB SOCIETY NOODLES  yield 6 servings

This is adapted from a recipe printed in our 1960 cookbook, MORE SAVORY SEASONINGS. It is an easy dish for family gatherings.

1 tablespoon butter or vegetable oil
1 medium onion, chopped
1 small garlic clove, minced
1 cup creamy cottage cheese
1 cup dairy sour cream
1 teaspoon Worcestershire sauce
¼ teaspoon white pepper
1 teaspoon minced fresh tarragon (or ¼ teaspoon crushed dried tarragon)
8 ounces fine-cut noddles, cooked and drained

Garnish: ¼ cup sliced black olives and 2 tablespoons minced fresh parsley

Preheat oven to 325°F. Butter a 2-quart casserole.

In a small frying pan heat butter or oil. Add onion and garlic and cook until soft, about 3 minutes.

Place cottage cheese and sour cream in a mixing bowl, stir to blend. Add seasonings, cooked noodles and onion-garlic mixture. Stir gently to combine. Taste to adjust seasoning. Spoon into prepared casserole and bake for 30 minutes. Sprinkle garnishes over top and serve immediately.

NOTE: Other herbs, such as sweet marjoram or thyme, may be substituted for tarragon. This dish may be prepared ahead and then baked just before serving.

CABBAGE AND NOODLES

yield 4 - 6 servings

A lighter version of the traditional Old World family dish. Amounts are not critical; therefore, this may be prepared for 1 or 2 servings or large family-size portions. Leftovers may be reheated in microwave.

1 small head cabbage*
1½ cups dry noodles
2 tablespoons butter or margarine
½ cup chicken broth
ground pepper, to taste
Paprika for garnish (optional)

Shred cabbage. Cook and drain noodles according to package instructions.

In Dutch oven or large frying pan melt butter over medium-high heat. Add shredded cabbage. Stir-fry until cabbage "wilts down" and butter is absorbed, about 5 minutes.

Add ½ cup chicken broth and drained noodles. Reduce heat to simmer. Cook about 5 minutes more, or until most of the broth has been absorbed.

Add ground pepper to taste; sprinkle with a little paprika, if desired. Serve hot.

*Quick-cooking is the secret to a sweeter taste and no lingering cabbage odor.

NOTE: Ingredients which may be added include 1 teaspoon crushed caraway seed, ½ cup shredded carrot, ¼ cup chopped onion or ½ cup chopped cooked ham.

LINGUINI IN HERB GARDEN SAUCE

yield 4 servings

Fresh picked herbs and a garden-ripe tomato create this tasty sauce for pasta.

12 ounces linguini, cooked and drained
½ cup butter
2 tablespoons minced parsley
2 tablespoon minced basil leaves
1 tablespoon minced rosemary leaves
2 teaspoons minced marjoram leaves
2 small sage leaves, minced
1 cup light cream, divided
1 large ripe tomato, peeled and chopped
freshly ground pepper

Over low heat melt butter in a saucepan that will be large enough to hold the cooked linguini. Add the herbs and chopped tomato. Let simmer in the butter for 3 minutes. Stir in ¼ cup of the cream to heat, but not boil.

Add cooked linguini and remaining cream. Toss to coat. Allow to remain over low heat until linguini is thoroughly reheated; then place in a serving dish. Add freshly ground pepper and serve immediately.

COUNTRY STYLE PASTA

3 slices lean bacon
1 medium onion, chopped
¼ pound fresh mushrooms, sliced
2 ripe tomatoes (medium size), peeled and chopped
½ teaspoon crushed marjoram
¼ cup sliced black olives
salt and pepper, to taste
16 ounces pasta shells, cooked and drained
¼ cup butter
½ cup grated Parmesan cheese, divided
½ cup grated Fontinella cheese, divided

Cut bacon crosswise into thin slices. Place in a frying pan and cook until beginning to crisp. Add onions and mushrooms. Cook until soft. Stir in chopped tomato and marjoram. Simmer for 10 minutes. Add the black olives and simmer for 5 more minutes. Season with salt and pepper.

Place hot cooked pasta in a serving bowl, add the sauce, butter, and half of the cheeses. Toss until well mixed. Sprinkle remaining cheese on top of each serving.

CREAMY PASTA SAUCES

Two sauces to use with easy pasta dishes.

UNCOOKED CREAMY PASTA SAUCE   yield 2½ cups

Prepare 30 minutes before serving. This sauce should be served at room temperature.

2 cups low-fat cottage cheese
½ cup low-fat milk
¼ teaspoon garlic powder
¼ teaspoon white pepper
⅛ teaspoon grated nutmeg
¼ cup grated Parmesan cheese
(additional milk to thin sauce, if necessary)

Place cottage cheese and ½ cup milk in food processor work bowl (or food blender). Process until creamy-smooth, about 1 minute. Add remaining ingredients. Process for 10 seconds. Let stand in work bowl for 30 minutes to reach room temperature. If necessary, thin with about ½ cup milk just before serving.

This recipe makes enough for 8 ounces of cooked fettucine.

COOKED CREAMY PASTA SAUCE   yield about 2 cups

2 tablespoons margarine
2 tablespoons all-purpose flour
1½ cups low-fat milk
¼ teaspoon white pepper
⅛ teaspoon grated nutmeg
¼ cup white wine
1 tablespoon lemon juice
⅓ cup grated Parmesan cheese

Garnish: fresh chopped parsley and additional Parmesan cheese

In small sauce pan over medium heat melt margarine; whisk in flour and let cook about 2 minutes. Gradually add milk, whisking until smooth. Add pepper and nutmeg. Cook until slightly thickened. Stir in wine, lemon juice and Parmesan cheese until blended.

Keep warm over very low heat until ready to serve.

Beverages

The knot is a sixteenth century garden form developed in England whose interest derives not from color but from pattern. Interlaced herbs kept closely clipped produce a structured beauty that compensated for England's lack of variety in its native flowers. The knot is further embellished by five old millstones.

LACED WITH LAVENDER PUNCH

yield 15 - 20 servings

A special champagne punch for a June party. Fresh lavender is required for the syrup, which may be made several days before serving.

2 cups lavender syrup
2 bottles dry champagne, chilled
1 quart club soda, chilled

Combine ingredients in a punch bowl. Serve over ice. May be decorated with fresh flowers.

LAVENDER SYRUP

1 cup, packed, fresh lavender blossoms and stems
2 cups sugar
2 cups water
⅓ cup blueberry syrup (commercial brand or homemade)

Wash lavender and pat dry. Cut the stems into small pieces.

Place ingredients in a saucepan and bring just to a boil. Remove from heat immediately. Stir until sugar is dissolved. Cool to room temperature. Let steep for several hours before straining into a glass jar. Refrigerate until ready to use.

GREAT THYME COOLER

yield 20 - 25 servings

Fresh lemon thyme is preferable. French or English thyme would also be satisfactory. Allow 2 days for the thyme to permeate the wine.

750 ml bottle white wine (Rhine, Chablis or Sauterne)
5 sprigs lemon thyme (about 6 inches long)
2 quarts sparkling soda (such as Sprite)

Garnish: If in bloom, float purple violets in the punch bowl. Or create small ice rings with tiny sprigs of thyme and violets.

Two days before serving: Wash thyme and pat dry. Lightly bruise the thyme leaves and place sprigs in the bottle. Recap and let wine stand for 2 days.

When ready to serve, place ice rings (if using) in punch bowl. Strain wine over ice into punchbowl and discard thyme sprigs. Add sparkling soda.

NOTE: For a special occasion surround the punch bowl tray with tiny bouquets of thyme and violets tied with lavender ribbons.

ROSEMARY RHUBARB SHRUB

yield 12 - 15 servings

Tender springtime rhubarb is preferred for this unusual beverage with a delicate rosy tint.

8 cups rhubarb, cut in 1-inch pieces
6 cups water
2 tablespoons dried rosemary
2 cups sugar, or to taste
1 quart sparkling club soda

Tie the dried rosemary in a paper coffee filter. Place rhubarb, rosemary and water in a large stainless steel saucepan. Bring to a boil. Reduce heat to simmer and cook until rhubarb is soft, about 20 minutes.

Discard rosemary bag. Strain rhubarb through sieve or colander to make about 1 quart of liquid. Add sugar to warm rhubarb juice and stir until dissolved. Chill until ready to serve.

To serve place rhubarb juice in a tall pitcher or punch bowl. Add club soda. Serve over ice.

STRAWBERRY GAZPACHO CUP

yield 12 - 15 servings

This is an elegant and refreshing fruit cup for a special party. Make the thickened fruit syrup a day or two ahead.

¼ cup granulated sugar
¼ cup cornstarch
4 cups cranberry-apple juice
4 cups fresh strawberries, washed, stems removed
2 cups white wine

Garnish: Select an assortment of chopped fresh fruits such as green grapes, kiwi, strawberries, honeydew melon, orange sections and cantaloupe to place in individual bowls.

Combine sugar and cornstarch in saucepan. Gradually stir in juice until cornstarch is dissolved. Bring to a boil over medium heat, stirring constantly until mixture is clear and thickened. Remove from heat. Pour into container. Chill.

When ready to serve, process fresh strawberries in electric blender until liquified. Add liquid strawberries and wine to chilled fruit syrup. Ladle into serving bowls. Let guests select their choice of chopped, fresh fruit toppings.

THE ROSE BOWL

yield 20 - 25 servings

A delightful beverage for a special occasion.

2 cups rose petal syrup
8 cups pink champagne or white zinfandel wine
1 2-litre bottle club soda

Combine ingredients over ice in a punch bowl. For a special touch float a few fresh rose petals in the punch.

ROSE PETAL SYRUP

The secret to this fragrant pink syrup is to gather petals from old-fashioned roses, the highly scented roses which bloom only in June. Hybrid roses will not create the desired essence. Be sure to gather petals only from unsprayed rose bushes.

2 cups water
2 cups sugar
4 cups rose petals

In a saucepan bring water and sugar to a boil and cook until sugar is dissolved. Remove from heat. Add rose petals and stir until all petals are wet. Slightly crush the petals while stirring. Cover pan and allow to cool. Strain rose petals and discard. Store syrup in a glass jar. Syrup may also be frozen.

APRICOT SLUSH

yield 1 gallon

1 (16-ounce) can frozen orange juice concentrate, thawed
1 (12-ounce) can frozen lemonade concentrate, thawed
2 cups double-strength brewed tea
6 cups water
750 ml bottle apricot brandy
1 quart 7-Up, chilled

Combine all ingredients, except 7-Up, in a gallon container and blend thoroughly. Transfer to quart-size containers for freezing. (Freezer-proof glass canning jars would be convenient.) Allow 1-inch expansion room at top of each container. Freeze overnight or until ready to serve.

Let container stand at room temperature until slush can easily be spooned into brandy glasses or dessert cups. Pour chilled 7-Up over slush and serve.

ROSE GERANIUM FRUIT FIZZ

yield 15 - 20 servings

Fresh leaves are required for this beverage.

2 cups rose geranium leaves, washed
4 cups cold water

In a saucepan place leaves and water. Bring just to a boil, but do not allow to boil. Remove from heat and let cool. Strain into a large glass jar. Discard leaves.

Add: **1 cup sugar**
8 cups cranapple juice
4 cups orange juice
2-liter bottle lemon-lime soda (such as 7-Up)

Serve over ice.

FRUIT CORDIALS

yield 2 quarts

Raspberry is a favorite. Other fresh fruits may also be used.

1 quart red raspberries, washed (fresh or frozen)
4 cups granulated sugar
1 (750 ml) bottle vodka

Place ingredients in a *glass* gallon jar with a lid. Stir until sugar is dissolved. Cover with lid and let age for at least 3 months. Occasionally give the jar a gentle shake to redistribute fruit.

When ready to use, strain through paper coffee filters into glass decanters.

NOTE: The "tipsy" fruit makes a fine topping for ice cream, pound cake and other desserts.

SHARE A SMOOTHIE

yield 4 - 6 servings

Select favorite yogurt flavors for this creamy, cool drink.

1 (8-ounce) carton fruit-flavored yogurt
1 (6-ounce) can frozen orange juice concentrate, undiluted
2 cups milk
ice cubes

In electric blender place half of the yogurt and orange juice concentrate, plus 1¼ cups of the milk. Add ice cubes (about 4 or 5) to bring ingredients to 3-cup marking level on blender container.

Process until smooth and creamy. Pour into pitcher then repeat with remaining ingredients. Serve immediately.

FRESH ICED MINT TEA FOR A CROWD

yield 20 - 25 servings

Use both stems and leaves for this strong mint tea concentrate. It is good alone over ice or mixed with fruit juices or alcoholic beverages as a punch. May be diluted with ginger ale, 7-Up or a similar soft drink.

2 quarts, packed, fresh mint, washed
5 quarts cold water

Place mint in an 8 or 10-quart stainless steel pan and add cold water. Over high heat just bring to a boil, but do not boil. Remove from heat and steep until cool. Strain into containers. Discard mint.

NOTE: Borage flowers are attractive garnish for mint teas and other cooling drinks. Violets, when in bloom, also add a special touch.

MINTED LEMON COOLER

yield 6 servings

This is a good way to use leftover mint tea.

1 cup fresh lemon juice
1¼ cup sugar
4 cups strong mint tea

Combine ingredients. Refrigerate until chilled. Serve over ice. Decorate with fresh mint leaves, if desired.

MINTED LEMON SHRUB: Add 1 cup light rum to the recipe and serve over ice.

MARY, MARY

yield 6 - 8 servings

1 (46-ounce) can vegetable-tomato juice
⅓ cup dry mint flakes, powdered
1 teaspoon sugar
1 tablespoon lemon juice

Combine ingredients in a saucepan. Over medium heat bring to a simmer for 5 minutes for flavors to blend. Serve hot or chilled.

GROWN-UP BROWN COW

yield 4 servings

4 tablespoons chocolate liqueur (such as Vandermint)
4 tablespoons chocolate syrup
3 to 4 cans club soda, chilled
1 pint vanilla ice cream
1 pint chocolate ice cream

Garnish: Whipped cream and fresh mint sprigs

Use 4 tall glasses, ice tea spoons and drinking straws. In each glass combine 1 tablespoon each of chocolate liqueur and chocolate syrup. Fill each glass about half full with club soda. Add scoops of vanilla and chocolate ice cream. Add more club soda to fill the glass. Top each serving with whipped cream and a sprig of mint.

CAFE SCHOKOLADE

yield 6 - 8 servings

The street cafes of old Vienna inspired the creation of this dessert coffee. Freeze the coffee ice cubes a day ahead.

6-8 cups double-strength brewed coffee.
Cool and pour into ice cube trays. Freeze until solid.

6-8 cups double-strength brewed coffee, chilled (additional)
½ cup chocolate syrup
½ pint whipping cream, whipped

Garnish: Ground cinnamon

Use tall parfait or Pilsener glasses.

To serve, half fill each glass with chilled coffee. Stir in 2 tablespoons chocolate syrup per glass. Add 2 coffee ice cubes per glass. Top each serving with a dollop of whipped cream. Sprinkle with cinnamon. Serve immediately.

GLÖGG

A spicy-warm beverage traditionally offered during the winter holiday season. This is a member's family recipe from Sweden.

One week before the Glögg is to be served, combine spices, fresh ginger and ¼ cup of the vodka in a covered glass container. Let stand at room temperature.

7 whole cardamom (use only the seeds; remove and discard husks)
4 whole cloves
2 cinnamon sticks (2-inch pieces)
1 slice fresh ginger (¼-inch thick)
¼ cup vodka

3½ cups Burgundy wine
¼ cup vodka (additional)
¼ cup sugar (more may be added to taste)

¼ cup raisins
¼ cup blanched almonds

When ready to serve, drain vodka from spice mixture. In a stainless steel pan combine spiced vodka, Burgundy, the additional vodka and sugar. Cover pan and warm over *low heat*. Make sure mixture does not boil.

To serve, place several raisins and almonds in each cup. Ladle warmed Glögg into cup. Serve warm.

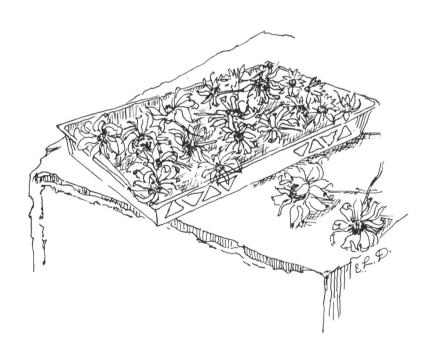

HARVEST HEAT

yield 16 - 20 servings

4 cups water
1 cup packed brown sugar
2 tablespoons dried orange peel, slivered
6 sticks cinnamon (3-inch pieces)

Place the following spices in coffee filter and secure with string to form a spice bag:

4 teaspoons whole cloves
2 teaspoons whole allspice
2 teaspoons coriander seed
½ teaspoon ground nutmeg

1 gallon apple cider
1 cup orange juice
⅓ cup lemon juice
2 cups rum (optional)

In a 5-quart saucepan place water, sugar, dried orange peel, cinnamon sticks and spice bag. Bring to a boil; then reduce heat to simmer for 20 minutes. Remove spice bag.

Add cider, orange juice, lemon juice and rum (if using). Allow to heat through. Serve warm.

WASSAIL

This sprightly holiday punch may be prepared a day ahead of serving.

6 small baking apples (use unwaxed apples)
1 cup packed brown sugar
1 cup water
2 tablespoons cognac (optional)
1 cup water (additional)

Place the following spices in coffee filter and secure with string to form spice bag:
   6-inch cinnamon stick, broken in pieces
   1 teaspoon whole allspice, crushed
   6 whole cloves

6 cups apple cider
2 cups cranberry juice
1 (46-ounce) can unsweetened pineapple juice
1 (12-ounce) can frozen orange juice concentrate
1 (6-ounce) can frozen pink lemonade concentrate

Preheat oven to 350°F. Lightly oil a 1½ quart casserole.

Wash apples and place in casserole. Do not peel or core. In a small saucepan combine brown sugar and water. Over medium heat bring to a boil, stir to dissolve sugar, and simmer for 5 minutes. Stir in cognac. Pour syrup over apples and bake for 35 minutes. Lift apples out of syrup with slotted spoon and set aside.

In a 5-quart saucepan place syrup from apples, the additional cup of water, spice bag, along with remaining ingredients. Simmer for 15 minutes or until heated through.

When ready to serve, transfer hot Wassail to a large heat-proof punch bowl. Float the baked apples for decoration.

NOTE: Clove-studded orange slices may also be floated in the Wassail Bowl.

HERBAL TEAS FROM YOUR GARDEN

HERBAL TEAS are soothing as well as refreshing. Herbs and flowers may be combined to create tea blends to suit the taste. Plants suitable for teas include:

HERBS AND PARTS USED	BEST TIME TO HARVEST
Basil, leaves (Spicy Globe, bush basil)	July-August
Bergamot flowers, leaves	June-August
Chamomile flowers (see note)	June
Elder flowers	June
Lemon balm leaves	June-August
Lemon thyme leaves	June-August
Lemon verbena leaves	June-September
Lemon geranium leaves (Rober's lemon rose)	August-September
Linden flowers, leaves	May-June
Mints, leaves (apple, Blue Mountain, orange, orange bergamot, peppermint, spearmint)	May-August
Lavender flowers	June-July
Rose geranium leaves	August-September
Rosemary leaves	August-September
Rosebuds	June-September
Rose petals (old-fashion fragrant)	June
Raspberry and strawberry leaves	Before flowering
Sweet woodruff leaves, flowers	May

NOTE: Use caution with chamomile: If a person is allergic to ragweed, then it would be wise to avoid herbal teas containing chamomile flowers for a similar reaction might result. This is unfortunate because chamomile makes a soothing herbal tea and has been used for centuries.

FRESH HERBAL TEAS

The ideal herbal tea is made with fresh herbs, cut directly from the garden. Cut one sprig per cup of one variety or use a combination of herbs. Wash the sprigs and pat dry. Rinse out the teapot with boiling water. Then place herb sprigs in the warm teapot. Pour fresh boiling water over the herbs. Cover teapot with a tea cozy and steep up to 20 minutes. The longer brewing brings out more flavor. Herbal teas will be a pale green color.

It is necessary to rely on a harvest of dried herbs during the winter months when most fresh herbs are not available.

HARVESTING AND DRYING HERBS FOR TEAS

1. Be sure that sprays and pesticides have not been used.

2. Pick plant materials on a sunny day, ideally after two consecutive days of sunshine. The flavor will be stronger.

3. Discover the prime time for each plant. Usually this is just before flowers form. When herb flowers are used, pick them in bud or early bloom.

4. Immediately after picking, wash plant material in lukewarm water. Use a large container filled with water. Change water three to four times for thorough cleaning. When clean, place herbs in a terry towel and gently pat dry.

5. Dry herbs on screens in an area away from light and where air circulates. Dry until *crisp.*

6. Before drying scented geranium or large basil leaves, use scissors to remove the large center vein in each leaf.

7. Strip dried leaves from stems before storing. To ensure evenly dried leaves, place in a shallow pan and put in a warm oven (150°) for up to 10 minutes. Keep oven door slightly open.

8. To create tea blends, rub the leaves through a coarse sieve. A food processor may also be used to crumble herb leaves. Use quick on/off pulses to achieve uniformity. Guard against over-processing or powdering the leaves.

9. Store material in glass jars, tightly capped, in a dark, cool cupboard. Label and date the containers. Refresh supply each year.

NOTE: Follow these same steps for harvesting and drying herbs for culinary uses.

DRIED HERBAL TEA BLENDS

UNE TISANE FRANCAISE BLEND   yield 3½ cups dried

The Western Reserve Herb Society has been creating this classic blend since 1981. The lavender blossoms bestow a certain peaceful quality. It is a soothing tea to sip after dinner or just before bedtime.

2 cups crushed lemon balm leaves
1 cup crushed mint leaves
½ cup dried lavender blossoms

Combine dried ingredients. Store in airtight container.

HOT TISANE FRANCAISE   yield 6 servings

3 tablespoons tea blend
6 cups boiling water

Place tea blend in a paper coffee filter. Tie with string to form bag. Place in a scalded teapot. Add boiling water. Cover pot with tea cozy and let steep for 20 minutes.

GOOD BEE TEA BLEND   yield 4 cups dried

The scarlet petals of bergamot combined with lemon verbena create a pleasant, rich-tasting tea. The color will be rosy red.

2 cups red bergamot flower petals, dried
2 cups dried crushed lemon verbena leaves

Combine dried material. Store in airtight container.

HOT GOOD BEE TEA   yield 6 servings

3 tablespoons tea blend
6 cups boiling water

Place tea blend in paper coffee filter. Tie with string to form bag. Place in scalded teapot. Add boiling water. Cover pot with tea cozy and let steep for 20 minutes.

LONGING-TO-BE-LEAN TEA BLEND

yield 8 cups dried

This dessert tea was created in 1983. the aroma of orange and vanilla reminds one of forbidden desserts. The combination of finely chopped vanilla bean and Spicy Globe basil is an interesting flavor.

2 cups crushed orange bergamot mint
1 cup crushed Blue Mountain mint*
2½ cups crushed Spicy Globe basil (bush basil)
2 cups dried chopped orange peel
10-12 vanilla beans

The vanilla beans must be finely chopped, then dried, before adding to the other dried ingredients.

Combine dried ingredients. Store in airtight containers.

*Blue Mountain mint is a highly aromatic peppermint.

HOT LONGING-TO-BE-LEAN TEA

yield 6 servings

3 tablespoons tea blend
6 cups boiling water

Place tea blend in paper coffee filter. Tie with string to form bag. Place in scalded teapot. Add boiling water. Cover pot with tea cozy and let steep for 20 minutes.

LOVE OF LEMON TEA BLEND

yield 4½ cups dried

A delicately scented tea which has been a favorite since it was created by WRHS members in 1979.

1 cup crushed lemon verbena leaves
1 cup crushed lemon balm leaves
1 cup crushed lemon-scented geranium leaves
  (such as Rober's Lemon Rose)
1 cup crushed lemon thyme leaves
3 tablespoons dried lemon rind pieces
1 generous tablespoon dried calendula petals

Combine dried ingredients. Store in airtight container.

HOT LOVE OF LEMON TEA

yield 6 servings

3 tablespoons tea blend
6 cups boiling water

Place tea blend in paper coffee filter. Tie with string to form bag. Place in scalded teapot. Add boiling water. Cover pot with tea cozy and let steep for 20 minutes.

APPLE CINNAMINT TEA BLEND

yield 4 cups dried

*Save apple peel from **unwaxed** red apples to dry for tea blends.*

3 cups apple mint leaves, crushed
½ cup dried apple peel, broken into small pieces
½ cup coarsely cracked cinnamon sticks (about 4-inch sticks)

Combine dried ingredients. Store in airtight container.

HOT APPLE CINNAMINT TEA

yield 6 servings

3 tablespoons tea blend
6 cups boiling water

Place the tea blend in a paper coffee filter. Tie with string to form bag. Place in scalded teapot. Add boiling water. Cover pot with tea cozy and let steep for 20 minutes.

APPLE DAZZLE COOLER

yield 6 servings

4 cups brewed Apple Cinnamint tea, cooled
1 cup apple cider or apple juice
1 cup sparkling soda

Combine ingredients and serve over ice.

TWIN ROSE TEA BLEND

yield 6½ cups dried

Black tea and cloves are combined with dried rose petals and rose geranium, creating an aromatic blend to serve hot or as a rosy, clove scented punch.

3 cups crushed dried Rober's Lemon Rose geranium leaves
2 cups black tea leaves
⅓ cup whole cloves
1½ cups dried rose petals

Combine dried ingredients. Store in airtight container.

HOT TWIN ROSE TEA

yield 6 servings

3 tablespoons tea blend
6 cups boiling water

Place tea blend in paper coffee filter. Tie with string to form bag. Place in scalded teapot. Add boiling water. Cover with tea cozy and steep for 15-20 minutes.

TWIN ROSE TEA PUNCH

yield 20-25 servings

4 cups cold water
¼ cup tea blend
2 tablespoons sugar
2 quarts ginger ale (or 7-Up)

In a saucepan combine water, tea blend (use paper coffee filter to form tea bag), and sugar. Bring water just to a boil. Turn off heat and steep until cool.

When ready to serve, strain tea into punch bowl over ice. Add choice of carbonated beverage.

TWIN ROSE WINE COOLER: Prepare tea as directed for punch. Add a light white wine in place of carbonated beverage. Serve chilled.

Breads

The medicinal garden, a charming area, is a favorite of students and faculty from the area's nearby hospitals. These interesting plants have medicinal properties attributed to them from ancient times.

NO KNEAD REFRIGERATOR BREAD

yield 2 loaves

A sweet dough with a water base which allows yeast action to continue for up to 5 days while chilled. This recipe has been in a family collection for over 70 years. It has been adapted slightly for electric mixer method.

2 packages active dry yeast
1 teaspoon granulated sugar
¼ cup warm water (110° to 115°)
1¾ cups boiling water
2 tablespoons butter or margarine
½ cup granulated sugar
1 teaspoon salt
2 eggs, slightly beaten
8 cups all-purpose flour, spoon lightly into measuring cup

Soften yeast in warmed water, stir in sugar to dissolve and let stand until mixture is foamy.

Place boiling water in large electric mixing bowl. Add butter and allow to melt slightly before stirring in sugar and salt. When cooled to 120° (test with instant-read or candy thermometer), stir in yeast mixture and beat in eggs until blended.

Add 4 cups of flour and beat on medium speed for 5 minutes. Change to dough hook and gradually beat in remaining 4 cups of flour until thoroughly incorporated.

Transfer dough to large greased bowl. Turn dough over to grease top or spray top lightly with vegetable oil spray. Cover with waxed paper and a kitchen towel. Let rise in a warm place until doubled in bulk.

Punch down dough and turn out onto lightly floured surface. At this point dough may be divided into portions for chilling. Use lightly greased covered containers or plastic bags for storing dough in refrigerator.

About 2 hours before serving time place dough on floured work surface. Allow to rest for 30 minutes before shaping into rolls or loaves. Place in greased baking pans. Cover and let rise until nearly doubled in bulk.

Preheat oven to 400°F. Bake rolls for 10 to 15 minutes and loaves for 15 to 20 minutes, or until the loaf sounds hollow when tapped. Remove from pans to cool on racks.

BLUE RIBBON EGG BREAD

9 x 5 x 3-inch bread pans

This basic recipe produces a tender loaf with good keeping qualities and may be used for a variety of breads and rolls.

1 package active dry yeast
¼ cup warm water (110° to 115°)
¼ teaspoon sugar
¼ teaspoon ground ginger

¾ cup skim milk
5 tablespoons vegetable oil
4 to 4½ cups all-purpose flour
2 teaspoons salt
⅓ cup granulated sugar
2 eggs, slightly beaten

In a small bowl soften yeast in ¼ cup warm water, add sugar and ginger, stir to dissolve, and let stand until mixture is foamy.

In small saucepan warm milk and oil (120° to 130°).

Combine 1½ cups flour, salt and sugar in a large electric mixing bowl. Stir in warmed milk and oil, yeast mixture and beaten eggs. Blend at low speed until flour is moistened. Beat 3 minutes on medium speed.

Change to dough hook and continue beating, adding ½ cup of flour at a time until dough begins to ball-up around dough hook. May not require entire amount of flour. Beat dough at medium speed for 7 to 10 minutes, or until texture is smooth and elastic.

Place dough in a large well-greased bowl, turning to grease all sides. Cover and let rise in warm place until doubled in bulk, 1 to 1½ hours.

Punch dough down. Turn out onto floured work surface. Let dough rest 5 minutes. Knead for several turns, then divide into 2 loaves and place in greased 9 x 5 x 3-inch loaf pans. Cover and let rise again until almost doubled in bulk, 45 minutes to 1 hour.

Preheat oven to 375°F. Bake loaves for 35 to 40 minutes, or until crust is golden brown and bread pulls away from sides of pan. Bottom crust should sound hollow when tapped. Remove bread from pans and cool on racks.

NOTE: For a shiny, golden crust, brush tops of loaves with egg yolk glaze just before baking. Combine 1 slightly beaten egg yolk with 1 teaspoon water. Brush gently over top of bread.

In place of egg glaze, brush crusts with melted butter as soon as removed from oven.

66

VARIATIONS:

* * *

CINNAMON-RAISIN BREAD: 1 recipe Blue Ribbon Egg Bread. Add 1½ teaspoons ground cinnamon to the flour, salt and sugar mixture. Mix in 1½ cups raisins after first 5 minutes of kneading. Bake as directed. If desired, frost with a confectioners' sugar frosting as suggested for Holiday Fruit Bread.

* * *

HOLIDAY FRUIT BREAD: 1 recipe Blue Ribbon Egg Bread.

1 cup candied fruit
1 tablespoon all-purpose flour
1½ teaspoons ground cardamom
⅓ cup slivered almonds
egg yolk glaze

Coarsely chop candied fruit. Place in a small bowl and coat with 1 tablespoon flour. Set aside.

Mix dough as directed. Add ground cardamom to flour, salt and sugar. Proceed with mixing directions. Add candied fruit after 5 minutes of kneading. Continue to knead until dough is smooth.

After first rising, divide dough into 3 equal portions. Roll and shape each portion into a strand, 15-inches long. Place strands on a greased cookie sheet and braid to form a long loaf.

Brush with egg yolk glaze. Sprinkle with slivered almonds and press them *lightly* into dough. Cover and let rise until doubled in bulk. Bake in preheated 350°F. oven for 30 minutes or until golden brown. Place on rack to cool. Prepare frosting.

FROSTING:

1 cup confectioners' sugar
1 teaspoon vanilla extract
3 teaspoons orange juice
2 tablespoons softened butter

Combine ingredients in mixing bowl and beat until smooth. Spread over top of bread while still slightly warm.

BASIC WHITE BREAD

This will produce a fine-textured loaf. An herb bread is among the variations from this good basic recipe.

2 packages dry active yeast
½ cup warm water (110° to 115°)
½ teaspoon sugar
¼ teaspoon ground ginger

1 cup water
½ cup milk
4 tablespoons butter or margarine

2 tablespoons sugar
2 teaspoons salt
5 to 6½ cups all-purpose flour

In a small bowl soften yeast in warmed water, add sugar and ginger, stir to dissolve, and let stand until mixture is foamy.

In a small saucepan heat water, milk and butter, 120° to 130°F. Butter need not melt completely.

Combine sugar, salt and 2 cups of flour in large electric mixer bowl. Add warmed liquids. Beat on low speed until flour is moistened. Add yeast mixture and beat for 5 minutes on medium speed.

Change to dough hook. Begin adding ½ cup of flour at a time and continue beating until dough is smooth and elastic. Turn out onto floured work surface. Let rest for 5 minutes. Knead for several turns to break up bubbles in dough. Place dough in a large greased bowl, turn to coat all sides. Cover and let rise in warm place until nearly double in bulk, about 1 hour.

Punch dough down. Turn out onto floured work surface. Cover with towel and let rest 10 minutes; then knead for several turns. Divide dough into 2 equal portions and shape into loaves. Place in greased loaf pans, cover and set in warm place for second rising, about 40 minutes, or until nearly doubled in bulk.

Preheat oven to 375°F. Bake loaves for 35 to 40 minutes, or until crust is golden brown. Bottom crust should sound hollow when tapped. Remove loaves from pans to cool on rack.

VARIATIONS:

* * *

HERB BREAD: 1 recipe Basic White Bread. With first addition of flour add 2 teaspoons crushed sage, 2 teaspoons crushed rosemary, 2 teaspoons celery seed, 1 teaspoon crushed thyme, and ½ teaspoon ground nutmeg. Continue mixing and bake as directed. (Experiment with other herb combinations.)

* * *

CHEESE BREAD: 1 recipe Basic White Bread. Add 2 cups grated sharp cheddar cheese after dough has been kneaded for 5 minutes. Continue mixing and bake as directed.

* * *

WHOLE WHEAT BREAD: 1 recipe Basic White Bread. Substitute 1 cup cracked wheat and 2 cups whole wheat flour for the listed amount of all-purpose flour. Whole grain flours require more time to absorb moisture than all-white flours. After first mixing allow dough to rest for 30 minutes *before* kneading. Continue to follow recipe instructions and bake as directed.

* * *

BUTTER CRUST BREAD: 1 recipe Basic White Bread. Shape dough into loaves and place in prepared loaf pans. With a very sharp knife or razor blade, cut an 8-inch slash along top of dough. Drizzle 2 tablespoons melted butter into slash. Let dough rise and bake as directed.

* * *

BREADSTICKS: 1 recipe Basic White Bread. Use a 1-pound portion of the dough. Divide the dough into 15 to 18 pieces. On floured work surface roll each piece into 10-inch long stick. Place on lightly greased cookie sheet. Bake plain or brush with egg glaze and sprinkle with sesame, poppy or caraway seeds. Cover and let rise in warm place for 20 minutes. Bake in preheated 400°F. oven for 15 minutes, or until golden brown. Cool on racks.

* * *

TO FREEZE BREAD DOUGH: 1 recipe Basic White Bread. After mixing divide dough into 2 equal portions. Flatten each portion into a 6-inch disc. Place disc in a lightly-floured 1 gallon plastic freezer bag, 1 portion per bag. Seal bag, allowing enough extra space for dough to raise slightly. Label and date bag for freezing up to one month.

TO THAW FROZEN BREAD DOUGH: Place frozen wrapped dough in refrigerator overnight, or let stand at room temperature until soft enough to work with, about 4 hours.

TO BAKE: After dough has thawed and is pliable, shape into loaves or rolls. Place in greased pans. Cover and let rise until nearly doubled; bake as directed.

BRIOCHE

Here is a simplified version of the traditional French buttery-rich rolls with the topknots.

NOTE: Dough must be refrigerated overnight. The mixing method differs from other yeast doughs. A heavy-duty mixer simplifies the process.

1 package active dry yeast
¼ cup warmed water (110° to 115°)
¼ teaspoon sugar

½ cup warmed milk (120° to 130°)
½ cup (1 stick) butter, softened
¼ cup sugar
1 teaspoon salt

3 large eggs
3½ cups bread flour (or all-purpose)

2 tablespoons melted butter for brushing tops of rolls

Soften yeast in warmed water, stir in sugar, and let stand until mixture is foamy.

In large mixer bowl, cream the butter until fluffy. Add sugar and salt. Beat on medium speed 1 minute.

Add yeast mixture and warmed milk. Beat on medium speed 2 minutes.

Add one egg at a time, beating thoroughly after each addition.

Add flour and beat on low speed to incorporate, then beat on medium speed for 2 minutes.

Cover bowl with plastic wrap. Let dough rise in warm place until doubled in bulk, about 2 hours.

With an *oiled* wooden spoon stir down the dough. At this stage the dough will be very sticky.

Place dough hook on mixer and beat dough at medium speed for 2 minutes.

Cover bowl with foil, press around edge for tight seal. Refrigerate overnight.

NOTE: Dough can remain in refrigerator until you are ready to bake the rolls. Plan accordingly for hot dinner rolls. After rolls are formed, second rising takes about 1 hour. Baking time is about 20 minutes. Brioche may also be baked a day ahead and reheated in oven.

BRIOCHE (Continued)

After dough has chilled overnight, beat down with mixing spoon.

Grease muffin cups, 2¼-inch size, or custard cups.

Turn dough out onto a lightly floured work surface. Cut dough into 2 pieces, one section about ¾ the size of the other.

Roll the largest section into a long tube. With a sharp knife cut into 20 pieces. Form into smooth balls. Place in greased muffin cups.

Roll smaller portion of dough into long tube. Cut into 20 pieces. Form small balls. (These will create the topknots.)

Make an indentation in center of each larger ball. Brush one side of each small ball *lightly* with water and press moistened side into the indentation.

Lightly oil one side of a sheet of waxed paper. Place oiled side over the formed rolls. Cover with a cloth. Let rolls rise in a warm place, about 1 hour, or until doubled in size.

Preheat oven to 375°F.

Lightly brush each topknot with melted butter. Bake rolls for 20 to 25 minutes, or until tops are golden brown.

* * *

VARIATIONS:

Add 2 tablespoons finely grated orange rind to creamed mixture after eggs have been incorporated. Continue with baking instructions.

OR mix ½ cup sugar with 1 teaspoon ground cinnamon. Place a teaspoonful in each greased muffin cup. Shake to distribute around bottom and sides. Form rolls and place in sugared cups. Place several slivered almonds on top of each roll. Dust with cinnamon-sugar. Bake as directed.

BERRY OAT BREAD

The wheat berries and cracked wheat add crunch to the crust. Multi-grain breads make fine toast.

**½ cup wheat berries
water to cover**

**2 packages dry yeast
½ cup warm water (110° to 115°)
¼ teaspoon sugar**

**1½ cups rolled oats
½ cup cracked wheat
3 tablespoons margarine or salad oil
2 cups boiling water**

**½ cup molasses
2 teaspoons salt
5½ to 6 cups all-purpose flour**

2 tablespoons melted butter for brushing tops of baked loaves

In a small saucepan cover wheat berries in cold water. Soak overnight. The next morning bring to a low boil and cook until berries are tender, about 60 minutes. Cooking water may be drained and combined with amount of liquid given in recipe.

For better texture, slightly chop wheat berries.

BERRY OAT BREAD (Continued)

In a small bowl soften yeast in warmed water, stir in sugar to dissolve, and let stand until bubbles form.

In a large mixing bowl place rolled oats, cracked wheat and margarine. Add boiling water. Stir to combine. Let soak for 20 minutes. *Temperature of water should cool to 120° to 130° before adding yeast mixture.*

Stir in chopped wheat berries, yeast mixture, molasses, salt and 3 cups flour. Mix for 3 minutes then let rest for 30 minutes.

Beat for 5 minutes with heavy-duty mixer. Change to dough hook. Add remaining flour in small amounts and continue beating on medium speed until dough is elastic, about 10 minutes. This dough will be slightly sticky.

Turn out onto floured work surface. Let rest for 5 minutes. Knead by hand for several turns to release bubbles.

Place dough in a large well-oiled bowl. Turn to coat all sides. Cover and let rise in warm place for about 1 hour, or until almost doubled in bulk.

Punch down the dough. Turn out on lightly floured work surface, and let rest for 5 minutes. Knead several times; then divide into 2 portions. Form loaves and place in well-greased loaf pans. Cover and let rise for about 1 hour.

Preheat oven to 375°F. Bake loaves 40 to 45 minutes or until loaves sound hollow when tapped. When top of loaves begin to brown, cover loosely with foil to prevent over-browning.

Turn loaves out on to racks. Brush tops with melted butter. This bread will be easier to slice if allowed to cool for 30 minutes.

SWEDISH LIMPA

This version is flavored with anise seed and a finely ground orange.

1 whole orange (medium size)

1 package active dry yeast
¼ cup warm water (110° to 115°)
¼ teaspoon sugar

1½ cups warm water (120°to 130°)
2 tablespoons butter
1 teaspoons salt

½ cup packed brown sugar
½ cup unsulphured molasses
2 teaspoons crushed anise seed
3 to 3½ cups bread flour (or all-purpose flour)
2 cups medium rye flour

Cut orange in half, remove any seeds. Cut into quarters and grind to a fine texture in food processor (rind included). Set aside.

In a small bowl soften yeast in warm water. Stir in sugar and let stand until mixture is foamy.

Place water, butter and salt in a small saucepan and heat to 120° to 130°.

In large electric mixer bowl place brown sugar, molasses and anise seed. Pour heated liquid over mixture; stir to combine. Add 1 cup of bread flour. Beat on low speed until flour is moistened. Add grated orange, yeast mixture, and 2 cups rye flour. Switch to medium speed and beat dough for 3 minutes.

Change to dough hook. Add remaining bread flour (small amounts at a time) and continue beating until dough is smooth and glossy, about 7 to 10 minutes.

Place dough in a large greased bowl, turning to grease all sides. Cover and let rise in a warm place until doubled in bulk. Punch dough down and let rise again until doubled. Punch down once more and divide into 2 portions. On a lightly floured surface shape each portion into a round loaf about 8 inches in diameter. Place on greased baking sheets. Cover and let rise until doubled in size.

Preheat oven to 375°F. Bake loaves for 40 to 45 minutes, or until loaves sound hollow when tapped. Place on racks to cool.

NOTE: Dough may be shaped for baking in 2 greased 9 x 5 x 2½ loaf pans.

CHILI BREADSTICKS

yield 20 breadsticks

A heavy-duty food processor and fast-acting yeast will have these ready before the chili, (or may be mixed by hand).

1¾ to 2¼ cups all-purpose flour
1 cup yellow corn meal
¼ cup sugar
½ teaspoon salt
¼ teaspoon cumin
1 teaspoon crushed oregano
½ teaspoon chili powder
1 package fast-acting dry yeast
¼ cup cold butter or margarine, cut in pieces
1 cup warm water (120°to 130°)

¼ cup melted butter (additional)
2-3 tablespoons corn meal (additional)

In food processor with metal blade place 1¼ cups flour. Add remaining dry in-gredients, including yeast. Pulse on/off to combine. Add the pieces of butter, and pulse to a crumbly mixture, about 5 seconds.

With machine running, pour warmed water through feed tube. Process until blended, about 20 seconds.

Add 1 cup flour and process another 10 seconds, or until stiff dough forms. May not need all of the flour.

Scrape dough into a well-greased bowl. Mold into a ball, turn to grease all sides. Cover with waxed paper and a kitchen towel. Let rise in a warm place until doubled in bulk. Fast-acting yeast will raise this amount of dough in about 15 minutes.

Preheat oven to 375°F. Grease 2 large cookie sheets. Sprinkle lightly with corn meal.

After dough has doubled in bulk, punch down; then turn out onto a lightly floured work surface. Divide into 20-24 pieces. Roll each piece into a 10-inch long stick. Place on cookie sheet, about 2-inches apart. Brush with extra melted but-ter and sprinkle with corn meal. Bake in preheated oven for 12 to 18 minutes, or until golden brown. Serve warm or cool on rack to reheat later.

COTTAGE CHEESE DILL BREAD

yield 2 loaves
8 x 4 x 2½-inch loaf pans

Dill and onion add special aroma and flavor to this easy bread.

1 package active dry yeast
¼ cup warm water (110°to 115°)
1 teaspoon sugar

1 cup cottage cheese
¼ cup water
¼ cup butter
3 tablespoons sugar
1 tablespoon minced onion
1 tablespoon crushed dillweed
1 teaspoon salt
¼ teaspoon baking soda
1 egg, slightly beaten
2½ to 3 cups bread flour (or all-purpose flour)
2 teaspoons melted butter (for brushing crusts after baking)

In a small bowl soften yeast in ¼ cup of warm water. Stir in sugar and let stand until mixture is foamy.

In a small saucepan combine cottage cheese, water, butter, sugar, onion, dillweed, and salt. Over low heat warm to 120° to 130°. Stir in baking soda and beaten egg.

In a large electric mixing bowl place 1½ cups flour. Add cottage cheese and yeast mixtures. Blend on low speed until flour is moistened. Blend in 1 more cup flour. Switch to medium speed and beat dough for 3 minutes.

Change to dough hook. Continue to beat on medium speed, adding small amounts of flour until dough begins to ball-up around dough hook. Beat for 7-10 minutes, or until texture is smooth.

Place dough in a large well-greased bowl, turning to grease all sides (or spray top of dough with vegetable oil spray). Cover with waxed paper and a kitchen towel. Let rise in a warm place until doubled in bulk. Punch dough down and let rise again.

Divide dough between 2 greased loaf pans. Cover and let rise until almost doubled in bulk. Preheat oven to 375°F. Bake loaves for 35 to 40 minutes or until crusts are golden brown and bottom crusts sound hollow when tapped. Place loaves on racks to cool. Brush melted butter over top crust of warm loaves.

FOCACCIA

This Italian flat bread is said to be the predecessor of pizza. The dough may be mixed by hand; however, a heavy-duty food processor seems easier.

1 package active dry yeast
¼ cup warm water (110° to 115°)
¼ teaspoon sugar
2 to 2½ cups all-purpose flour
¾ teaspoon sugar
1 teaspoon salt
3 tablespoons olive oil
½ cup warm water (115° to 120°)
3-4 tablespoons olive oil, additional
2 teaspoons coarse salt
½ cup finely chopped onion (optional)
1 tablespoon finely-minced fresh rosemary (optional)
3 tablespoons grated Parmesan cheese (optional)

In a small bowl soften yeast in ¼ cup warmed water, stir in sugar to dissolve. Let stand until mixture is foamy.

Measure flour, ¾ teaspoon sugar and salt into processor work bowl. Pulse on/off to combine. Add olive oil and process for 5 seconds.

Add yeast mixture. Process until well blended, about 5 seconds. With machine running, add warmed water *very slowly* through feed tube. Add just enough water to make dough ball up and clean sides of work bowl. Process for 20 seconds. Turn off processor and let dough rest for 2 minutes. If dough seems sticky, add a tablespoonful of flour, pulse on and off to incorporate.

Grease a jelly roll pan (10 x 15 x 1-inch), or a 14-inch pizza pan.

Turn dough out onto pan. Shape into ball. Cover with waxed paper and kitchen towel. Let stand for 10 minutes.

Dough may be kneaded once more by hand on a lightly floured work surface. This extra kneading will develop gluten for a crisper crust.

Preheat oven to 425°F.

Pat and stretch dough to cover pan. With small spoon make indentations about 1 inch apart over surface of dough. Brush with 3 or 4 tablespoons olive oil. Sprinkle lightly with coarse salt. At this stage dough may be baked plain, or arrange the chopped onion, rosemary and Parmesan cheese over the dough.

Let rise, uncovered, for 15 minutes. Bake in preheated oven for 12-15 minutes, or until golden brown.

NOTE: Focaccia dough may be turned into a quick pizza. Cover dough with favorite toppings and bake for 25 minutes. Sausage toppings should be pre-cooked before baking.

ROLLED-UP PIZZA BREAD

yield 2 14-inch long rolls

Commercial frozen bread dough may be used if this is more convenient.

2 pounds white bread dough

FILLING:

1 pound bulk Italian sausage, sweet or hot
1 green pepper, finely chopped
1 onion, finely chopped
2 teaspoons crushed oregano
½ pound pepperoni, coarsely chopped
½ pound mozzarella cheese, shredded
½ cup grated Parmesan cheeese
2 tablespoons melted butter (additional)

In a large frying pan fry sausage until lightly browned. Stir to break up into little pieces. Remove from pan with slotted spoon to a bowl lined with paper towels. Press out excess fat.

Drain fat from frying pan. Place green pepper and onion in same pan. Cook over low heat until tender, about 3 minutes. Stir to loosen any sausage bits remaining in pan.

In a bowl combine sausage, vegetables, oregano, pepperoni, and cheeses. Stir to blend and set aside.

Grease a large cookie sheet.

On a lightly floured work surface, roll out 1 portion of bread dough to a 12 x 14-inch rectangle. Spread with ½ of the meat filling. Starting with longer side, roll up. Pinch seam together and place seam side down on prepared baking sheet. Repeat with remaining dough and filling.

Cut slits across top of each roll, about 1-inch apart, using a sharp knife or razor blade. Cover with waxed paper and a kitchen towel. Let rise in a warm place for 30 minutes.

Preheat oven to 350°F. Bake rolls for 25-35 minutes, or until crust is golden brown. Remove from oven, brush melted butter over top crusts. Place loaves on rack to cool for about 10 minutes before cutting in slices. Serve warm.

BREAKFAST IN BREAD

yield 8 - 10 servings

An easy breakfast treat if you assemble the ingredients the night before.

1 pound white bread dough (may use frozen dough)
2 cups finely chopped cooked ham
¼ cup minced chives or green onions
2 tablespoons minced fresh parsley
1 cup shredded Gruyere or Monterey Jack cheese (about 4 ounces)
1 cup shredded sharp cheddar cheese (about 4 ounces)

If using frozen bread dough, allow ample time for thawing.

Chop ham and combine with chives and parsley. Refrigerate in covered container. Shred cheese and refrigerate in covered container.

In the morning allow bread dough to come to room temperature. Grease a jelly roll pan (10 x 15 x 1-inch), gently stretch and pat dough to cover bottom of pan.

Sprinkle ham and herb mixture over dough. Top with shredded cheese. Leave about an inch on all sides free of filling. Starting with longer side of dough, roll up firmly. Pinch seam along bottom and at each end to keep filling from seeping out.

Place seam side down on pan. Bread roll may be baked immediately or it may stand, covered with a towel, for 30 minutes.

Preheat oven to 350°F. Bake for 25-30 minutes, or until crust is golden brown. Remove from oven and place on rack. Let stand for 10 minutes before cutting into slices for serving.

QUICK BREADS

TEATIME ROSE GERANIUM BISCUITS   yield 8 - 10 biscuits

The fresh leaves of a rose-scented geranium are necessary for this easy recipe. Use large leaves from the top part of the plant.

Preheat oven to 400°F. Use an 8 or 9-inch cake pan or pie plate.

12 fresh rose geranium leaves
2 tablespoons butter
2 tablespoons brown sugar
1 tube ready-mix buttermilk biscuits, 8 to 10-biscuit size

Wash and dry rose geranium leaves. With scissors cut out heavy center vein of each leaf. Finely mince tender leaf portions.

Place butter in baking pan and let melt in oven, while preheating. Remove pan from oven and stir in brown sugar. Return pan to oven to melt brown sugar until it just begins to bubble. *Watch carefully.*

Remove from oven and sprinkle the minced rose geranium leaves over sugar mixture. Separate biscuits and place on top of mixture. Bake for 10 minutes or until lightly browned.

Remove pan from oven and invert over serving platter, sugary side up. Serve warm.

MILLSTREET BREAD   yield 2 loaves

This quick bread has the good flavor of a whole wheat yeast bread.

2 cups whole wheat flour
1 cup all-purpose flour
1 teaspoon salt
⅓ cup granulated sugar
2 teaspoons baking soda (dissolve in buttermilk)
2 cups buttermilk (shake carton before measuring)

Preheat oven to 350°F. Grease two 8 x 4 x 2-inch loaf pans.

In a large mixing bowl combine flours, salt and sugar. Dissolve baking soda in buttermilk and stir into dry ingredients until completely moistened.

Spoon into prepared loaf pans. (May also be shaped into mound on greased baking sheet.)

Bake for 50 minutes until golden brown, or until cake tester comes clean from center of loaves. Remove from oven and turn out onto rack to cool. This bread is also very good toasted.

BOSTON BROWN BREAD

yield 2 loaves

This moist and spicy bread is not steamed but baked in the oven. The recipe is adapted from one which appeared in our 1960 cookbook, MORE SAVORY SEASONING.

1½ cups all-purpose flour
⅔ cup sugar
1 teaspoon salt
½ teaspoon ground ginger
½ teaspoon ground allspice
2 teaspoons baking soda (dissolve in buttermilk)
2 cups buttermilk (shake carton before measuring)
1½ cups dark molasses
2 eggs, lightly beaten
2 cups whole-wheat flour
1½ cups raisins

Preheat oven to 350°F. Grease two 9 x 5 x 3-inch loaf pans.

In a large bowl combine flour, sugar, salt and spices.

Dissolve baking soda in buttermilk. Add to dry ingredients along with molasses and eggs. Stir until blended.

In separate bowl combine whole-wheat flour with raisins, toss to coat raisins. Stir into batter. Blend thoroughly but do not beat.

Pour batter into prepared pans and bake until well browned and sides shrink slightly from pans, about 40 minutes, or until center tests clean.

Remove from pans and place on rack to cool before slicing.

WELSH TEA CAKES

yield approximately 2 dozen

In Wales March 1 is St. David's Day which would be a good day to try these scone-type cakes with a cup of hot tea.

2 cups all-purpose flour
¼ teaspoon salt
½ cup sugar
2 teaspoons baking powder
1 teaspoon crushed lemon thyme (optional)
½ cup butter (1 stick)
2 eggs, slightly beaten
¼ cup milk
1 teaspoon lemon extract
½ cup dried currants
Confectioners' sugar for dusting baked cakes

In a large bowl combine dry ingredients. Cut in butter with pastry cutter until mixture is crumbly. (This step may be done quickly in food processor.)

In a small bowl whisk eggs, milk and lemon extract. Add to dry ingredients. Stir until flour mixture is just moistened. Fold in dried currants.

Turn dough out onto lightly-floured work surface. Roll or pat to ½-inch thickness. Use a 2-inch biscuit cutter to form cakes. Keep reforming dough until all is used.

Bake on a hot, greased griddle for about 5 to 8 minutes per side. Make sure cakes do not become too brown. Dust with powdered sugar. Serve hot.

QUICK HERB & CHEESE BISCUITS

yield 12 biscuits

*This food processor method is speedy. The trick is to process dough until flour is **just** moistened.*

1 cup all-purpose flour
1 cup pastry flour
1 tablespoon baking powder
½ teaspoon crushed sage
1 teaspoon caraway seed
½ teaspoon salt
¼ cup cold butter (½ a stick), cut in pieces
½ cup grated cheddar cheese
⅔ cup milk

Preheat oven to 425°F. Use *ungreased* cookie sheet or jelly roll pan.

In food processor with steel blade combine dry ingredients in work bowl. Whirl to blend. Add butter. Blend in on-off pulses for 15 seconds, or until mixture is crumbly.

Add grated cheese, pulse several times to blend.

With machine running, add milk through feed tube; blend for 7 seconds. DO NOT OVERMIX.

Turn dough out on a lightly-floured work surface. Gently press into a ½-inch thick circle. Use 2-inch, floured biscuit or cookie cutter to form biscuits. Place on ungreased baking sheet. Gently reform dough until all has been used.

Bake for 10 to 15 minutes, or until tops are light golden brown. Serve hot.

APRICOT BREAD

yield 2 small loaves

2 cups chopped dried apricots (about 12 ounces)
1 cup boiling water
¼ cup butter, softened
1½ cups granulated sugar
2 eggs, slightly beaten
3 cups all-purpose flour
2 teaspoons baking soda
½ teaspoon salt
¼ teaspoon ground cardamom
1 cup chopped nuts (pecans or walnuts)

Preheat oven to 325°F. Grease two 7 x 3 x 2-inch loaf pans, or one 9 x 5 x 2-inch pan.

Place chopped apricots in a small bowl and cover with boiling water. Let stand for 15 minutes.

In large mixing bowl cream butter and sugar until fluffy. Add eggs and beat thoroughly .

Sift dry ingredients and blend into creamed mixture. Stir to combine but do not beat.

Add *undrained* apricots and chopped nuts and stir to blend. Spoon into prepared pans and bake for 50 minutes or until centers test clean.

Turn loaves onto rack. Cool completely before slicing.

ORANGE BREAD

yield 1 loaf

This recipe is adapted from SAVORY SEASONING, published in 1957 by the Western Reserve Herb Society.

(Preparation of the orange rind may be done a day ahead of baking.)

2 large navel oranges
½ cup granulated sugar
½ cup water

Remove rind from the oranges. Cut in strips; then with a sharp knife, scrape off the white pithy layer. (Or remove rind with a sharp vegetable peeler.) Shred or finely chop the rind. Place in a small saucepan along with the sugar and water. Bring to a slow boil and cook until mixture is slightly thickened and the rind is tender, about 15 minutes. Remove pan from burner and allow mixture to cool. (Refrigerate if not using the same day.)

Bread batter ingredients:

2 cups all-purpose flour
4 teaspoons baking powder
½ teaspoon salt
½ cup granulated sugar
2 eggs
½ cup orange juice
3 tablespoons vegetable oil
½ cup chopped pecans (optional)

Generously grease an 8½ x 4½ x 2½-inch loaf pan.

Combine dry ingredients and sift together. Set aside.

In a large mixing bowl whisk eggs until frothy. Add orange juice and oil, whisk until blended. Stir in cooled orange rind mixture. Gradually stir in dry ingredients and mix until just moistened and well combined. Stir in chopped pecans, if using.

Spoon batter into prepared pan. *Let stand for 20 minutes.*

Preheat oven to 350°F. Bake bread for 50 to 60 minutes, or until center tests clean. (Test after 50 minutes of baking time.)

Remove bread from pan and place on rack. Allow bread to cool completely before slicing. May be served with a softened cream cheese spread. (This bread freezes well.)

CRANBERRY RELISH BREAD

yield 1 loaf

A food processor speeds up the work of chopping the nuts, orange and cranberries.

1 cup walnuts or pecans
2 cups all-purpose flour
1½ teaspoons baking powder
1 teaspoon salt
½ teaspoon ground cardamom
½ teaspoon baking soda
¼ cup cold butter or margarine cut into pieces

1 medium-size orange
2 tablespoons Grand Marnier
1½ cups cranberries, washed and sorted
1 cup sugar
1 egg, slightly beaten

In food processor work bowl with steel blade, coarse chop nuts. Remove to small bowl and set aside.

Measure dry ingredients into work bowl. Pulse on/off to mix. Add butter pieces and pulse on/off until mixture is crumbly. Scrape into a large mixing bowl. Set aside.

Cut orange (including rind) into quarters (remove seeds) and place in food processor. Pulse until finely chopped. Spoon into a measuring cup. Stir in Grand Marnier and enough water to equal 1 cup. Set aside.

Put cranberries in food processor work bowl and pulse until finely chopped. In a separate mixing bowl combine chopped orange mixture, cranberries and sugar. Stir in beaten egg and let stand for 30 minutes.

Preheat oven to 350°F. Grease a 9 x 5 x 3-inch loaf pan.

Pour orange-cranberry mixture into dry ingredients and stir until just moistened. Fold in chopped nuts.

Spoon batter into prepared pan. Bake for 50-60 minutes, or until center tests clean. Remove loaf to a rack and cool completely before slicing.

APPLE DATE MUFFINS

yield 12 muffins

1½ cups all-purpose flour
½ cup corn meal
½ cup granulated sugar
½ teaspoon ground cinnamon
¼ teaspoon ground cardamom
¾ teaspoon cream of tartar
½ teaspoon baking soda
½ teaspoon salt

1 large egg
¼ cup salad oil
¾ cup evaporated milk (undiluted)
½ cup chopped pecans
½ cup snipped dates
2 teaspoons all-purpose flour
½ cup chopped apple
Cinnamon-sugar for topping

Preheat oven to 425°F. Grease 12-cup muffin tin.

Sift dry ingredients and set aside.

In a large mixing bowl place egg, oil and milk. Beat with rotary beater or hand-mixer until frothy.

Gradually stir in dry ingredients and blend until just moistened. Do not beat.

Mix the pecans and dates with 2 teaspoons flour. Fold into batter along with the chopped apple.

Spoon into prepared muffin tin. Sprinkle cinnamon-sugar topping over each muffin. Bake for 15 minutes in preheated oven. Centers should test clean. Serve warm.

CINNAMON-SUGAR TOPPING:

4 tablespoons granulated sugar
1 teaspoon ground cinnamon

Combine ingredients in a small bowl and stir until blended. Store unused portion in a shaker-top container for other uses.

PRUNE MUFFINS

yield 12 muffins

2 cups all-purpose flour
1 tablespoon baking powder
½ teaspoon salt
¼ teaspoon ground nutmeg
1 egg
½ cup packed brown sugar
¼ cup salad oil
¾ cup milk
⅔ cup chopped pitted prunes
cinnamon-sugar topping*
¼ cup chopped walnuts for topping

Preheat oven to 400°F. Grease 12-cup muffin tin.

In a small bowl combine dry ingredients. Stir to blend.

In a large bowl lightly beat egg. Stir in sugar, oil and milk. Blend thoroughly.

Gradually stir in dry ingredients and mix until just moistened. Fold in chopped prunes.

Spoon batter into prepared muffin tin, filling about ⅔'s full. Sprinkle cinnamon-sugar topping and chopped nuts over batter.

Bake for 15 to 20 minutes or until centers test clean.

Remove muffins from baking pan and serve warm.

*CINNAMON-SUGAR

4 tablespoons granulated sugar
1 teaspoon ground cinnamon

Combine ingredients in a small bowl and stir to blend.

BROWN SUGAR PECAN MUFFINS
OR COFFEECAKE

yield 24 muffins or one
9 x 13 x 2-inch coffee cake

2 cups all-purpose flour
1½ cups packed brown sugar
¾ cup (1½ sticks) butter or margarine
⅔ cup finely chopped pecans
1 cup all-purpose flour (additional)
2 teaspoons baking powder
2 teaspoons ground nutmeg
1 teaspoon ground cinnamon
½ teaspoon salt
½ teaspoon baking soda (dissolve in buttermilk)
1 cup buttermilk (shake carton before measuring)
2 eggs, slightly beaten
1 cup chopped pecans (additional)
1 cup raisins (optional)

Preheat oven to 350°F. Generously butter muffin tin or baking pan.

In large mixing bowl (or food processor) place flour, brown sugar, and butter. Blend until mixture resembles coarse meal.

Remove ¾ cup for topping. Place in small bowl and stir in ⅔ cup finely chopped pecans. Set aside.

Add 1 cup additional flour to mixing bowl along with baking powder, nutmeg, cinnamon and salt. Blend thoroughly. (If using food processor, blend ingredients; then transfer to a larger mixing bowl.)

Dissolve baking soda in the buttermilk, combine with beaten egg and gradually blend into dry ingredients. Stir until just moistened. Fold in pecans and raisins.

FOR MUFFINS: Spoon batter into prepared muffin cups, filling ½ full. Sprinkle each muffin with 1½ teaspoons of reserved topping. Bake in preheated oven for 20-25 minutes or until centers test clean. Remove muffins from pans as soon as baked. Serve warm.

FOR COFFEECAKE: Spoon batter into prepared baking pan. Sprinkle reserved topping evenly over batter and lightly press in. Bake for 45-50 minutes or until center tests clean. Cool in pan. Cut into squares.

GRANDMA'S APPLE CORN BREAD

yield 6 - 8 servings

2 cups buttermilk (shake carton before measuring)
¼ cup sugar
1 teaspoon salt
2 cups yellow corn meal
2 tablespoons butter or margarine
2 eggs, lightly beaten
1 teaspoon baking soda
1 tablespoon cool water
1 cup chopped tart apple

Preheat oven to 400°F. Grease a 9 x 9 x 2-inch baking pan.

In the top of a double boiler pan combine buttermilk, sugar, salt, corn meal and butter. Place over boiling water and cook about 10 minutes. Stir frequently until mixture thickens, about 10 minutes.

Remove from hot water and allow to cool slightly before adding eggs. Dissolve baking soda in water before stirring into mixture. Add chopped apple and stir to blend.

Spoon into prepared pan and bake for 25 minutes or until center tests clean. Serve warm.

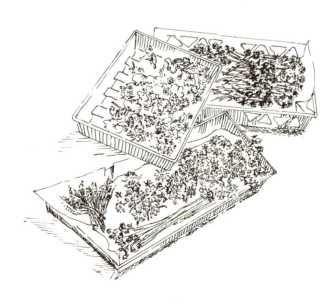

BLUE MAIZE MUFFINS

Stone-ground blue corn meal gives a subtle richness to these Southwestern-style muffins.

1 cup stone-ground blue cornmeal*
1 cup all-purpose flour
2 teaspoons baking powder
1 teaspoon cinnamon
½ teaspoon salt
1 cup milk, room temperature
1 egg, slightly beaten
¼ cup melted butter
4 tablespoons honey

Preheat oven to 400°F. Grease a 12-cup muffin tin.

Combine dry ingredients in small bowl. Stir to blend.

In a large bowl combine milk and eggs. Beat with whisk until frothy. Stir in melted butter and honey.

Gradually add dry ingredients and stir until just moistened. Spoon into prepared muffin cups, filling about ⅔'s full.

Bake for 20-25 minutes or until golden brown and centers test clean.

*Yellow or white stone-ground corn meal may be substituted.

CROUSTADES

Little boxes or cases made of bread to use in place of patty shells for serving creamed foods or appetizer fillings.

Croustades may be any size or shape you desire, limited only by the dimensions of the bread you have available. You need a pound loaf of *unsliced* bread of the fine texture (no large holes). If bread is extremely fresh, freeze before slicing.

Cut slices from 1 to 1½-inch thick. Remove crusts. Trim bread to desired shape: square, round, eliptical, etc. With small scissors or a small sharp knife carefully remove the center, leaving ½-inch on sides and bottom.

Brush croustades with melted butter. Place on cookie sheet and bake in preheated 375°F. oven until lightly browned.

May be used immediately or cooled and stored in airtight tin for several days. Rewarm croustades before filling.

CROUSTADE CHEESE PUFFS

yield 30 - 40 appetizers

May be prepared ahead and chilled until baking time.

1 pound loaf unsliced bread

Cut 1-inch slices and prepare small croustades, about 1½-inch in diameter. Cut in squares or circles. Do not bake before filling.

CHEESE PUFF FILLING:

1 (8-ounce) package cream cheese, softened
1 large egg, slightly beaten
1½ teaspoons baking powder
½ teaspoon onion salt
¼ cup melted butter, approximately
Paprika

Preheat oven to 350°F.

In mixing bowl combine cream cheese, egg, baking powder and onion salt. Beat until mixture is smooth and fluffy.

Dip tops of croustades in melted butter then fill with a generous teaspoon of cream cheese mixture. Place croustades on cookie sheet. Dust with paprika. Bake until cheese mixture is puffy and golden brown, about 15 minutes. Serve hot.

HERB CROUTONS

yield 3 cups

3 cups bread cubes
¼ cup melted butter
½ teaspoon onion powder
¼ teaspoon garlic powder
1 teaspoon crushed oregano
1 teaspoon crushed thyme
½ teaspoon rubbed sage
¼ teaspoon crushed rosemary

Preheat oven to 325°F. Use 9 x 13 x 2-inch baking pan.

Place bread cubes in baking pan and warm in oven for 10 minutes.

Melt butter in a small pan, stir in remaining ingredients.

Remove baking pan from oven and pour melted butter mixture over bread cubes. Toss to coat. Return to oven and bake until bread cubes are crisp, about 20 minutes. Stir once or twice and test frequently to prevent over-baking. Allow croutons to cool before storing in airtight container.

NOTE: Experiment with other herb combinations to suit the soup or salad the croutons will complement.

TOASTY MARMALADE ROLLS

yield 12 to 16 pieces

1 pound loaf fresh, sliced white bread (such as thin-sliced sandwich bread)
½ cup butter or margarine, softened
1 (18-ounce) jar orange marmalade (should not be too thick)

Preheat oven to 225°F. Use a large cookie sheet.

Trim crusts from bread. With rolling pin roll each slice between sheets of waxed paper until thin, but still flexible.

Spread one side of each slice with butter and then a generous layer of marmalade. Roll up firmly and secure with toothpick.

Place on cookie sheet. Bake in oven for 1 hour or until lightly golden. Remove toothpick from each roll. Return to oven and bake another 30 minutes. May be served warm or at room temperature. If prepared ahead, cool completely before storing in airtight container.

SESAME HERB TOASTS

yield about 64 pieces

2 tablespoons sesame seeds, toasted
½ pound butter or margarine, softened
1 tablespoon lemon juice
1 tablespoon crushed parsley
1 teaspoon crushed summer savory
1 teaspoon crushed marjoram
½ teaspoon crushed rosemary
1 teaspoon onion powder
1-pound loaf thin-sliced sandwich bread, whole wheat or white

Preheat oven to 350°F.

Spread sesame seeds in a pie pan and place in oven for 10 to 15 minutes; stir twice for even browning. When golden brown remove from oven and set aside. Watch carefully to prevent overbrowning.

Herbs may be crushed to a fine powder just before mixing with other ingredients.

In a mixing bowl cream softened butter with lemon juice until fluffy. Add herbs, onion powder and sesame seeds. Stir until combined.

Spread butter mixture on one side of each bread slice. Cut in strips or quarters. Place on cookie sheet and bake until light golden brown, about 15 minutes. May be served warm or at room temperature. If preparing for later use, cool completely before storing in airtight container.

DUTCH BABIES WITH APPLE TOPPING

yield 2 - 4 servings

This type of pancake puffs up grandly as it bakes; then begins to deflate when removed from oven. Plan to serve immediately.

APPLE TOPPING: (prepare first)

2 medium apples, peeled and chopped (about 2 cups)
¾ cup apple cider or apple juice
1 tablespoon cornstarch
¼ teaspoon cinnamon
¼ teaspoon nutmeg
Sugar, to taste

In a small saucepan dissolve cornstarch in cool apple cider. Stir in chopped apple and spices.

Cook over medium heat, stirring, until mixture thickens and apples are tender, about 5 minutes. Taste for sweetness. Add sugar to taste. Keep warm while preparing Dutch Babies.

DUTCH BABIES

Preheat oven to 425°F. Use a 10-inch frying pan with sloping sides and ovenproof handle.

2 eggs
½ cup milk
¼ teaspoon vanilla extract
½ cup all-purpose flour
¼ teaspoon baking powder
2 tablespoons sugar
¼ cup butter or margarine

In a mixing bowl, combine eggs, milk, and vanilla. Beat with rotary beater until frothy. Add flour, baking powder and sugar. Beat until well blended.

Put butter in frying pan and place in oven until butter is melted and bubbly. Watch carefully. Do not let butter brown.

Remove pan from oven, tilt to coat sides with butter. Pour batter into *hot* butter. Return to oven and bake until puffed and golden brown, about 20 minutes. Serve immediately with warm Apple Topping.

SCARBOROUGH WAFFLES

. . . parsley, sage, rosemary and thyme. These herb-flavored waffles may be topped with creamed turkey, chicken or seafood.

2 cups all-purpose flour
1 tablespoon baking powder
½ teaspoon salt
2 eggs, separated
6 tablespoons butter, melted
1¾ cups milk
1 tablespoon minced fresh parsley
½ teaspoon rubbed sage
½ teaspoon crushed thyme
¼ teaspoon finely crushed rosemary
1 tablespoon finely minced onion

Preheat waffle iron.

In a small bowl combine dry ingredients. Stir to blend.

In a large bowl whisk egg yolks until foamy. Add melted butter, milk, herbs and onion. Beat with rotary beater until well blended.

Stir in flour mixture until just moistened.

In a small mixing bowl beat egg whites with electric hand-mixer until stiff peaks form; then gently fold into waffle batter.

Pour batter onto waffle iron and bake according to manufacturer's directions.

If serving immediately, keep baked waffles warm in oven while preparing remaining batter.

Baked waffles may be frozen up to 1 month. Thaw frozen waffles, then reheat in oven (350°) for 10 minutes, or until crisp.

Cakes & Cookies

The stone watering trough came to the Herb Garden from a member's family farm. It is placed between the medicinal and culinary gardens and is shaded by an amelanchier tree.

CHOCOLATE NUT TORTE

yield 8 - 10 servings

¼ cup dry, white bread crumbs (1 slice, crusts removed)
1 cup unblanched almonds
4 ounces semisweet chocolate
½ cup butter, softened
⅔ cup granulated sugar
1 tablespoon cocoa powder
3 eggs, slightly beaten
grated rind of 1 orange
4 tablespoons Grand Marnier or Triple Sec

Preheat oven to 350°F. degrees. Butter one 9-inch round cake pan.

In food processor (or blender) process bread slice to fine crumb. Remove and set aside.

Place almonds in work bowl and process until finely chopped. Set aside.

Melt chocolate in small saucepan. Set aside to cool slightly.

In electric mixer bowl cream butter and sugar until fluffy; then beat in cocoa powder. Add eggs, one at a time, beating well after each addition. Beat in melted chocolate and grated orange rind. By hand, stir in bread crumbs and chopped almonds until thoroughly combined.

Pour into prepared cake pan. Bake for 25 minutes or until center tests clean. Do not overbake. Cool on rack for 30 minutes *before* removing torte from pan. Turn out onto serving platter. Sprinkle top with liqueur. Let torte cool completely before spreading with glaze.

CHOCOLATE GLAZE:

2 ounces semisweet chocolate
2 ounces unsweetened chocolate
¼ cup butter
2 teaspoons honey

Garnish: ½ cup toasted unblanced almond slices

Combine glaze ingredients in small saucepan. Over low heat, melt chocolate, stirring until smooth and thickened. Remove from burner. Let cool slightly before spreading over top and sides of torte. Garnish with toasted almonds. Chill before serving. Torte may be wrapped and frozen up to 1 month.

VARIATION: Spread a thin layer of raspberry jam over top of torte. Let jam set a few minutes; then spread chocolate glaze over top and sides of torte. For a special touch, arrange fresh raspberries on top of glaze. Chill before serving.

FRUIT-FILLED COFFEE CAKE

16 servings

¼ cup chopped walnuts
¼ cup dried chopped dates
¼ cup dried chopped apricots
1 tablespoon all-purpose flour
¾ cup (1½ sticks) butter or margarine, softened
1½ cups sugar
2 eggs, slightly beaten
1 teaspoon vanilla extract
2¼ cups all-purpose flour
2 teaspoons baking powder
½ teaspoon baking soda
½ teaspoon salt
1 cup dairy sour cream
2 tablespoons sugar
1 teaspoon cinnamon

Preheat oven to 350°F. degrees. Grease and flour a 9 x 13 x 2-inch baking pan (or a 10-inch tube pan).

In a small bowl combine walnuts, dates, apricots and 1 tablespoon of flour. Toss to coat and set aside.

In a large mixer bowl cream butter and sugar. Add eggs and vanilla, beating until light and fluffy.

Combine dry ingredients in small bowl and stir to blend. Gradually add to creamed mixture; then beat thoroughly to combine. Add sour cream and beat until smoothly blended. By hand, stir in walnuts and fruit mixture.

Spoon batter into prepared pan. Combine sugar and cinnamon and sprinkle evenly over batter. Bake for 45 minutes or until center tests clean.

If using tube pan, cool for 15 minutes before removing to serving plate. If baked in 9 x 13-inch pan, let cool in pan; then cut into squares.

GLAZED ORANGE CAKE

3 cups sifted *cake* flour
1 tablespoon baking powder
¼ teaspoon salt
1 cup butter, softened
2 cups granulated sugar
½ teaspoon vanilla extract
2 tablespoons grated orange rind
5 eggs, room temperature
¾ cup milk, room temperature

Preheat oven to 350°F. degrees. Grease a 10-inch tube pan.

Sift dry ingredients together. Set aside.

In large electric mixer bowl cream butter and sugar until fluffy. Beat in vanilla and orange rind. Add eggs, one at a time, beating well after each addition.

Gradually mix in dry ingredients and milk. Beat on medium speed for 2 minutes. Pour batter into prepared tube pan. Bake for 1 hour or until cake tester comes clean from center.

Cool to room temperature before removing cake from pan; then invert onto serving platter to spread with glaze.

ORANGE CAKE GLAZE:

¼ cup butter
⅔ cup granulated sugar
⅓ cup orange juice

Combine ingredients in a saucepan and cook, stirring continuously, over medium heat until sugar is dissolved; then pour slowly and evenly over cake. Let cake stand several hours before serving.

BUTTERMILK POUND CAKE
yield 2 loaves

Save one loaf for making our scented-geranium cake.

2¾ cups granulated sugar
1 cup butter (2 sticks), softened
6 eggs, separated
2 teaspoons vanilla
3 cups all-purpose flour
½ teaspoon salt
½ teaspoon ground nutmeg
¼ teaspoon baking soda, dissolved in
1 cup buttermilk (shake carton before measuring)

Preheat oven to 350°F. Grease two 9 x 5 x 3-inch loaf pans, dust with flour and shake out excess (may also be baked in 10-inch tube pan).

In large electric mixer bowl (4-quart minimum) cream sugar and butter. Add egg yolks, one at a time, beating well after each addition. Beat in vanilla.

Sift together flour, salt and nutmeg. Dissolve baking soda in buttermilk. Gradually add flour to creamed mixture, alternating with buttermilk; then beat on medium-high speed until batter is smooth.

In a clean bowl beat egg whites until stiff, but not dry. Gently fold into batter and spoon into prepared pans. Bake for 1 hour or until top is firm and center tests clean. Allow cakes to cool for 30 minutes in pans before removing. Place on racks to finish cooling.

NOTE: There will be about 9 cups of cake batter. Smaller size loaf pans may be used. Fill about two-thirds full and reduce baking time to about 40 minutes, or until centers test clean.

VARIATIONS: Pleasing Pelargonium Pound Cake (scented-geranium cake) is next in this section.

GINGERED POUND CAKE — For one loaf, measure out 4½ cups of batter into a separate bowl. Mix 1 tablespoon flour with ½ cup finely-diced candied ginger. Stir into batter and bake as directed.

APRICOT POUND CAKE — Snipped dried apricots may be substituted for candied ginger. Bake as directed.

PLEASING PELARGONIUM POUND CAKE

yield 6 - 8 servings

1 baked pound cake (9 x 5-inch loaf)
¼ cup brandy
20 fresh rose geranium leaves (approximately)

Wash geranium leaves and pat dry. With kitchen scissors remove stem and thick center vein from each leaf.

Place a cooled pound cake loaf on a large sheet of plastic wrap. With a pastry brush generously brush brandy onto one side of cake. Press on rose geraniums leaves to cover side of cake. Gently bruise the leaves while applying to cake. Repeat brushing on brandy and applying leaves to each side of loaf. Apply leaves immediately after brushing on brandy. The alcohol will absorb the rose flavor and hold it to the cake.

As soon as all sides are completed, tightly wrap the plastic around the cake and let stand at room temperature for 18-24 hours. When ready to serve, unwrap cake and discard leaves. Cut loaf into slices. The taste of the scented geranium will remain pronounced for about 2 days after unwrapping.

VARIATIONS: Use Triple Sec or Grand Marnier liqueur in place of brandy; then wrap in leaves of Rober's Lemon Rose geranium.

ALMOND CAKE

yield 10 - 12 servings

1 cup butter or margarine, softened
2 cups granulated sugar
3 teaspoons almond extract
4 eggs, slightly beaten
2 cups all-purpose flour
¼ teaspoon salt (optional)
⅓ cup slivered almonds
1 tablespoon sugar

Preheat oven to 350°F. degrees. Grease a 9 x 13 x 2-inch baking pan.

In electric mixer bowl cream butter and sugar until fluffy. Mix in almond extract. Add eggs, one at a time, beating well after each addition. Gradually beat in flour and salt until well blended.

Pour into prepared pan. Mix almonds with sugar; then distribute over top of batter. Bake for 30 minutes. DO NOT OVERBAKE. Let cake cool before cutting into squares. This cake is served without frosting. It is often used as a base for strawberry shortcake.

SPICY GINGERBREAD

This is adapted from the heritage recipe included in SAVORY SEASONING, Western Reserve Herb Society's first cookbook printed in 1957.

2 cups all-purpose flour
1 teaspoon ground cinnamon
1 teaspoon ground ginger
½ teaspoon ground cloves
¼ teaspoon ground nutmeg
½ teaspoon salt
1 egg
½ cup butter, softened
½ cup unsulphured molasses
½ cup granulated sugar
1 teaspoon baking soda
¾ cup, plus 2 tablespoons hot water

Preheat oven to 350°F. Generously grease a 9 x 9 x 2-inch baking pan.

Sift dry ingredients together and set aside.

In a large mixing bowl, slightly beat egg before stirring in butter, molasses, and sugar. Beat with a large spoon until thoroughly blended.

Dissolve baking soda in the hot water. Alternate adding liquid and dry ingredients to creamed mixture. Stir thoroughly after each addition.

Spoon batter into prepared pan and bake for 35 to 40 minutes, or until center tests clean. (Test after 35 minutes of baking time.) Cut into squares and serve warm with whipped cream or Orange Fluff Sauce.

ORANGE FLUFF SAUCE:

⅓ cup butter
2 teaspoons grated orange rind
¼ teaspoon salt
5 cups sifted confectioners' sugar
½ cup orange juice
1 tablespoon lemon juice

Cream butter, grated orange rind and salt. Gradually blend in sugar and fruit juices; then beat until light and fluffy. Spread over top of gingerbread.

CASSATA CAKE

This is a rich and easy version of the Sicilian dessert.

1 loaf pound cake, purchased or homemade
1 pound carton ricotta cheese
½ cup granulated sugar
⅓ cup milk or cream
2 tablespoons rose water
2 ounces semisweet chocolate, chopped
½ cup chopped toasted almonds
⅔ cup finely diced mixed candied fruit
2 tablespoons orange-flavored liqueur

Chill or freeze the pound cake for easier cutting. Slice into 2 or 3 horizontal layers, about ½-inch each. Set aside.

In food blender or processor place ricotta, sugar, milk and rose water. Process until creamy smooth. Spoon into a mixing bowl and stir in chopped chocolate, almonds and candied fruit. Cover and chill for an hour.

To fill, place a cake layer on serving platter. Spread with ½ of filling. Repeat with second layer. Place third layer on top of filling and brush with liqueur. Cover and return to refrigerator to chill before spreading with frosting.

CASSATA CAKE FROSTING:

2 tablespoons butter, softened
2 cups sifted confectioners' sugar
2 tablespoons cocoa powder
1 teaspoon almond extract
1 tablespoon sweet Marsala wine (or strong coffee)

Combine ingredients in mixing bowl and beat until smooth and of spreading consistency. If necessary, add a bit more wine or coffee. Spread frosting over top and sides of cake. Decorate with chocolate curls or pieces of candied fruit, if desired. Place several toothpicks halfway into top of cake to keep plastic wrap from sticking to frosting. Cover and chill for 12-24 hours before serving. Keep leftover cake refrigerated.

BLITZ TORTE

Two meringue-type layers form the basis for a variety of fresh fruit fillings.

½ cup butter, softened
1½ cups granulated sugar, divided
4 large eggs, separated (at room temperature)
1 cup cake flour
1 teaspoon baking soda
5 tablespoons milk
½ cup slivered almonds, divided

Preheat oven to 325°F. Line bottoms of 2 round 9-inch cake pans with waxed paper. Lightly oil with baking spray.

In a large mixing bowl cream butter with ½ cup of the sugar. Add egg yolks and beat until thick, about 3 minutes at medium speed.

Sift cake flour with baking soda. Gradually mix into batter along with milk and beat until well blended. Divide batter evenly between the two pans. Set aside.

In clean mixing bowl beat egg whites until foamy. Gradually beat in remaining 1 cup of sugar. Beat until stiff peaks form. Divide and spread evenly over batter in each pan. Sprinkle ¼ cup of almonds over each batter. Bake for 40 minutes or until meringue is golden in color. Do not allow to brown. Let meringues cool in pans before removing to serving plate.

Just before serving place filling between the layers. Use sliced fresh fruit such as strawberries or peaches with sweetened whipped cream and extra slices of fruit for garnish. Custard fillings may also be used.

ALMOND BONBONS

½ cup butter, softened
½ cup granulated sugar
½ teaspoon vanilla extract
¼ teaspoon salt
1¼ cups all-purpose flour

Preheat oven to 350°F. Butter a 9 x 13 x 2-inch baking pan.

In a large mixing bowl cream butter, sugar, vanilla and salt until light and fluffy. Gradually beat in flour until just combined. Spoon batter into prepared pan and press evenly over bottom of pan. Bake for 12 to 15 minutes or until edges begin to pull away from sides of pan. Remove from oven and spread with filling.

FILLING:

1 (7-ounce) roll of almond paste (or use 8-ounce can)
¼ cup granulated sugar
¼ cup butter, softened
2 eggs, slightly beaten
48 red candied cherries

In a mixing bowl cream almond paste, sugar and butter. Add eggs and beat thoroughly. Spread mixture evenly over cake base. Arrange cherries on filling in rows of 8, evenly spaced. Do not press cherries into filling. Return pan to oven and bake for 20 to 25 minutes. Remove from oven and allow to cool in the pan before covering with glaze.

GLAZE:

1 ounce (1 square) unsweetened chocolate
1 tablespoon butter
½ cup sifted confectioners' sugar
1 tablespoon milk
½ teaspoon vanilla extract

In a small saucepan over low heat melt chocolate and butter, stir until smooth. Remove pan from burner and stir in confectioners' sugar, milk and vanilla; then beat until well blended and smooth. Pour evenly over cooled bonbons. When glaze is set, cut into 48 pieces.

ALMOND OAT SQUARES

yield about 30 squares

½ cup, plus 2 tablespoons butter, melted
⅔ cup granulated sugar
1⅓ cups old-fashioned rolled oats
⅔ cup chopped almonds
½ cup semisweet chocolate chips

Preheat oven to 350°F. Use ungreased 9 x 9-inch baking pan.

In a large mixing bowl combine melted butter, sugar, oats and almonds. Stir until thoroughly blended. Spread mixture in ungreased pan. Bake for 20 minutes, or until top is lightly browned. Remove from oven. (The cookie crust will begin to firm up as it cools.)

Sprinkle chocolate chips over hot crust. When chocolate softens, spread evenly over top. Let stand for 10 minutes before cutting into squares. If squares are not cutting easily, return to oven for a few minutes to soften crust. Serve with ice cream for an easy dessert.

The squares may be wrapped and frozen up to 1 month.

SNAPPY GINGER COOKIES

yield about 5 dozen

2 cups all-purpose flour
½ teaspoon salt
2 teaspoons baking soda
1 teaspoon ground cinnamon
1 teaspoon ground ginger
⅔ cup cooking oil
1 cup granulated sugar
1 large egg, slightly beaten
¼ cup molasses
⅓ cup granulated sugar for coating cookies

Preheat oven to 350°F. Use ungreased cookie sheet.

Measure flour, salt, baking soda and spices into a bowl. Sift or stir to combine. Set aside.

In large mixing bowl combine oil and sugar. Add egg and beat thoroughly. Stir in molasses. Gradually beat in dry ingredients until well blended.

Place additional sugar in a small dish. Form a teaspoonful of dough into a ball (keep hands slightly moistened) and roll in sugar to coat. Place balls on prepared baking sheet about 3 inches apart. Bake for 15 minutes. Remove from baking sheet and cool on rack.

These cookies will keep well in a covered container.

LEMON CARAWAY COOKIES yield about 60 cookies

This recipe was included in the Herb Society's first cookbook, SAVORY SEASON-ING, published in 1957.

2½ cups cake flour
½ teaspoon salt
½ teaspoon baking soda
1 egg
1 cup granulated sugar
½ cup butter, softened
2 tablespoons lemon juice
1 teaspoon caraway seed, crushed

Sift dry ingredients and set aside.

In a large mixing bowl lightly beat egg. Gradually beat in sugar until mixture is fluffy; then beat in butter, lemon juice and crushed caraway seed. Stir in dry ingredients; then beat until well blended.

On sheets of waxed paper form cookie dough into rolls, 2 inches in diameter. Wrap and chill until firm. When ready to bake, preheat oven to 375°F. Lightly grease cookie sheets. Cut chilled dough into thin slices, place an inch apart on cookie sheet. Bake for 6-8 minutes, or until lightly browned. Remove from pan and cool on racks.

PEPPERMINTED BROWNIES yield about 16 bars

The recipe for peppermint sugar is in the Sweets and Sours section, see index.

⅓ cup butter or margarine
1 (1 ounce) square unsweetened chocolate
2 eggs
1 teaspoon vanilla extract
⅓ cup peppermint sugar
⅓ cup granulated sugar
⅔ cup all-purpose flour
½ teaspoon baking powder
¼ teaspoon salt
½ cup chopped pecans or walnuts

Preheat oven to 350°F. Grease an 8-inch square baking pan.

Place butter and chocolate in a 1½-quart saucepan. Over medium heat stir until chocolate is melted and smooth. Remove from burner to cool.

In a small bowl whisk eggs until frothy; then add to cooled chocolate mixture. Stir in vanilla and sugars. Beat with large spoon until well combined.

Mix together dry ingredients and nuts; then stir into chocolate mixture until blended. Spread batter in prepared pan and bake for 20-25 minutes. These are fudge-type brownies so do not overbake. Cool before cutting into squares.

PEANUT COOKIES

yield 4½ dozen

⅓ cup butter or margarine, softened
1 cup firmly packed brown sugar
1 teaspoon vanilla extract
1 egg, slightly beaten
1 tablespoon milk
1 cup all-purpose flour
¾ teaspoon baking powder
¾ teaspoon baking soda
¼ teaspoon salt
1¼ cups rolled oats
1 cup salted peanuts, chopped

Preheat oven to 375°F. Lightly grease cookie sheets.

Cream butter and sugar in mixing bowl. Add vanilla, egg and milk. Beat until light and fluffy.

Sift together dry ingredients; then gradually add to creamed mixture, beating thoroughly. Stir in rolled oats and chopped peanuts.

Use one generous teaspoonful of dough for each cookie. Lightly moisten hands to prevent dough from sticking to fingers. Form into small ball, place about 1½ inches apart on cookie sheet. Bake for about 8 minutes or until light golden brown. Remove from oven and let stand 1 minute before removing from pan. Allow cookies to cool completely before storing.

RAISIN OAT BARS

1 cup granulated sugar
3 tablespoons all-purpose flour
1½ cups raisins
1½ tablespoon minced fresh lemon thyme leaves (optional)
1 cup water

In a 1-quart saucepan combine sugar and flour, add raisins, thyme leaves (if using), and water. Bring to a boil. Reduce heat to simmer and cook for 3 minutes, stirring occasionally. Remove from heat and cool to room temperature. Prepare cookie base.

COOKIE BASE:

1 cup packed brown sugar
1¼ cups all-purpose flour
½ teaspoon baking soda
1¼ cups rolled oats (quick-cooking preferable)
¾ cup margarine
1 teaspoon vanilla
1 tablespoon water
½ teaspoon salt

Preheat oven to 350°F. Grease a 9 x 13 x 2-inch baking pan.

In a large mixing bowl combine brown sugar, flour, soda and rolled oats.

In a small saucepan melt margarine over low heat. Stir in vanilla, water and salt. Pour over dry ingredients and stir to blend.

Spread half of the cookie base in prepared pan. Spread raisin mixture over top of base. Sprinkle remaining base mixture over raisins. Press in gently. Bake for 30 minutes, or until top is lightly browned. Let cool before cutting into bars.

SUMMER COOKIES

Old-fashioned ice box cookies make summer baking easier.

3½ cups sifted all-purpose flour
1 teaspoon baking soda
1 teaspoon ground cinnamon
¼ teaspoon ground cardamom
¼ teaspoon salt
1 cup butter (2 sticks) softened
1 cup packed brown sugar
1 cup granulated sugar
2 large eggs, slightly beaten
1 teaspoon vanilla extract
1 tablespoons warm water
⅔ cup *finely* chopped nuts (walnuts or pecans)

Sift dry ingredients together and set aside.

In large mixing bowl cream butter and sugars until fluffy. Beat in eggs, vanilla and water until well blended. Gradually mix in dry ingredients; then stir in nuts until combined.

Place portions of dough on sheets of waxed paper. Shape into a roll about 2 inches in diameter. Wrap and refrigerate overnight. Dough must be chilled for easy slicing.

When ready to bake, preheat oven to 350°F. With sharp knife cut chilled dough into ¼-inch slices. Place 1½ inches apart on ungreased cookie sheet. Bake 10-15 minutes or until lightly browned.

Unbaked rolls of cookie dough may be wrapped and kept frozen up to six months.

LEFTOVER FRUITCAKE COOKIES

yield about 5 dozen

This is a tasty way to use up that last bit of fruitcake. Dried mixed fruit may take the place of fruitcake.

1 cup margarine (2 sticks), softened
1½ cups granulated sugar
2 large eggs, slightly beaten
1½ cups all-purpose flour
½ teaspoon salt
½ teaspoon *each:* ground cinnamon, nutmeg and allspice
½ teaspoon baking soda, dissolved in
1 tablespoon hot water
2 cups rolled oats
1½ cups coarsely chopped fruitcake*
½ cup chopped nuts (optional)

In large mixing bowl cream margarine and sugar. Add eggs and beat well.

Measure flour, salt and spices into a small bowl and stir with fork to combine. Gradually mix into creamed mixture. Dissolve baking soda in water and add to batter. Beat until well blended.

Stir in rolled oats, chopped fruitcake and nuts; mix until combined.

Chill dough for 2 hours. (Dough may also be frozen in portions for later use.)

When ready to bake, preheat oven to 350°F. Lightly grease cookie sheets.

Use a teaspoonful of dough for each cookie and drop 2 inches apart onto prepared pan. Bake for 10-12 minutes. Do not overbake. Place cookies on rack to cool. Store in covered container.

Substitute 1½ cups chopped dried mixed fruit for the fruitcake; or use 1½ cups coarsely chopped plum pudding to make this spicy moist cookie which keeps well.

ANZAC BISCUITS

yield about 52 cookies

This is a crisp little cookie that is popular in Australia and New Zealand.

1 cup rolled oats
1 cup unsweetened flaked coconut
1 cup all-purpose flour
1 cup granulated sugar
½ cup butter
1 tablespoon Lyle's Golden Syrup*
1 teaspoon baking soda
2 tablespoons hot water

Preheat oven to 325°F. Lightly grease cookie sheets.

Measure dry ingredients into large mixing bowl and set aside.

In a small saucepan melt butter with syrup. Dissolve baking soda in hot water; then stir into butter mixture. It will foam slightly. Remove from burner.

Make a well in center of dry ingredients and pour in butter mixture. With a large mixing spoon stir until well blended and dry ingredients are moistened.

Measure by rounded teaspoonful and place in a mound on prepared baking sheet. Bake until golden brown, about 12 minutes. Do not overbake. Remove from oven and allow cookies to cool a minute before removing to rack to cool. If using only one baking sheet, allow it to cool slightly before adding next batch of cookies.

*Lyle's Golden Syrup is available in specialty stores and most supermarkets. A light unsulfured molasses may be substituted.

112

Desserts & Pies

The culinary garden has been arranged for easy and close inspection of its plant material. The stepping stones, some of them old grindstones, are both decorative and practical.

HONEY LAVENDER ICE CREAM
yield 1 quart

Heavenly rich and delicately flavored with lavender blossoms.

½ cup granulated sugar
1½ teaspoons lavender flowers
1 cup whipping cream
2 cups half-and-half cream
6 egg yolks
3 tablespoons liquid honey

Garnish: (optional) For a special touch use candied violets or mint leaves.

Place sugar and lavender flowers in blender; run at high speed until lavender is pulverized and blended with sugar. Set aside.

In a 1½-quart saucepan heat the two creams to just below scalding point. Remove from heat.

In a medium-size bowl whisk egg yolks until smooth, but not foamy. Stir in lavender sugar. Whisk a small amount of hot cream mixture into egg yolks and sugar. Blend completely, then return mixture to saucepan. Cook over medium high heat, stirring constantly, until mixture coats spoon. Stir in honey and remove from burner.

Chill the mixture by placing pan in a bowl of ice water and whisk until mixture is cool. Overnight refrigeration will mellow the mixture, although it can be frozen immediately.

Pour the mixture into ice cream maker and freeze according to manufacturer's directions.

Scoop into serving dishes and garnish with candied violets or mint leaves, if desired.

FRUIT SLUSH
yield 10 - 12 servings

1 (12-ounce) can frozen orange juice concentrate
8 ripe bananas, diced
1 (20-ounce) can crushed pineapple
1 tablespoon minced fresh lemon thyme (optional)

Dilute orange juice with 3 cans of water according to package directions. Place in a large mixing bowl and stir in remaining ingredients.

Place in freezer unit and freeze until slushy, stirring several times. Spoon into freezer containers and return to freezer.

Before serving, let stand at room temperature for 20 minutes. Fruit slush may be frozen up to 1 month.

CANTALOUPE SORBET WITH MINT SAUCE
yield 6 servings

Recipes for sugar syrup and peppermint sugar are in Sweets and Sours section (see index). Both may be prepared ahead and stored until needed.

1 large ripe cantaloupe
1 cup sugar syrup

Garnish: fresh mint leaves or candied violets. (Instructions for making candied violets are in Sweets and Sours section, see index.)

Peel and seed cantaloupe. Cut into small chunks and puree in food blender or processor to make 2½ generous cups. Add enough sugar syrup to make 3 cups. Chill mixture; then place in ice cream freezer or sorbet machine. Freeze according to manufacturer's directions.

(Cantaloupe puree may also be frozen in freezer section of refrigerator. Stir several times to break up ice crystals. When frozen, place puree in covered container and freeze for up to 2 hours.)

MINT SAUCE:
1 tablespoon cornstarch
1 cup water
⅓ cup peppermint sugar
1 or 2 drops green food coloring

In a small saucepan dissolve cornstarch in cool water. Stir in sugar; then place over medium heat and stir until mixture thickens. Add a drop or 2 of green food coloring to enhance mint color.

Allow sauce to cool slightly; then strain through fine sieve to remove any peppermint leaf bits. Store in covered container in refrigerator. Will keep for 5 days or more.

To serve, place scoops of sorbet in dessert dishes and top with mint sauce. Garnish with fresh mint leaves or candied violets.

AUNT BAL'S FRESH FRUIT COBBLER yield 6 - 8 servings

This heritage recipe was printed in SAVORY SEASONING, the Herb Society's first cookbook published in 1957.

Preheat oven to 375°F. Grease a 12 x 8 x 2-inch baking dish.

3 cups sliced fresh peaches*

Place fruit in prepared baking dish and set aside. Prepare topping.

TOPPING:
½ cup granulated sugar
2 tablespoons softened butter
¼ teaspoon salt
2 teaspoons baking powder
1 cup all-purpose flour
½ cup milk plus 2 tablespoons

1 cup granulated sugar (additional)
½ cup water

In a mixing bowl, cream sugar and butter. Stir in dry ingredients and milk; blend thoroughly. Spread creamed mixture over fruit.

Sprinkle the additional 1 cup sugar over batter; then pour ½ cup water evenly over all.

Bake for 45 minutes. When done there will be a crunchy, sugary topping on cobbler. Serve at room temperature.

*Cobbler may be prepared with other fresh fruits: sweet or sour cherries, blueberries, sliced apples, plums or rhubarb.

APPLE CRISP

yield 6 - 8 servings

6 to 8 tart baking apples
1 tablespoon water
1 tablespoon lemon juice
1 cup packed brown sugar
½ cup (1 stick) butter or margarine
¾ cup all-purpose flour
1 teaspoon cinnamon
⅛ teaspoon salt

Preheat oven to 350°F. Butter a 12 x 8 x 2-inch baking dish.

Peel and core apples. Cut into thick slices and arrange in prepared baking dish. Sprinkle with water and lemon juice.

In mixing bowl (or food processor work bowl) place the remaining ingredients and blend until crumbly. Spread mixture evenly over apples. Bake for 45 minutes or until topping is crispy and golden brown. Serve warm with ice cream, if desired.

LEMON PUDDING CAKE

yield 6 - 8 servings

A cakelike layer covers the lemon pudding. This is a heritage recipe from a family cookbook.

2 eggs, separated
1 cup granulated sugar
3 tablespoons all-purpose flour
½ teaspoon salt
1 cup milk
juice of 1 lemon (about ¼ cup)
1 tablespoon butter, melted

Preheat oven to 300°F. Butter a 1-quart casserole.

In a large electric mixing bowl beat egg yolks until thick. Combine sugar, flour and salt. Gradually blend into egg mixture; then beat for 3 minutes on medium high speed. Beat in milk, lemon juice and butter.

In a clean mixing bowl beat egg whites until stiff peaks form; then fold into pudding mixture. Spoon into prepared baking dish. Bake 1 hour. Serve warm or chilled.

CREAMY FROZEN FRUIT

1 (8-ounce) package cream cheese, softened
⅔ cup granulated sugar
1 (20-ounce) can pineapple tidbits, well drained
1 (10-ounce) package frozen strawberries, thawed
½ cup chopped pecans or walnuts
1 cup whipping cream, whipped

Garnish: (optional) fresh mint sprigs, additional chopped nuts and chocolate sauce.

Line two loaf pans (9 x 5 x 3-inch) with plastic wrap. Use pieces long enough to overlap top of salad to serve as cover while freezing.

In a large bowl combine cream cheese and sugar. Beat until thoroughly blended.

In another bowl combine pineapple, strawberries, nuts, and bananas. Stir to combine.

Fold whipped cream into cheese and sugar mixture; then carefully stir in fruit mixture. Spoon into prepared pans. Cover and freeze until firm. (May be frozen up to 1 month.)

Before serving, remove pans from freezer and let stand for 10 minutes before cutting into slices. Serve on dessert plates with choice of garnish.

PEACHES AMARETTO OVER ICE CREAM

1 (16-ounce) can sliced peaches, drained
5 tablespoons Amaretto liqueur
1 teaspoon lemon juice
1 quart vanilla ice cream
½ chopped toasted almonds or pecans

Place drained peaches and Amaretto in food blend or processor. Whirl until peaches are pureed. Spoon mixture into a sauce pan and over medium heat bring to a simmer. Cook for 2 minutes and remove pan from burner. Stir in lemon juice. Allow to cool slightly; then place in covered container and chill.

To serve, place scoops of ice cream in serving dishes, top with peach sauce and garnish with almonds.

NOTE: In place of canned peaches use 5 or 6 fresh ripe peaches when available.

SPICED PRUNES IN PORT WINE

yield 4 servings

1 cup pitted prunes
1¼ cups water
1 3-inch stick cinnamon
3 whole cloves
¼ cup packed brown sugar
½ cup port wine (such as Tawny Port)

In a saucepan combine prunes, water and spices. Bring to a boil; then reduce heat to a simmer and cook until prunes are tender, about 15 minutes. Add brown sugar and stir until dissolved. Simmer for 5 minutes.

Remove from heat and stir in port wine. Transfer to glass bowl and let stand until cool. Remove cinnamon stick and cloves before serving. For a special dessert, serve with crackers and Camembert cheese.

PEARS IN RASPBERRY VINEGAR SYRUP

yield 4 servings

4 fresh, firm-ripe pears (such as Anjou)
3 cups water
1½ cups granulated sugar
4 tablespoons raspberry vinegar

Garnish: ½ cup fresh red raspberries

Peel and core pears, cut in half lengthwise. Set aside.

Combine water and sugar in saucepan. Bring to a boil, stirring until sugar dissolves. Add raspberry vinegar and boil for 3 minutes.

Place pears in syrup, reduce heat to a simmer. Cover pan and poach pears for 10 to 15 minutes. Do not overcook. Transfer pears and syrup to shallow glass dish. Cover and refrigerate until chilled.

To serve, place pear halves in dessert dishes, spoon over a small amount of syrup. Garnish with red raspberries.

PEARS IN BAY LEAF CUSTARD

yield 6 servings

6 firm-ripe pears (such as Anjou)
¾ cup granulated sugar
¾ cup water
1 slice lemon, quartered
red food coloring (optional)

Cut pears in half, core and peel. Set aside.

In a large frying pan combine sugar, water and lemon. Cook over medium-high heat, stirring until sugar dissolves and mixture is bubbly. Place pears, cut side down, in syrup. Cover and cook for 5 minutes or until pears are lightly glazed. Baste with syrup several times. Remove from heat.

Transfer pears to deep bowl. Add 1 or 2 drops of food coloring to syrup, if desired; then pour syrup over pears. Syrup should cover pears completely. Let cool to room temperature; then cover and refrigerate until chilled. Prepare custard sauce.

BAY LEAF CUSTARD SAUCE

1½ cups milk
2 bay leaves
2 egg yolks
3 tablespoons sugar

In the top of a double boiler place milk and bay leaves. Heat milk to scalding point, but do not allow to boil.

In a small mixing bowl combine egg yolks and sugar. Whisk until frothy.

Remove bay leaves from milk. Gradually whisk ½ cup of hot milk into egg mixture; then stir into milk in double boiler. Cook over hot (not boiling) water, stirring constantly until mixture thickens and coats spoon. Remove from heat to cool slightly. Cover and refrigerate until chilled.

To serve, drain chilled pears and place 2 halves in each serving dish. Pour sauce over each serving.

GRECIAN RICE PUDDING

yield 4 - 6 servings

1½ tablespoons cornstarch
⅓ cup granulated sugar
¼ teaspoon ground nutmeg
¼ teaspoon ground cardamom
3 eggs, slightly beaten
2 cups milk
1¾ cups *cooked* rice
1 teaspoon vanilla
2 tablespoons butter
⅔ cup raisins (optional)

In 2-quart saucepan mix cornstarch, sugar, and spices. Add beaten eggs and milk. Over medium heat bring to a slow boil, stirring constantly, until mixture thickens slightly.

Stir in cooked rice, vanilla and butter. Continue stirring and cook for 1 minute; then remove from heat. Stir in raisins, if using, and let stand for 5 minutes. May be served warm or chilled.

NOTE: ⅔ cup long-grain white rice cooked in 1⅔ cups boiling water will yield 1¾ cups cooked rice.

APRICOT MOUSSE

yield 6 servings

1 (17-ounce) can apricot halves (packed in syrup)
½ cup apricot nectar (approximately)
1 (6-ounce) package apricot-flavored gelatin
1½ cups boiling water
4 tablespoons apricot brandy
2 large egg whites
1 cup whipping cream, whipped

Garnish: semisweet chocolate curls

Drain juice from apricots into measuring cup. Add apricot nectar to equal 1 cup. Set aside.

Puree apricots in food blender or processor and set aside.

In a large bowl dissolve gelatin in boiling water. Stir in drained apricot juice and brandy. Chill until slightly thickened, about 30-45 minutes.

In clean bowl beat egg whites to stiff-peak stage. Fold in whipped cream and apricot puree; then gently stir into gelatin mixture. Pour into 6-cup mold or individual dessert dishes. Chill until firm. When ready to serve garnish with chocolate curls.

SPICED RHUBARB WHIP

yield 6 - 8 servings

4 cups fresh rhubarb, diced (about 6 stalks)
½ cup water
1¼ cups sugar
¼ teaspoon ground cardamom
¼ teaspoon ground allspice
2-3 drops red food coloring (optional)

2 envelopes unflavored gelatin (2 tablespoons)
½ cup cold water

1 cup whipping cream
1 teaspoon vanilla extract

In a 1-quart stainless saucepan, cook rhubarb with water, sugar, and spices until rhubarb is tender, about 8 minutes. Stir in red food coloring to achieve a rosy pink color.

Soften gelatin in ½ cup cold water. Add to hot mixture and stir until dissolved. Taste for sweetness; more sugar may be needed. Remove from burner and set aside to cool.

Whip the cream with the vanilla extract to soft-peak stage. Fold into cooled rhubarb mixture. Pour into serving bowl. Chill until firm.

VARIATION: Spiced Rhubarb Whip may be poured into a cooled, baked pie shell and chilled. Garnish with extra whipped cream, if desired.

ROSEMARY TANGERINE

8 tangerines
1 cup granulated sugar
2 cups water
2-inch piece vanilla bean
3 sprigs fresh rosemary (each 3 inches long)

Garnish: sour cream or lemon-flavored yogurt.

Peel tangerines, (remove white fibers) and break into segments. Set aside.

In a large frying pan combine sugar, water, vanilla bean and rosemary. Cook over medium-high heat, stirring until sugar dissolves. Let mixture cook at a low boil for about 5 minutes or until consistency of light syrup.

Place tangerine segments in syrup, cover pan and poach for 5 minutes. Remove from heat.

Remove vanilla bean and rosemary sprigs from syrup. Pour syrup and tangerines into a deep bowl. Syrup should cover tangerines. Cover and refrigerate until chilled.

To serve, transfer tangerine segments with slotted spoon to serving dishes. Add a small amount of syrup to each serving. Garnish with a dollop of sour cream or flavored yogurt.

SPICE DRIED FRUIT COMPOTE

4 cups water
1¼ cups granulated sugar
1 teaspoon ground cinnamon
½ teaspoon ground cardamom
2 lemon slices, ¼-inch thick
1 cup dried apricots
1 cup dried peaches
1 cup dried pears
½ cup dried apple slices
¼ cup toasted walnuts, coarsely chopped
¼ cup orange-flavored liqueur (or use fresh orange juice)

Combine water, sugar, spices and lemon slices in large saucepan. Bring to a boil over medium-high heat, stirring until sugar dissolves. Add dried fruit, reduce heat to simmer and cook until fruit is tender, about 25 minutes. Stir occasionally. With a slotted spoon transfer fruit to a bowl. Set aside.

Bring syrup to a rapid boil for 6 minutes, or until slightly thickened. Stir in nuts and liqueur (or orange juice) and pour over fruits. May be served warm or chilled.

BASIC PIE PASTRY

2 cups all-purpose flour
½ teaspoon salt
½ cup (1 stick) chilled butter or margarine
3 tablespoons vegetable shortening
⅓ cup ice water

In a mixing bowl combine flour, salt, butter (cut into pieces), and shortening. Cut in shortening with pastry cutter until mixture resembles coarse meal. (This step may be done quickly in a food processor; then follow processor instructions for completing the procedure.)

Sprinkle ice water over flour mixture and gently incorporate with a fork until dough begins to ball up. Turn out dough onto a sheet of waxed paper or plastic wrap. Pull the waxed paper up around the dough and gently press in any loose pieces of dough until a soft ball is formed. Divide into two equal portions. Chill for 30 minutes before rolling out.

For prebaked pie crust: On lightly floured work surface roll out dough to fit 9-inch pie pan. Ease dough, without stretching, into pan. Pat gently into place. Crimp edges. Prick sides of pie shell.

Place a 12-inch square of foil on top of pie dough. Fill with pie weights.* Pull up edges of foil so it is not touching crimped edge of dough.

Bake in preheated oven, 425°F., for 15 minutes. Remove from oven. Lift out foil with pie weights. Reduce oven temperature to 375°F. Return pie shell to oven and bake for another 5 to 10 minutes, or until bottom of crust is golden brown. Cool before adding precooked filling.

Pie weights may be purchased in kitchen specialty stores. These small pellets of aluminum can be used indefinitely.

PURELY PEACH PIE

Use very sweet, juicy-ripe peaches for this chilled pie.

1 9-inch pie crust, baked and cooled

8 large fresh ripe peaches
3 tablespoons cornstarch
3 tablespoons lemon juice (divided)
½ cup cold water
½ cup granulated sugar
1 tablespoon butter
3 tablespoons sugar (additional)

Garnish: 1 cup whipping cream or 1 quart frozen vanilla yogurt

Peel and slice 4 peaches. Place in food blender and puree. There should be 1½ cups puree.

In a saucepan combine cornstarch with 2 tablespoons lemon juice and cold water. Stir until smooth; then add pureed peaches. Cook over medium heat, stirring constantly, until mixture begins to bubble.

Taste for sweetness before adding sugar. Continue to stir until sugar is dissolved and mixture begins to thicken. Blend in butter and remove from heat. Cool to room temperature then chill in refrigerator for 30 minutes.

Peel and slice remaining peaches. Place in mixing bowl and sprinkle with remaining lemon juice and 3 tablespoons sugar. Toss to combine. Arrange peach slices in bottom of pie crust. Spread chilled puree over top. Refrigerate until ready to serve.

Garnish each serving with whipped cream or a scoop of frozen yogurt.

VARIATION: Use 1 pint fresh strawberries for puree. Orange juice may be used instead of lemon juice. Cook according to directions for peaches. Use about 3 pints of strawberries to fill pie crust.

BUTTERMILK PIE

This richly flavored custard-type pie was included in SAVORY SEASONING, the Western Resereve Herb Society's first cookbook printed in 1957.

1 cup granulated sugar
¼ teaspoon salt
3 tablespoons all-purpose flour
2 large eggs, separated
2 teaspoons vanilla extract
2 cups buttermilk (shake carton before measuring)
½ cup melted butter
½ teaspoon powder basil*
grated rind from ½ a lemon
1 unbaked 9-inch pie shell

Preheat oven to 425°F.

In a mixing bowl combine sugar, salt and flour. Lightly beat egg yolks and add to dry ingredients. Stir in vanilla, buttermilk, melted butter, powdered basil and lemon rind. Beat with a rotary beater until well blended.

In a clean mixing bowl beat egg whites until stiff peak stage. Fold into buttermilk mixture; then pour into pie shell. Bake for 10 minutes at 425°F. Reduce temperature to 325°and bake for 40 minutes or until center is firm. Test with knife. Top of pie should be a light golden color.

Crush basil leaves to a fine powder and then measure.

CHOCOLATE FLUFF PIE

yield 6 - 8 servings

Plan to bake the meringue crust on a day when the humidity is low. It will keep in an airtight container for up to 2 days.

MERINGUE PIE SHELL:

2 egg whites, at room temperature
⅛ teaspoon cream of tartar
½ cup granulated sugar
½ teaspoon vanilla extract
¼ cup chopped pecans, toasted.

Preheat oven to 275°F. Generously butter a 10-inch pie pan.

In electric mixer bowl beat egg whites with cream of tartar until frothy. Add sugar, a tablespoon at a time, and beat until smooth and glossy. Add vanilla and continue beating until stiff peak stage.

Spread meringue in prepared pan. Keep meringue from spreading on rim of pie pan. Sprinkle chopped nuts over bottom of meringue. Bake 1 hour. Cool completely before adding filling.

CHOCOLATE FLUFF FILLING:

1 cup semisweet chocolate chips
¼ cup hot water
1 cup whipping cream
1 tablespoon granulated sugar
1 teaspoon vanilla extract

Place chocolate chips in top of double boiler over hot water. Stir until melted. Add hot water and stir until mixture is smooth and thickened. Remove from heat and set aside to cool.

In mixing bowl beat whipping cream, sugar and vanilla until thick and soft peaks form. Gradually fold chocolate sauce into whipped cream. Spoon into meringue shell. Refrigerate for 3 hours or overnight.

PEANUT BUTTER PIE

1 9-inch pie crust, baked and cooled

PEANUT BUTTER CRUMBS:
⅔ cup confectioners' sugar
⅓ cup crunchy-style peanut butter

In a mixing bowl combine ingredients and stir with a fork until mixture resembles fine crumbs. Sprinkle half of the mixture in the bottom of pie crust. Reserve remaining crumbs for topping.

PIE FILLING:
⅓ cup sugar
1 tablespoon all-purpose flour
1 tablespoon cornstarch
2 egg yolks, slightly beaten
2 cups milk
1 tablespoon butter
1 teaspoon vanilla extract

Garnish: 1 cup whipping cream

Place sugar, flour and cornstarch in a saucepan. Stir in beaten egg yolks and mix until smoothly blended.

Place saucepan over medium heat and gradually add milk. Stir continuously until mixture thickens. Remove from burner and stir in butter and vanilla. Cool for 15 minutes before spooning into pie crust. Allow filling to cool for another 15 minutes before sprinkling with remaining peanut butter crumbs. Refrigerate until chilled.

Just before serving, whip cream until stiff; then spread over top of filling. Keep leftovers refrigerated.

CRUSTY COOKIE

This makes a good base for fresh strawberries and whipped cream. It may also be used as a pie crust for a chilled filling.

Preheat oven 325°F. Lightly grease a cookie sheet or 9 x 13-inch baking pan. For pie crust use 2 8-inch pie pans.

2 cups all-purpose flour
½ cup packed brown sugar
½ teaspoon ground cinnamon
1 cup (2 sticks) butter or margarine, softened
2 teaspoons grated lemon or orange rind (optional)

Place flour, brown sugar and cinnamon in mixing bowl and stir to combine. Blend in butter and citrus rind (if using) until mixture is thoroughly combined.

Scrape mixture onto prepared baking pan and press into a circle or rectangle ½ inch thick. Bake for 20-25 minutes or until lightly browned. Let cool; then cut into wedges or squares for shortcake base.

For pie crust: divide mixture between the prepared pie pans. Press and pat to form crusts. Bake for 15-20 minutes or until lightly browned. Allow to cool before adding a prepared, chilled filling.

Eggs & Cheese

A corner of the historical rose garden. An Austrian pine, one of several, helps enclose the garden and provides a nice background for these large, old rose bushes.

GARDEN SCRAMBLE

2 tablespoons butter or cooking oil
1 small zucchini (4-5 inches long)
½ cup asparagus tips
½ cup shredded carrot
¼ cup diced red bell pepper
2 green onions, finely sliced
4 eggs (egg substitutes may be used*)
¼ cup milk
½ teaspoon crushed basil
½ teaspoon crushed summer savory
1 tablespoon butter or cooking oil (additional)
¼ cup shredded Swiss or Gruyere cheese

In a 10-inch frying pan melt butter or oil over medium high heat. Add vegetables and stir-fry until tender-crisp. Remove from pan and keep warm.

In a small mixing bowl beat eggs with rotary beater until frothy. Add milk and seasonings. Beat to combine.

Melt additional butter or oil in frying pan. Pour egg mixture into pan and stir gently until almost set; then stir in reserved vegetables. Sprinkle cheese over top and continue cooking until eggs are set. Serve hot.

*Egg substitutes will cook more successfully in a lightly oiled, non-stick frying pan.

NOTE: Other vegetable choices may be used. Broccoli and cauliflower florets should be parboiled (2 minutes) and drained before stir-frying.

EGG FOO YUNG

yield 4 - 6 servings

Egg substitutes may be used in this Chinese omelet.

2 tablespoons cooking oil
2 cups bean sprouts, rinsed and drained
6 green onions finely sliced
¼ cup diced red bell pepper
½ cup finely diced cooked ham
¼ cup diced water chestnuts
6 eggs, slightly beaten*
1 tablespoon light soy sauce
½ teaspoon Oriental sesame oil
¼ teaspoon ground ginger
¼ teaspoon pepper

In a frying pan heat oil over medium high heat. Add bean sprouts, green onions, and red bell pepper. Stir-fry until tender-crisp. Add cooked ham and water chestnuts; stir-fry for 2 more minutes.

In a mixing bowl, beat eggs with rotary beater until frothy; add remaining ingredients and beat until combined. Pour over vegetable mixture, reduce heat; stir carefully to distribute ingredients, and cook until eggs are set. Serve hot with additional soy sauce, if desired.

*Egg substitutes will cook more successfully in a lightly-oiled, non-stick frying pan.

NOTE: In place of ham use chopped cooked shrimp.

CURRIED DEVILED EGGS

6 large eggs
2 tablespoons mayonnaise
½ teaspoon lemon juice
1 teaspoon spicy prepared mustard
½ teaspoon Worcestershire sauce
1 tablespoon minced parsley (or chive)
½ teaspoon curry powder (or to taste)

Garnish: paprika and 2 tablespoons toasted sesame seed

Place eggs in a single layer in a saucepan. Add cool tap water to cover 1 inch above eggs. Cover pan and bring to a rapid boil. Turn off heat. (If using electric range, remove pan from burner.) Let eggs stand in the hot water for 15 minutes. Drain hot water from pan and immediately run cold water over eggs, or place eggs in ice water until cooled. Dry shells, crack and peel.

Cut eggs in half lengthwise. Remove yolks to a small mixing bowl and set whites aside.

Mash eggs yolks with a fork. Stir in remaining ingredients. Use about 1 tablespoon of yolk mixture to fill each egg white half. Garnish with a dusting of paprika and a sprinkle of sesame seeds. Chill for 3 hours.

VARIATIONS: Many other ingredients may be combined with the mashed egg yolk mixture including chopped crabmeat, deviled ham, minced onion or chive, chopped olives, or pimiento. Herb seasoning blends will also vary the flavor. See Herb Scents section.

OVEN-BAKED FRENCH TOAST

yield 4 - 6 servings

¼ cup butter
20 slices French bread (about ½-pound loaf)
4 eggs (or egg substitute equivalent)
1¼ cups milk
½ teaspoon vanilla extract
⅛ teaspoon ground nutmeg

Preheat oven to 375°F. Use a 9 x 13 x 2-inch baking pan.

Place butter in baking pan and put in oven while preheating. Remove pan from oven as soon as butter is melted. Tilt pan to spread butter evenly over bottom. Arrange bread slices close together in pan. If necessary, cut slices in half to fill entire pan.

In a mixing bowl combine eggs*, milk, vanilla and nutmeg. Beat with rotary beater until frothy. Pour evenly over bread slices. Bake in oven until bread is golden brown, about 20 minutes.

Serve hot with maple syrup or fruit topping.

*If using egg substitutes, beat vigorously before combining with other ingredients.

MAKE-AHEAD CHEESE SOUFFLE

yield 4 servings

4 slices firm white bread cubed (trim crusts)
¾ pound sharp cheddar cheese, grated
4 eggs, beaten
2 cups milk
¼ teaspoon dry mustard
¼ teaspoon salt
2 tablespoons sherry wine

Generously butter a 9 x 9-inch baking dish. Place bread cubes and grated cheese in pan in alternate layers.

In a mixing bowl combine eggs, milk, and seasonings. Beat thoroughly with rotary beater. Pour over bread and cheese. Refrigerate for 12 hours. When ready to bake, preheat oven to 350°F. Place baking dish in a pan filled with ½ inch of water. Bake for 50 to 60 minutes, or until top is golden brown and mixture is set. Serve plain or with Marsala Mushroom Sauce, see page

CHEESE STRATA-VARIOUS

yield about 4 - 6 servings

Egg substitutes may be used in this recipe.

6 slices day-old whole wheat or white bread
1 cup chopped cooked ham
2 cups shredded cheese (Swiss or sharp cheddar)
4 fresh mushrooms, chopped
¼ cup chopped green or red bell pepper
2 tablespoons chopped onion or chive
1 tablespoon chopped fresh parsley
4 eggs, slightly beaten*
1 cup milk
2 teaspoons Dijon-style mustard
½ teaspoon crushed summer savory
¼ teaspoon white ground pepper
¼ teaspoon ground nutmeg

Preheat oven to 375°F. Butter an 8 x 12 x 2-inch casserole.

Cut bread slices into 1-inch cubes. Place half of the cubes in bottom of prepared dish. Combine ham, cheese and vegetables; distribute evenly over bread cubes. Top with remaining bread cubes.

In a mixing bowl combine eggs, milk and seasonings. Beat with rotary beater until frothy. Pour evenly over other ingredients. Bake for 20-25 minutes, or until golden brown. Serve immediately.

*If using egg substitutes, beat vigorously before combining with other ingredients.

NOTE: Other combinations of cooked meats (or poultry), vegetables, and herbs may be selected.

MACARONI CASSEROLE

4 eggs, hard-cooked, diced
1 cup dry elbow macaroni, cooked and drained
4 ounces Danish Saga Blue cheese, crumbled
1 cup diced celery
¼ cup chopped red bell pepper
2 green onions, finely sliced (use part tops)
¼ cup slivered almonds, toasted

Garnishes: 2 tablespoons chopped fresh parsley, paprika

SAUCE:

2 tablespoons lemon juice
1 cup sour cream
¼ teaspoon salt
¼ teaspoon white pepper

Preheat oven to 350°F. Grease a deep 1½-quart casserole.

In a mixing bowl combine first 7 ingredients. Set aside.

In a small bowl blend together sauce ingredients. Add to macaroni mixture and stir to combine. Spoon into prepared casserole. Bake for 15 minutes or until hot and bubbly. Do not overbake.

Just before serving sprinkle with parsley and a dusting of paprika.

This recipe may be prepared ahead and refrigerated. Reheat in oven (325°F.) until sauce is bubbly.

TEAROOM RAREBIT

yield 3 - 4 servings

A 1925 recipe file produced this good cheese sauce to serve over toast.

¼ cup all-purpose flour
½ teaspoon dry mustard
½ teaspoon salt
¼ teaspoon sweet paprika
¼ cup butter, melted
1 cup milk
1 cup cream
1 tablespoon Worcestershire sauce
2-3 drops hot pepper sauce
2 cups grated sharp cheddar cheese (about ½ pound)

Garnishes: 4 hot toast points per serving, ½ cup slivered toasted almonds, 4 bacon slices, cooked crisp, drained and crumbled

In a saucepan combine flour, mustard, salt and paprika. Whisk in melted butter. Cook over medium heat, stirring continuously, until mixture begins to bubble. Remove from heat. Gradually stir in milk and cream, whisk until smooth.

Return pan to burner and cook, while stirring, until sauce is thickened and smooth. Add Worcestershire sauce, hot pepper sauce and cheese. Stir until cheese melts. Remove from burner.

Serve over warm toast. Sprinkle each serving with toasted almonds and crumbled bacon. A fresh fruit salad is a good choice for an accompaniment.

NOTE: This cheese sauce may be used with macaroni, noodles and other pastas.

135

HOT BROWNS

yield 4 servings

A tasty sandwich to serve anytime, but especially during half-time on TV football afternoons.*

8 slices bacon, cooked crisp, drained
8 slices toast (whole wheat or white bread)
12 generous slices cooked turkey (or chicken)
8 tomato slices

Have ready 4 broiler-proof individual serving dishes, such as gratins.

CHEESE SAUCE:

2 tablespoons butter
2 tablespoons flour
1 cup milk
few grains cayenne pepper
2 cups shredded sharp cheddar cheese (about 8 ounces)

In a small saucepan, over medium heat, melt butter; stir in flour. Continue to stir until flour is blended and cooked, about 2 minutes. Gradually whisk in milk and cayenne pepper. Stir until mixture is thickened and smooth.

Add shredded cheese, stir until melted; then remove pan from burner.

For each serving, arrange 2 slices of toast in serving dish, top with layer of turkey, 2 slices of tomato, and 2 slices of cooked bacon. Spoon cheese sauce generously over each serving. Place dishes under preheated oven broiler and broil until cheese is bubbly and slightly browned. Serve immediately.

*The name, however, is not football-inspired. According to long-time residents of Louisville, Kentucky, the sandwich was created by a cook at the city's old Brown Hotel.

Entrees

A view of the dye garden as seen from outside the hawthorn hedge. A small garden with a plant collection whose useful qualities will always exceed their aesthetic ones.

TENDER STEAK FAJITAS

yield 4 servings

1 pound sirloin, or other tender beef cuts
2 tablespoons lime juice
1 tablespoon olive oil
1 clove garlic, minced
1 tablespoon olive oil (additional)
1 small onion, thinly sliced
1 medium sweet green pepper, seeded and cut into slivers
4 flour tortillas (7 or 8-inch size)
1 large tomato, peeled, seeded and chopped

Garnishes: Salsa, shredded Monterey Jack cheese, chopped green onions, minced cilantro leaves, guacamole sauce.

Cut steak into thin slices. Place in shallow glass dish. Combine lime juice, oil and garlic. Pour over steak and marinate for two hours in refrigerator.

Just before serving warm tortillas according to package directions.

Heat additional oil in large frying pan over medium-high heat. Quickly brown steak slices on both sides until medium done. Remove to platter and keep warm. Add onion and pepper slices to frying pan and cook about 2 minutes. Fill warmed tortillas with steak, onion, pepper, and chopped tomato. Serve hot with Salsa and choice of garnishes.

NOTE: Pork or chicken may be used in place of beef.

SALSA:

yield about 2½ cups

2 tablespoons olive oil
1 tablespoon white or red wine vinegar
¾ cup chopped sweet green pepper
1 cup chopped tomato, peeled
½ cup chopped onion
2 cloves garlic, minced
2 tablespoons minced cilantro leaves
½ teaspoon crushed dry oregano
½ teaspoon salt (or to taste)
cayenne or black pepper, to taste
¼ cup chopped fresh or canned green chilies (optional)

Combine all ingredients until well blended. This sauce can be served fresh or simmered about 10 minutes; then cooled to room temperature.

MRS. WELLINGTON'S BEEF

yield 4 - 6 servings

The mushroom paté and pastry may be prepared a day ahead. The meat mixture may be done early in the day before serving.

MUSHROOM PATÉ:

1 pound fresh mushrooms
2 tablespoons butter
6 shallots, minced
½ rib celery, minced
1 tablespoon all-purpose flour
½ cup cream
salt and pepper, to taste

Chop mushrooms very fine. Squeeze out moisture with paper towel. The mushrooms should be very dry.

In a small frying pan melt butter over medium-high heat. Saute shallots and celery until soft. Add mushrooms and cook until all moisture has evaporated.

Stir in flour, cream and seasoning. Bring to a boil for 2 minutes, stirring constantly. Remove from heat. Allow to cool slightly then refrigerate until ready to use.

PASTRY:

1½ cups all-purpose flour
½ teaspoon salt
½ cup shortening
1 medium egg, slightly beaten
¼ cup ice water
1 egg (additional, for glazing crust)

In mixing bowl combine flour and salt, cut in shortening until crumbly. Make well in center, add beaten egg and water. Mix lightly with fork until dough holds together. Form ball, wrap and chill until ready to use.

BEEF MIXTURE:

1 egg, slightly beaten
¼ cup milk
1 tablespoon cognac or brandy
1 teaspoon salt
½ cup fresh bread crumbs
1 pound lean ground beef

In mixing bowl lightly beat egg, add milk, cognac and salt. Mix in bread crumbs. Let stand 5 minutes. Then mix in ground beef until thoroughly combined. Mixture may be chilled until ready to assemble.

MRS. WELLINGTON'S BEEF (Continued)

To assemble: Preheat oven to 425°F. Lightly grease a jelly roll pan.

Roll out pastry to a 9 x 8-inch rectangle, about ¼-inch thick. Save pastry scraps. Place dough on prepared baking sheet.

Spread paté on pastry to within 1 inch of each side.

Shape meat mixture into a roll 3 inches thick and center over paté. Fold pastry over meat roll and overlap edges. Moisten edges with water and seal. Turn up short ends of pastry, envelope-style, moisten edges and seal. Carefully turn over and place seam side down.

Beat additional egg until frothy and lightly brush egg glaze over pastry. With a nutpick, create 3 evenly spaced holes in center of pastry roll.

Pastry scraps may be formed into decorative designs to place on top of pastry roll. Brush with egg glaze.

Bake for 20 minutes at 425°F., then reduce oven temperature to 400°F. and bake another 25 minutes. After removing from oven allow to stand for 15 minutes before slicing.

MEAT ROLL WITH
SPINACH CHEESE STUFFING

yield 6 - 8 servings

2 eggs
½ cup tomato juice
2 cups soft bread crumbs (reserve 2 tablespoons for filling)
1 tablespoon Dijon-style mustard
1 medium onion, finely minced
½ teaspoon crushed thyme
1½ teaspoon salt
¼ teaspoon black pepper
2 pounds ground lean beef

FILLING:

1 (10-ounce) package frozen chopped spinach, thawed, drained
1 egg, slightly beaten
2 tablespoons reserved bread crumbs
4 large mushrooms, finely diced
½ cup finely minced onion
½ cup shredded Gruyere cheese
½ teaspoon freshly ground nutmeg

Preheat oven to 350°F. Use a 13 x 9 x 2-inch baking pan.

In large mixing bowl lightly beat eggs with fork. Add tomato juice, bread crumbs, mustard, onion, thyme, salt and pepper. Combine and let stand 5 minutes. Add ground beef and mix thoroughly.

Place a 20-inch long piece of foil on work area. Place meat loaf mixture on foil. Cover with a 20-inch long piece of waxed paper. Flatten the mixture into a 16 x 11-inch rectangle. Set aside.

Press excess moisture from spinach and combine with remaining filling ingredients.

Remove waxed paper, straighten edges of meat. Spread filling evenly over meat, leaving 1 inch from edge on all sides. Begin rolling from shorter end. Use foil as aid to make a firm roll and to keep edges even; then wrap foil around meat roll and seal.

Place foil-wrapped roll in baking pan. Punch several small holes in foil along sides of meat roll to allow fat to drain. Bake for 1¼ hours. Let stand 15 minutes before slicing.

BEEF BRISKET

This easy entree may be prepared a day ahead. Select a thick cut of brisket.

4 to 5 pounds beef brisket
¼ cup tarragon vinegar

½ cup all-purpose flour
½ teaspoon salt
¼ teaspoon black pepper

½ to 1 cup boiling water (to be used during baking)

Cut off any excess fat from brisket and place in a shallow glass dish. Sprinkle with tarragon vinegar. Let stand for about an hour, turning several times.

Preheat oven to 350°F. Lightly grease a roasting pan.

Combine flour, salt and pepper.

Drain the meat; then dredge in seasoned flour. Place brisket in prepared pan, fat side up. Roast, uncovered, for 1 hour.

Remove from oven, and add boiling water to the pan to about ¼-inch depth. Cover pan tightly with foil. Reduce heat to 250°F. and roast for about 3½ hours. Test after 3 hours. Brisket should be easily pierced with fork.

Remove from oven. Roll back foil to allow steam to escape. Cool to room temperature then refrigerate overnight.

When thoroughly chilled, cut the brisket into slices across the grain and return to pan.

A half hour before serving preheat oven to 300°F. Spoon pan juices over the meat. (Or, pan juices may be removed at this point to make gravy.) Cover pan tightly with foil and place in oven to heat through. Arrange slices on platter and spoon any remaining liquid over the meat and serve. If gravy is made, place in separate bowl.

BIFF A LA LINDSTROM

yield 4 - 6 servings

1 tablespoon margarine
2 tablespoons finely chopped onion
1 whole egg
1 tablespoon capers, drained and chopped
1 teaspoon salt
¼ teaspoon black pepper
2 teaspoons white vinegar
1 pound lean ground sirloin (finely ground)
½ cup light cream
¼ cup finely chopped canned beets (drain well before chopping)
1 tablespoon oil

SAUCE:

½ **cup beef broth**
¼ **cup light cream**

Melt margarine in large frying pan, over medium-high heat. Add chopped onion, cook until soft.

In a large mixing bowl lightly beat egg, add capers, salt, pepper and vinegar. Then add ground sirloin and cooked onion. Mix thoroughly. Add cream and chopped beets.

Shape mixture into 12 round patties about ⅜-inch thick. Heat oil in frying pan over medium-high heat. Add patties and cook about 3 minutes per side or until nicely browned. Keep in warm oven until all are brown and sauce is ready.

Add beef broth to hot frying pan, scraping any meat bits from bottom. Cook until reduced by about half, add cream and continue to cook, stirring for about 3 more minutes. Pour sauce over meat patties. Serve hot.

PORT ORANGE BEEF STEW

2 pounds round steak
½ teaspoon black pepper
1 teaspoon paprika
¼ teaspoon garlic powder
⅔ cup all-purpose flour
3 tablespoons cooking oil
1 large onion, coarsely chopped
2 carrots, diced
⅓ cup Tawny Port wine
1 cup beef broth, divided
¼ cup tomato juice
¼ teaspoon ground allspice
½ teaspoon crushed lemon thyme
½ teaspoon crushed rosemary
1 large navel orange
⅓ cup *toasted* chopped walnuts

Garnish: 2 tablespoons chopped fresh parsley or chives

Cut round steak into bite-size pieces. Trim excess fat. Combine pepper, paprika, garlic powder and flour. Coat beef pieces in seasoned flour. Shake off excess flour.

Heat oil in 4-quart Dutch oven over medium high heat. Add meat pieces, a few at a time, and brown on all sides. As meat browns transfer to a plate.

Add ¼ cup of the beef broth to pan. Stir to incorporate any browned bits in pan. Add chopped onion and carrots; cook until softened, about 5 minutes, and stirring occasionally. Add remaining beef broth, wine, tomato juice, allspice and herbs. Return browned meat to pan.

Preheat oven to 350°F.

In order to save all of the orange juice, use a shallow bowl in which to cut *unpeeled* orange into small pieces (remove white pith in center). Add orange pieces and juice to pan. Cover and bake for 1 hour. Remove from oven and stir in toasted walnuts. Return to oven and bake **uncovered** for another 30 minutes. Add garnish and serve.

OVEN BARBECUED BEEF

yield 16 servings

4 pounds boneless chuck
1 large onion, finely chopped
6 ribs celery, coarsely chopped
4 medium carrots, shredded
2 cloves garlic, minced
1 (19-ounce) bottle barbecue sauce or ketchup (about 2 cups)
½ cup beef broth or Burgundy wine

16 sandwich buns for serving

Preheat oven to 300°F. Lightly spray a large Dutch oven with vegetable oil.

Cut chuck into large pieces. (Remove gristle and excess fat.) Place meat in Dutch oven and roast uncovered for 1½ hours. Add remaining ingredients, stir to combine, **cover** pan and bake for another 1½ to 2 hours or until meat can be easily shredded.

If there is excess liquid, bake uncovered for 15 to 20 minutes, or until reduced to sandwich-filling consistency.

May be prepared ahead to reheat just before serving.

VARIATION: Use 4 pounds boneless pork roast instead of beef. Substitute Madeira wine for Burgundy.

CHICKEN WITH BASIL SAUCE

yield 4 - 6 servings

6 chicken breast halves, skinned and deboned

CRUMB TOPPING:

¼ pound bacon, chopped
1 cup fresh bread crumbs
⅓ cup grated Parmesan cheese
1 tablespoon chopped parsley
⅓ cup vegetable oil
2 garlic cloves, crushed
2 teaspoons Worcestershire sauce
½ teaspoon dry mustard

BASIL SAUCE:

½ cup vegetable oil
¼ cup white wine vinegar
1 garlic clove, crushed
1 cup lightly packed fresh basil leaves, finely chopped
½ cup cream or half-and-half
1 egg yolk slightly beaten

Preheat oven to 375°F. Lightly grease 12 x 7 x 2-inch casserole.

In a small frying pan cook chopped bacon until crisp. Drain on paper towel. In a small bowl combine bread crumbs, Parmesan cheese and parsley. Add drained bacon to bread crumb mixture. Set aside.

In a shallow bowl mix vegetable oil with crushed garlic, Worcestershire sauce and mustard. Whisk to combine. Dip chicken halves in mixture and coat thoroughly. Arrange chicken pieces in prepared casserole. Sprinkle with bread crumb mixture. Bake uncovered for 25-30 minutes.

While chicken is cooking, make the Basil Sauce. In a small saucepan combine all sauce ingredients, except the egg yolk. Simmer over low heat, continue stirring until sauce just begins to bubble.

Place egg yolk in a cup and whisk until frothy. Stir a tablespoon of the hot sauce into the beaten egg. Then whisk beaten egg yolk into saucepan. Stir until mixture is thickened, but *do not* allow to boil.

Pour hot sauce over the chicken just before serving, or serve in a separate bowl.

SPINACH GRUYERE CUTLETS

yield 4 servings

May be prepared ahead to reheat just before serving.

2 whole chicken breasts, skinned and boned
1 10-ounce package frozen chopped spinach, thawed and drained
4 ounces Gruyere cheese, shredded
¼ teaspoon freshly grated nutmeg
4 tablespoons all-purpose flour
1 teaspoon paprika
2 tablespoons oil

SAUCE INGREDIENTS:

2 tablespoons butter or margarine
2 tablespoons all-purpose flour (additional)
¾ cup cream
1 can cream of mushroom soup
½ cup white wine
½ teaspoon crushed dry tarragon (or 2 teaspoons minced fresh)
¼ teaspoon garlic powder

Rinse chicken and pat dry. Cut in half to make 4 cutlets. Pound cutlets between waxed paper until about ¼-inch thick.

Press spinach to remove excess moisture. In a small bowl combine spinach, Gruyere cheese and nutmeg. Place a portion on each cutlet. Roll up and secure with toothpicks.

Combine flour and paprika and thoroughly coat each chicken roll. Cover and chill for 30 minutes.

Heat oil in large frying pan over medium-high heat. Add cutlets and brown on all sides. Remove to a warm plate.

Make Sauce: Add butter or margarine to frying pan, melt over medium-high heat. Whisk in 2 tablespoons flour. Cook and stir 2 minutes. Gradually add cream, soup, wine, tarragon and garlic powder. Stir and simmer until smooth and slightly thickened.

Return chicken cutlets to pan. Simmer about 20 minutes. Baste several times with sauce.

Preheat oven to 350°F. Butter a shallow 1½ quart baking dish.

Place cutlets in a prepared baking dish, add sauce and bake for 20-25 minutes, or until sauce is bubbly.

If prepared ahead, allow ingredients to cool slightly then cover and refrigerate. Reheat just before serving.

HERB SAVORY CHICKEN, OVEN-FRIED

yield 4 servings

2½ to 3 pounds of chicken pieces
1 cup buttermilk (shake carton before using)
1 tablespoon chicken bouillon granules
¼ teaspoon garlic powder
½ teaspoon crushed marjoram
¼ teaspoon crushed rosemary
⅛ teaspoon lemon-pepper seasoning
¾ cup all-purpose flour
¼ cup *cracked* wheat flour
2 tablespoons Parmesan cheese
¼ teaspoon paprika
¼ teaspoon pepper

Preheat oven to 375°F. Grease a 13 x 9 x 2-inch baking pan.

Remove skin and excess fat from chicken pieces. Wash and pat dry.

In a large deep bowl combine buttermilk with chicken bouillon granules, garlic, marjoram, rosemary and lemon-pepper seasoning. Let stand for 10 minutes, stir several times. Add chicken pieces to buttermilk mixture and let stand 15 minutes. Make sure all pieces are covered.

In a plastic bag combine the flours, Parmesan cheese, paprika and pepper.

Coat each chicken piece in flour mixture. Place in baking pan. Drizzle with melted butter or spray with vegetable oil. Bake until chicken is tender, 45 minutes to 1 hour. Coating should be a crisp golden brown.

GRILLED CHICKEN BYTES

yield 6 - 8 servings

4 whole chicken breasts, skinned and boned

MARINADE:
Juice from 3 lemons
1 medium onion, finely chopped
12-ounces beer
¼ cup soy sauce
2 cloves garlic, mashed
2 tablespoons vegetable oil

Cut chicken breasts in half. Rinse and pat dry.

In a small bowl combine marinade ingredients. Whisk to blend.

Place chicken breasts in shallow glass dish. Pour on marinade. Be sure chicken is completely covered. Refrigerate overnight.

Grill 5 minutes on each side or until chicken is tender and juices run clear. Baste with marinade during grilling.

ONION SMOTHERED CHICKEN

yield 4 - 6 serving

6 chicken thighs, or other favorite pieces
½ cup all-purpose flour
1 teaspoon poultry seasoning*
2 tablespoons vegetable oil
2 or 3 large onions, thinly sliced
½ cup chicken broth
salt and pepper, to taste

Rinse chicken. Remove skin and excess fat. (A paper towel makes a good grip for pulling off chicken skin.)

In a plastic bag combine flour and seasoning. Coat chicken pieces in flour.

Heat oil in large frying pan over medium-high heat. Cook chicken pieces until golden brown on each side. Remove to platter. Reduce heat.

Place a layer of onion slices in bottom of pan. Place chicken pieces on top then add remaining onions to cover chicken. Pour on broth. Season with salt, pepper and additional poultry seasoning. Cover pan and simmer until chicken is tender, about 45 minutes. Serve with mashed potatoes, hot rice or noodles.

See index for our Poultry Season Blend.

TURKEY ORLANDO

yield 4 - 6 servings

May be made a day ahead and reheated.

1 cup dry navy beans, rinsed and picked over
2 oranges
2 cups chicken broth
1 medium onion, chopped
1 tablespoon Dijon-style mustard
3 tablespoons molasses
½ teaspoon crushed summer savory
1 pound cooked turkey breast, cubed
salt and pepper, to taste

Soak beans overnight in water to cover. (Or use quick-cook method.)

To cook, drain beans and place in 4-quart Dutch oven.

Remove zest from oranges; cut into fine slivers. Reserve half for garnish. Juice the oranges.

Add orange juice, half of zest, 2 cups chicken broth, onion, mustard, molasses and summer savory to beans. Bring to a boil, then reduce to simmer, cover and cook for 1½ hours or until beans are just tender.

Add cubed turkey and simmer for 30 minutes more. Remove cover to allow liquid to reduce by half.

Serve with hot rice or noodles. Garnish with reserved orange zest.

DAD'S GREET CHICKEN

yield 4 - 6 servings

1 roasting chicken, 3½ to 4 pounds

SEASONED COATING:
¼ cup all-purpose flour
1 teaspoon crushed lovage or celery
½ teaspoon poultry seasoning*
¼ teaspoon rubbed sage
¼ teaspoon crushed thyme
¼ teaspoon paprika
¼ teaspoon pepper

1 stick margarine, melted for basting

Preheat oven to 425°F. Place roasting rack in large baking pan. Spray rack and pan with vegetable oil.

Wash and clean chicken. Combine flour and seasoning. Thoroughly coat chicken with seasoned flour. Sprinkle any excess flour inside chicken cavity. Place chicken, breast side up on rack.

Bake for 15 minutes in 425°F. oven. Reduce temperature to 350°F. and continue baking for 30 minutes. After this baking period, begin basting chicken every 15 minutes with melted margarine.

After 45 minutes carefully turn over chicken. Continue roasting and basting until chicken is tender and well browned. During last 15 minutes of baking time carefully turn chicken breast side up to crisp the skin. Save pan juices for gravy or stock.

See index for our Poultry Season Blend.

149

CHICKEN STEW VERACRUZ

yield 8 servings

A flavorful stew that can be assembled ahead of time, then baked in the oven.

2 whole chicken breasts, skinned and boned
⅓ cup all-purpose flour
1 teaspoon sweet paprika
¼ teaspoon ground cumin
⅛ teaspoon cayenne pepper
½ teaspoon salt
3 tablespoons olive oil
1 medium onion, chopped
1 medium green pepper, seeded and diced
1 medium sweet red pepper, seeded and diced
1⅓ cups chicken broth
1 (1 pound, 12-ounce) can stewed tomatoes, or 4 large ripe fresh tomatoes, peeled and chopped
¼ teaspoon ground cumin (additional)
½ teaspoon crushed oregano
salt and pepper, to taste
1 cup green peas, fresh or frozen
1 (10½-ounce) package frozen artichoke hearts, thawed

Cut chicken into bite-size pieces and coat with seasoned flour. Combine flour, paprika, cumin, cayenne pepper, and salt in small pan. Dredge each piece in flour mixture; then set aside while assembling remaining ingredients.

Preheat oven to 350°F. Lightly grease 3-quart casserole.

In a large frying pan heat olive oil over medium-high heat. Saute chicken pieces until golden brown. Place in casserole and set aside.

Add onion and peppers to frying pan and cook until soft. Add chicken broth, tomatoes, cumin, and oregano. Bring to a boil, scraping up bits in bottom of pan; then pour over chicken pieces.

Cover and bake for 30 minutes. Remove from oven, taste for seasoning. Add salt and pepper if needed. Remove cover and bake for 30 more minutes.

Just before serving stir in green peas and artichoke hearts. Return to oven for about 5 minutes or until peas and artichokes are heated.

RED SNAPPER IN HERB SAUCE

yield 3 - 4 servings

1 tablespoon margarine
1 pound red snapper fillets
1 tablespoon chopped fresh parsley
½ carrot, grated
1 rib celery, minced
¼ teaspoon crushed basil
¾ cup white wine
salt and pepper, to taste
lemon slices

Preheat oven to 350°F. Use a shallow baking dish.

Melt margarine in baking dish. Rinse fish and pat dry. Arrange fillets in a single layer in baking dish. Distribute parsley, grated carrot and celery over fish. Sprinkle with basil. Pour wine over all and bake uncovered for 20 minutes.

Arrange fillets on hot platter, spoon on sauce. Garnish with lemon slices.

NOTE: Fillets may be microwaved on HIGH setting for 6-8 minutes in a covered dish. Follow your microwave instructions.

HERBED BAKED FISH

yield 2 - 4 servings

4 firm, cleaned, fish fillets (such as orange roughy)
¼ cup butter or margarine
1 tablespoon lemon juice
½ cup fine dry bread crumbs
½ teaspoon crushed basil
½ teaspoon crushed oregano
¼ teaspoon garlic powder
¼ cup grated Parmesan cheese
salt and pepper, to taste

Preheat oven to 350°F. Use a shallow 12 x 8-inch baking dish.

Place butter in baking dish and while oven is preheating put dish in oven to melt butter. Remove from oven as soon as butter has melted. Stir in lemon juice.

Combine crumbs, herbs and Parmesan cheese in a shallow pan or plate.

When butter has cooled slightly, place fillets in baking dish, turn to coat with butter. Dip each piece in seasoned crumbs and return to baking dish.

Bake for 15-20 minutes or until fish turns opaque. Do not overbake.

BUTTERFLIED SHRIMP AND CRABMEAT FARCI

yield 4 - 6 servings

May be prepared early in the day; then baked just before serving. Allow 2-3 large shrimp per serving.

6 slices fresh bread, coarsely crumbed
½ cup milk
¼ cup butter
1 tablespoon minced shallots or green onion
1 tablespoon minced green pepper
1 tablespoon finely chopped celery
½ cup crabmeat, remove any cartilage bits
½ teaspoon crushed tarragon
salt and pepper
18 large raw shrimp
3 tablespoons butter (additional)
¾ cup white wine

Prepare crabmeat filling: Soak bread crumbs in milk.

In a small frying pan melt butter over medium-high heat. Saute shallots, green pepper and celery until soft, but not browned. Remove from heat, stir in bread and milk, crabmeat, tarragon, salt and pepper to taste. Set aside.

Preheat oven to 350°F.

Shell and devein shrimp. Then cut from underside toward back so that each piece will spread open or butterfly. Be careful not to cut clear through.

Butter a shallow casserole that will accommodate the shrimp. Place half of the shrimp back sides down in baking dish. Place a portion of filling on each shrimp, then cover with the remaining shrimp, back side up. (May now be refrigerated until ready to bake.)

Melt 3 tablespoons butter in pan, add white wine, stir to blend. Pour over shrimp. Cover dish with foil. Bake for 25 minutes. Serve hot.

TWO-MINUTE SHRIMP

yield 4 - 6 servings

This recipe, included in ANOTHER SAVORY SEASONING, published in 1969 by the Herb Society, uses the stir-fry method for quick preparation and good flavor.

1½ pounds raw shrimp
3 tablespoons butter
1 tablespoon chopped fresh parsley
1 tablespoon chopped fresh chive
1 teaspoon crushed basil
¼ teaspoon salt
¼ teaspoon pepper
¼ cup dry vermouth

Rinse shrimp in cold water; then peel and devein. Pat with paper towels to remove excess moisture. Set aside. (Refrigerate if prepared early in the day.)

In a large frying pan over medium-high heat, melt butter. Stir in herbs, lemon juice, salt and pepper. When butter begins to sizzle, add cleaned shrimp; stir continuously until shrimp become opaque and turns pink. Do not overcook. Stir in vermouth to blend and serve immediately.

NOTE: If fresh basil is available, use two large leaves, finely chopped, in place of the dried basil.

BROILED SWORDFISH STEAKS
WITH SWEET RED PEPPERS

yield 6 servings

1 large sweet red pepper
juice of 2 lemons
3 tablespoons fresh oregano (1 teaspoon dried)
1 cup olive oil
1 teaspoon salt
½ teaspoon black pepper
½ cup dry white wine
6 swordfish steaks (about 1-inch thick)

Preheat broiler unit.

Remove seeds and ribs from red pepper and coarsely chop. Place in bowl, add lemon juice, oregano, olive oil, salt and pepper. Set aside.

Pour wine to a depth of ⅛-inch in broiler pan. Place swordfish steaks in wine and broil for 3 minutes.

Spoon the seasoned pepper mixture over fish and broil for 3-4 minutes more, or until fish is cooked through and lightly browned. Remove steaks to platter. Keep warm.

Pour sauce into small saucepan and bring to a boil over high heat. Stir and cook for about 2 minutes, or until reduced.

Pour sauce over each serving portion. Serve hot.

FISH STIR FRY

2 large firm (cleaned), fish fillets (cod, haddock, orange roughy)
2 tablespoons Tamari sauce
2 tablespoons dry sherry (or rice wine vinegar)
½ teaspoon sugar
½ teaspoon Oriental sesame oil
¼ teaspoon ground ginger
pinch of cayenne pepper
1 thin slice fresh ginger (optional)
2 tablespoons peanut oil (or vegetable oil)
2 small zucchini, sliced
½ cup sliced fresh mushrooms
4 green onions, cut into thin diagonal slices
1 cup snow peas, remove strings and tips
2 cups sliced bok choy

Rinse fish fillets and pat dry. Cut into bite-size pieces.

In a shallow glass bowl combine Tamari sauce, sherry, sugar, sesame oil, ginger and cayenne pepper. Whisk to blend. Place fish pieces in marinade and let stand while preparing vegetables (or about 15 minutes).

In large frying pan (or wok) heat oil and slice of ginger (if using) over medium-high heat. Add vegetables and stir-fry until tender crisp, about 5 minutes. Discard ginger slice. Remove vegetables with slotted spoon to a bowl.

Add undrained fish to frying pan. Cover pan and let fish cook until opaque, about 5-8 minutes. Stir occasionally. When fish flakes, return vegetables to pan and stir gently to reheat vegetables.

Serve immediately with hot rice.

NOTE: Instead of adding more oil to a stir-fry mix as it is cooking, add a table-spoon of water. This "steam" effect will provide a buffer to prevent browning without adding extra oil.

SCALLOPS WITH ANGEL HAIR PASTA

3 tablespoons olive oil
3 tablespoons butter or margarine
1 pound bay scallops or sea scallops (cut sea scallops in quarters)
1 cup finely sliced green onions
1 clove garlic, minced
1 tablespoon chopped fresh basil
1 tablespoon chopped fresh tarragon
1 teaspoon minced fresh thyme
¼ cup white wine (or chicken broth)
5 large ripe tomatoes, peeled, seeded and chopped
½ cup light cream
2 teaspoons sugar (optional)
salt and pepper, to taste
1 pound angel hair pasta, cooked and drained

Garnish: Black olives, fresh basil leaves and chopped parsley

Heat oil and butter in large frying pan over medium heat. Add scallops to pan and saute until opaque, about 2 minutes. Transfer scallops to bowl and set aside.

Place onions and garlic in pan and cook until soft. Add herbs and wine, stir and cook about 2 minutes. Stir in chopped tomatoes and sugar. Bring to a boil and cook about 3 minutes or until tomatoes form sauce. Reduce heat and stir in cream.

Return scallops to pan. Stir gently to combine. Cook until just heated through.

Serve over hot pasta. Add garnishes.

SALMON QUICHE

CRUST:

1 cup whole wheat flour
⅔ cup shredded sharp cheddar cheese
¼ cup chopped almonds
¼ teaspoon salt
¼ teaspoon paprika
6 tablespoons vegetable oil

Preheat oven to 400°F. Use 9-inch pie pan.

In a mixing bowl combine flour, cheese, almonds, salt and paprika. Add oil and gently blend into dry ingredients.

Measure ½ cup of the crust mixture and press it into the bottom and sides of a 9-inch pie pan. To prevent crust from sliding down sides of pan during baking, cover crust with a piece of foil and fill with dry beans or pie weights.

Bake for 8 minutes then remove foil and weights. Return crust to oven and continue baking until lightly brown, about 3 minutes. After baking bottom crust, reduce oven temperature to 325°F.

FILLING:

3 eggs
¼ cup mayonnaise
½ cup shredded sharp cheddar cheese
¼ teaspoon dried dillweed
3 drops hot pepper sauce
1 tablespoon grated onion
1 (16-ounce) can red sockeye salmon

Break eggs into mixing bowl and beat until frothy. Stir in mayonnaise, cheese, dillweed, hot pepper sauce, and grated onion.

Drain salmon, remove skin and bones. Break up salmon into bite-size pieces and gently stir into egg mixture. Spoon mixture into the baked crust. Evenly distribute remaining crust mixture over top of salmon mixture. Bake at 325°F. for 45 minutes or until center tests firm. Let stand 5 to 10 minutes before cutting and serving.

SALMON STEAKS WITH FRESH HERB SAUCE   yield 4 servings

4 salmon steaks (1-inch thick)
¼ cup dry white wine
1 tablespoon lemon juice
¼ cup olive oil
½ cup chopped onion

Rinse salmon steaks and pat dry. Place in a single layer in a buttered shallow baking dish. Combine the wine, lemon juice and olive oil. Pour over steaks. Sprinkle with chopped onion. Cover and let stand about 30 minutes.

Bake in preheated 350°F. oven for about 30 minutes. Test for doneness after 20 minutes. Do not overcook.

FRESH HERB SAUCE:

1 cup medium white sauce (see Index)
½ cup chopped fresh herbs, using equal parts of parsley, chive and chervil
(may also add 1 tablespoon snipped dillweed, minced tarragon, or
**   chopped mint leaves)**
salt and pepper

After white sauce is prepared stir in fresh herbs. Cook over low heat until herbs are just slightly wilted. Taste for seasoning. Add salt and pepper. Serve warm over baked salmon steaks.

NOTE: Salmon steaks may also be char-broiled on outdoor grill. After marinating, follow instructions for cooking fish steaks on your type of grill.

NORTHCOAST CRAB CAKES

yield 4 servings

An imitation crabmeat product may be substituted for real crabmeat.

1 egg, slightly beaten
⅔ cup fresh bread crumbs
1 tablespoon all-purpose flour
1½ teaspoons Worcestershire sauce
1½ teaspoons lemon juice
¼ cup finely chopped onion
3 tablespoons minced fresh parsley
2 tablespoons mayonnaise
1 (8-ounce) package imitation crabmeat, thaw, if frozen*
4 tablespoons margarine

In a mixing bowl combine beaten egg with next 7 ingredients.

Coarsely chop the crabmeat. Add to crumb mixture and combine thoroughly. Let stand 15 minutes.

In large frying pan melt margarine over medium-high heat. Shape crab mixture into patties about ¾-inch thick. Place in hot margarine, press slightly with spatula into a round shape. Fry about 3 minutes per side, or until golden brown. Serve warm.

*Frozen products often contain excess moisture. Drain thoroughly before mixing with other ingredients, thus avoiding too much filler to hold the patties in shape.

HAM LOAF WITH RHUBARB SAUCE

yield 6 - 8 servings

2 eggs
½ cup chicken broth
½ cup orange juice
2 teaspoons Dijon-style mustard
¼ teaspoon ground coriander
¼ teaspoon ground allspice
¼ teaspoon ground cloves
1½ cups finely ground fresh bread crumbs
¼ cup chopped onion
1½ pounds smoked ham, finely ground
1 pound ground lean pork

Preheat oven to 350°F. Lightly grease 9 x 5 x 4-inch loaf pan.

In a large mixing bowl lightly beat eggs. Add liquids, mustard, spices and bread crumbs. Combine well. Let stand 5 minutes. Add onion and ground meat, combine thoroughly. Pack mixture in prepared loaf pan. Bake for 1 hour and 15 minutes. Drain fat from pan. Let loaf stand 15 minutes before cutting into slices. Serve hot with warm Rhubarb Sauce.

RHUBARB SAUCE

yield 1½ cups

1 cup diced rhubarb
1 cup water (divided)
⅓ cup sugar, or to taste
1 tablespoon cornstarch
¼ teaspoon salt
2 teaspoons lemon juice
red food coloring (optional)

In a stainless steel saucepan simmer rhubarb in ½ cup water until almost tender, about 5 minutes. Stir in sugar to taste.

Dissolve cornstarch in the other ½ cup cold water and gradually stir into rhubarb. Add lemon juice. Continue stirring until sauce is clear and slightly thickened. Stir in a drop or 2 of red food coloring if desired.

HAM KABOBS WITH
BRANDIED KUMQUAT SAUCE

1½ pound canned ham
1 (10-ounce) bottle brandied kumquats
⅓ cup juice drained from kumquats
⅓ cup red currant jelly
½ teaspoon cider vinegar
1 tablespoon brandy or cognac
¼ teaspoon grated nutmeg

½ pound fresh mushrooms
2 tablespoons butter

Garnish: Fresh parsley or watercress

Cut ham into 1-inch cubes. Place in a shallow glass dish and set aside.

Drain juice from brandied kumquats into a measuring cup. Should have ⅓ cup. Reserve kumquat pieces.

In a small saucepan combine reserved juice, jelly, vinegar and brandy. Warm over low heat until jelly melts. Pour over ham cubes. Dust with grated nutmeg. Marinate for an hour at room temperature. (If prepared early in the day, cover and refrigerate. Bring to room temperature before cooking.)

Prepare mushrooms: Cut stems from mushrooms and reserve for other use. Melt butter in frying pan over medium high heat. Add mushroom caps and cook until lightly browned.

To broil kabobs: Cut kumquat pieces into cubes and place on skewers alternately with ham cubes. Broil or grill until golden browned. Brush several times with marinade.

Place a kabob skewer on each plate, add mushroom caps and garnish with parsley or watercress.

ORANGE UPSIDE-DOWN HAM CAKES

yield 6 servings

1 egg, slightly beaten
½ cup orange juice
½ cup fresh bread crumbs
½ teaspoon paprika
½ teaspoon dry mustard
½ teaspoon Worcestershire sauce
⅛ teaspoon ground cloves
1 pound ground smoked ham
¼ pound mild bulk sausage (country style)
6 tablespoons brown sugar
½ teaspoon dry mustard (additional)
6 thin unpeeled orange slices, about 3 small oranges

Garnish: Fresh parsley sprigs and cooked carrots cut julienne

Preheat oven to 350°F. Butter 6 small ramekins or custard baking cups.

In a large mixing bowl slightly beat egg, add juice, bread crumbs and seasonings. Combine well. Let stand 5 minutes. Mix in ground ham and sausage, blend thoroughly.

Place 1 tablespoon brown sugar in each cup, sprinkle with a little of the mustard. Top with a slice of orange. Divide the meat mixture among the 6 baking dishes and pack firmly. Bake for 45 minutes. Let stand 5 minutes. Tilt each cup to drain off fat, then invert onto serving platter. Garnish with parsley sprigs and cooked julienne carrots.

NOTE: May be assembled ahead and baked just before serving.

SAVORY LAMB SHANKS

yield 4 servings

This flavorful entree is adapted from a recipe included in ANOTHER SAVORY SEASONING, the Western Reserve Herb Society's 1969 cookbook.

1 clove garlic, slivered
4 meaty lamb shanks
salt and pepper
¼ cup flour, for coating
2 tablespoons butter or cooking oil
¾ cup chicken broth
¼ cup white wine
2 small onions, sliced
1 tablespoons minced fresh parsley
½ teaspoon crushed marjoram
½ teaspoon crushed rosemary

Preheat oven to 300°F. Lightly grease a deep baking dish.

Tuck a sliver of garlic in each lamb shank. Season with salt and pepper and roll in flour.

Melt butter in frying pan over medium-high heat. Add lamb shanks and cook until well browned. Place in prepared baking dish.

Add broth to pan and bring to a boil, scraping up any browned bits in pan. Reduce heat and add wine, sliced onion and herbs. Simmer for 3 minutes. Pour pan juices over lamb shanks. Cover dish and bake until shanks are tender, about 1½ hours. Serve with pan juices over hot cooked rice.

LAMB AND HERB FRICASSEE

yield 4 - 6 servings

¼ cup olive oil
2 pounds lamb stew meat, cut into bite-size pieces
1 tablespoon all-purpose flour
1 clove garlic, minced
1 teaspoon crushed rosemary (or 1 tablespoon fresh, minced)
1 teaspoon rubbed sage (or 4 small fresh leaves minced)
½ cup white wine
½ cup chicken broth
salt and pepper, to taste

Heat oil in a large frying pan over medium-high heat. Add lamb cubes in small batches and saute until browned. After all the lamb cubes are browned, sprinkle flour over the mixture. Stir for 2 minutes while flour browns. Add garlic, rosemary and sage.

Stir in wine and broth. Season with salt and pepper. Cover pan. Reduce heat to a simmer and cook until meat is tender, about 1 hour. Stir frequently. Add more broth if necessary to maintain a gravy consistency.

Serve with hot noodles, pasta or rice.

GREEK LAMB LOAF

1 egg, slightly beaten
1 cup tomato sauce
1 cup fine-ground bulgur wheat (may use pre-cooked)
1 teaspoon ground allspice
½ teaspoon salt
¼ teaspoon black pepper
¼ teaspoon garlic powder
¼ teaspoon crushed dry thyme
¼ teaspoon crushed dry rosemary
1½ pounds ground lamb
1 cup minced onion
⅓ cup Zante currants
¼ cup pine nuts (divided)

Preheat oven to 350°F. Grease a 12 x 7 x 2-inch casserole.

In a large mixing bowl lightly beat egg, add tomato sauce and bulgur wheat. Stir in seasonings. Mix well. Let stand for 5 minutes to soften bulgur.

Add ground lamb, minced onion, currants and 2 tablespoons pine nuts. Mix with electric mixer until thoroughly blended.

Spoon mixture into prepared casserole. Sprinkle the remaining pine nuts evenly over top. Press gently into mixture. Bake for 35-40 minutes.

NOTE: Make a tasty sandwich with leftovers. Place slices of cold Greek Lamb Loaf in pita bread pockets, add chopped fresh tomato, plain yogurt and a sprinkle of crumbled Feta cheese.

CREAMY MINT LAMB CUTLETS

yield 4 servings

1 tablespoon sugar
2 tablespoons flour
1 heaping tablespoon finely chopped fresh mint
8 lamb cutlets
2 tablespoons butter or margarine
1 onion, peeled and sliced
1 cup apple cider
¼ pound mushrooms, sliced
½ cup sour cream (or plain yogurt)

Combine sugar, flour and chopped mint. Coat the cutlets with mixture. Reserve leftover coating mixture.

Melt the butter or margarine in a large frying pan. Add the onions and cook until slightly soft. Remove onions to a dish and set aside.

Add the cutlets to pan and brown on both sides. Stir in remaining flour mixture along with apple cider. Return onions to pan and add mushrooms. Cover pan and simmer for 10-15 minutes.

Stir in the sour cream (or yogurt) and heat gently for 5 minutes. Serve cutlets with the warm sauce.

INDONESIAN BRAISED PORK

yield 6 - 8 servings

Adjust the amount of hot red pepper flakes to preference. A smaller amount will not alter the flavor, just the fire, of this easy pork dish.

4 tablespoons cooking oil
4 pounds pork loin, cut into bite-size pieces
1 medium onion, chopped
4 cloves garlic, minced
2 tablespoons crushed hot red pepper flakes
1 tablespoon lime juice
⅔ cup soy sauce
3 tablespoons brown sugar

Heat oil in a large frying pan or Dutch oven over medium-high heat. Add pork, onion, garlic, red pepper flakes, and cook until pork is well browned, about 20 minutes. Stir frequently and adjust heat to prevent over-browning.

Stir in lime juice, soy sauce and brown sugar. Reduce heat to simmer, cover and cook for 15 to 20 minutes, or until pork is tender. Serve with hot cooked rice.

POZOLE

A version of the popular Southwestern stew of Pueblo Indian heritage.

1½ pounds pork loin, cut into small cubes
¼ cup all-purpose flour
2 tablespoons oil
1 medium onion, chopped
1 clove garlic, minced
½ cup chopped sweet red or green pepper
2 (15½-ounce) cans golden hominy (drain and reserve liquid)
1 teaspoon chili powder (or to taste)
¼ teaspoon salt
1 teaspoon crushed dry oregano
1 (4-ounce) can green chilies, drained and chopped (optional)

Dredge pork cubes in flour. Heat oil in large frying pan over medium-high heat. Add pork and cook until browned. Add onion and garlic, cook about 5 minutes.

Add reserved liquid from hominy plus enough water to cover pork. Stir in chili powder, salt, oregano and green chilies, if using. Cover pan and simmer about 25 minutes.

Add drained hominy and chopped pepper. Simmer until pork is fork-tender.

Serve hot in bowls. Blue cornmeal muffins would be a perfect Southwestern touch. See Index for our recipe.

APPLE ANNIE PORK CHOPS

yield 4 servings

1 tablespoon oil
4 pork chops, about 1-inch thick, trim excess fat
1 tablespoon margarine or oil, additional
2 medium onions, chopped
2 tart apples, peeled, cored and sliced
½ teaspoon crushed rosemary
½ teaspoon crushed summer savory
¼ cup chopped chutney (such as Major Grey's)
¼ cup apple juice or cider

Heat oil in large frying pan. Brown pork chops, about 4 minutes per side. Remove to platter. Melt 1 tablespoon margarine in same pan. Add onions, apples, rosemary and summer savory. Cook and stir over medium heat until onions are soft, about 3 minutes.

Return pork chops to pan. Spoon a portion of the onion-apple mixture over top of each chop. Place a tablespoon of chopped chutney on top of onion-apple mixture. Add apple juice to pan. Cover the pan with lid or foil and simmer until pork chops are fork-tender, about 30 minutes. Or, bake covered in 375°F. oven for 30 to 45 minutes.

PORK MEDALLIONS WITH PRUNES

yield 4 - 6 servings

1 cup pitted prunes
¾ cup dry red wine
12 pork tenderloin slices (2 pounds tenderloin)
2 tablespoons margarine
1 cup beef broth
¼ teaspoon ground ginger
1 clove garlic, minced
¼ teaspoon ground pepper and salt

In a small glass bowl marinate prunes in wine overnight.

Between sheets of waxed paper flatten pork slices to ½-inch thickness.

Melt margarine in large frying pan over medium-high heat. Add pork slices. Saute about 4 minutes per side or until nicely browned. Transfer to warm platter.

Drain prunes and save the wine. Add reserved wine to frying pan, stir to scrape any meat bits from bottom. Maintain heat at a brisk simmer until wine is reduced by half. Add broth, ginger and garlic. Simmer until liquid is reduced by half again. Season with salt and pepper.

Lower heat, add prunes and simmer until heated through, about 2 minutes. Pour sauce over warm medallions. Serve hot. Dish may be assembled and cooked ahead of time. When ready to serve, reheat in 325°F. oven for 20 minutes, or in microwave.

BRAISED PORK WITH MUSHROOMS

yield 4 - 6 servings

2 pounds pork loin, trimmed
¼ pound fresh mushrooms, trimmed and sliced
2 tablespoons cooking oil
1 cup chicken broth
½ teaspoon crushed summer savory
1 tablespoon minced onion
2 tablespoons Port wine

Seasoned flour:

  1 cup all-purpose flour
  1 teaspoon salt
  ¼ teaspoon black pepper

Preheat oven to 300°F. Lightly grease 1½-quart casserole.

Cut pork into 2 x ½-inch strips, cutting at right angle to the grain of meat. Dredge meat in seasoned flour. Heat oil in large frying pan over medium-high heat. Add meat and cook until well browned. Remove meat to prepared casserole.

Cook mushrooms in same frying pan, adding another tablespoon of oil if necessary. When browned transfer to the casserole.

Add chicken broth and wine to frying pan. Scrape up any remaining bits of meat. Add summer savory and onion. Simmer for 2 minutes, then pour over meat and mushrooms. Cover and bake for about 45 minutes, or until meat is very tender. Serve with hot cooked rice or noodles.

PLUM GOOD PORK CHOPS

6 boneless pork loin chops (about 1½ pounds)
2 tablespoons plum wine vinegar*
1 (16-ounce) can purple plums
1 tablespoon cooking oil
8 small onions, peeled and quartered
2 cloves garlic, minced
1 (16-ounce) can tomato sauce (divided)
2 tablespoons flour
½ teaspoon salt

Trim fat from chops. Save fat to render in frying pan. Sprinkle both sides of chops with plum vinegar. Let stand about 15 minutes.

Drain plums, reserving juice. Remove pits and roughly chop plums. Set aside.

In a large frying pan over medium-high heat render fat trimmings to obtain about 1 tablespoon melted fat. Remove trimmings from pan and discard. Add pork chops and brown on both sides. Remove to platter and set aside.

Add 1 tablespoon cooking oil to pan. Add onions and garlic. Cook until soft. Return chops to pan, add drained plum juice, 1¾ cups of tomato sauce and salt. Bring to a boil; then reduce heat, cover, and simmer about 25 minutes or until chops are fork-tender.

Add flour to remaining tomato sauce and blend until smooth; then stir into frying pan. Add chopped plums and raise heat to a gentle boil for several minutes, stirring until sauce has thickened slightly.

Serve with hot rice or noodles. Pass the extra sauce.

Plum wine vinegar is available in specialty stores and is often used in Oriental cooking.

BARBECUED SPARERIBS

2 tablespoons bacon drippings (or margarine)
4 pounds spareribs
1 cup ketchup
1 cup water
2 tablespoons Worcestershire sauce
¼ cup vinegar
¼ cup brown sugar
2 teaspoons dry mustard
1 teaspoon paprika
salt to taste
hot pepper sauce (optional)
1 cup sliced onion

Preheat oven to 350°F. Lightly grease large baking pan.

Melt fat in frying pan over medium high heat. Cut ribs into serving pieces and brown on both sides.

Combine ketchup, water and seasoning ingredients, except onions. Place a layer of ribs in baking pan. Cover with part of the sauce and sliced onions. Repeat layers with remaining ingredients.

Cover the pan and bake for 1¾ hours, or until meat is tender. Spoon the sauce over the ribs several times during baking. After ribs are tender, bake uncovered for 15 minutes.

BAKED VEAL CHOPS

⅔ cup water
¼ cup rice
2 tablespoons vegetable oil
4 veal chops
¼ cup minced onion
2 medium tomatoes
½ teaspoon crushed oregano
salt and pepper to taste
½ cup white wine

In a small saucepan bring water to a boil. Stir in rice and cook until tender. Set aside.

Preheat oven to 375°F. Grease a shallow baking dish.

Heat oil in a large frying pan. Add veal chops and brown on both sides. Transfer to prepared baking dish. Place a spoonful of cooked rice over each chop.

Cut 4 slices from one tomato and place a slice on top of the rice on each chop. Peel and chop the remaining tomato; combine with minced onion and spoon mixture around chops. Sprinkle with oregano, salt and pepper. Pour wine over ingredients. Cover and bake until chops are tender, about 30-45 minutes.

VEAL PATTIES IN MUSHROOM SAUCE   yield 4 - 6 servings

1 egg, slightly beaten
½ cup undiluted evaporated milk
½ cup dry bread crumbs
1 small onion, finely chopped
¼ cup finely minced celery
1 tablespoon minced fresh parsley
½ teaspoon salt
¼ teaspoon ground black pepper
1 pound ground veal
2 tablespoons margarine

In a large mixing bowl combine beaten egg, milk, crumbs, onion, celery, parsley, salt and pepper. Mix thoroughly. Let stand 5 minutes. Add ground veal and combine thoroughly.

Preheat oven to 350°F. Grease a shallow baking dish.

Heat margarine in large frying pan over medium heat. Form veal mixture into patties. Brown slowly on both sides. Transfer to prepared casserole. Pour Marsala Mushroom Sauce over patties and bake for 25 minutes or until sauce is bubbly. Serve with mashed potatoes or hot noodles.

MARSALA MUSHROOM SAUCE: yield about 1¾ cups

2 tablespoons butter
1½ cups sliced mushrooms
2 tablespoons Marsala wine
4 tablespoons margarine
¼ cup chopped onion
4 tablespoons all-purpose flour
1 cup rich chicken broth
½ cup milk
¼ teaspoon grated nutmeg
⅛ teaspoon ground white pepper

In a frying pan melt butter over medium-high heat. Saute mushrooms until golden brown on both sides. Reduce heat, add wine and simmer for 2 minutes. Remove pan from heat and set aside.

In a small saucepan melt margarine over medium heat. Add onions and cook until soft. Stir in flour and cook 2 minutes. Add chicken broth, milk, nutmeg and pepper. Stir until sauce is smooth. Add mushrooms to sauce and simmer for 3 minutes.

COUNTRY SAUSAGE
yield 6 - 8 servings

Herbs and spices season freshly ground pork for this easy breakfast treat.

2 pound lean ground pork
½ cup finely chopped onion
1 clove garlic, finely minced (optional)
1 tablespoon rubbed sage
1 teaspoon finely crushed marjoram
½ teaspoon crushed thyme
½ teaspoon ground cumin
½ teaspoon ground allspice
½ teaspoon paprika
1 teaspoon hot pepper flakes (optional)
¼ teaspoon cayenne pepper (optional)
1 teaspoon salt
1 teaspoon freshly ground black pepper

In a deep mixing bowl combine all ingredients and mix until light and fluffy. Divide mixture into two equal portions on sheets of waxed paper. Shape into rolls. Wrap in foil or plastic wrap and chill for at least 2 hours before slicing. Each roll should yield about 12 ½-inch slices.

To cook fry in a small amount of hot vegetable oil over medium-high heat. Cook slices about 4 minutes per side or until no longer pink. Drain on paper towels.

NOTE: Any unused portions should be cooked within 3 days. Sausage may be frozen up to 1 month.

CASSOULET

This is a simplified version of the succulent stew of French Provincial heritage which may be prepared up to 2 days before serving.

1 pound dried white beans, such as Great Northern
1 quart chicken broth

Bouquet garni: In a small square of muslin (or cheese cloth) place 4 sprigs parsley, 3 celery tops, 1 bay leaf and 2 whole cloves. Tie with string to form bag.

1 pound link sausage (bratwurst, Polish or Italian)
2 tablespoons vegetable oil
1½ pounds boneless pork, cubed
1 pound boneless lamb shoulder, cubed

2 cloves garlic, minced
1 medium onion, chopped
1 rib celery, diced
2 carrots, scraped and diced
½ cup white dry wine
1 cup tomato juice
1 teaspoon *each:* crushed thyme and marjoram
½ teaspoon crushed rosemary
¼ teaspoon black pepper
1½ cups dried bread crumbs

Soak beans overnight in water (or use quick-cooking method). Drain beans and place in large saucepan. Add chicken broth and bouquet garni. Bring to a boil, reduce heat to simmer. Cover pan and cook beans until just tender. Remove bouquet garni. Set pan aside. Do not drain cooking liquid.

Cut sausage in small sections and place in a frying pan. Add a ½-inch of water, bring to a gentle boil and steam sausage until no longer pink inside. Pierce sections with fork to release excess fat. Remove sausage to plate. Discard water. Remove casing from sausage and cut into bite-size pieces. Set aside.

Heat vegetable oil in frying pan. Brown pork and lamb cubes in small batches. Remove meat to a plate.

Add garlic, onion, and celery to pan. Cook until soft. Stir in carrots, wine, tomato juice, herbs and pepper. Simmer for 10 minutes.

Place a layer of beans and broth in bottom of 5-quart Dutch oven. Add a layer of meat. Alternate layers with remaining ingredients. Add vegetable and herb mixture.

(The cassoulet may be refrigerated at this point to bake later.)

To bake, preheat oven to 350°F. Cover top of ingredients with a layer of bread crumbs. Bake uncovered until crumbs form a thick golden brown crust, about 1 hour.

Serve hot with crusty bread, a favorite wine, and fruit for dessert.

CHOUCROUTE GARNIE

yield 6 - 8 servings

2 pounds sauerkraut, rinsed and drained
2 tablespoons butter or margarine
2 clove garlic, minced
2 medium onions, chopped
2 carrots, diced
1 cup chicken broth (divided)
1 cup white wine
1 teaspoon crushed dried thyme
1 bay leaf
1 teaspoon caraway seeds, crushed slightly
4 juniper berries
freshly ground black pepper, to taste
4 knockwurst links, cut into slices
1 pound mild Italian sausage links
½ cup water

Preheat oven to 350°F.

Drain sauerkraut in a colander. Rinse thoroughly under cool running water. Redrain.

In a 5-quart Dutch oven melt butter over medium-high heat. Add garlic, onions and carrots. Saute until vegetables are softened, about 3 minutes. Add ½ cup chicken broth, cover and simmer for 10 minutes. Stir in remaining broth, wine and seasonings. Add sauerkraut and knockwurst slices. Season with pepper to taste. Bring to a simmer; then cover pan and place in oven. Bake 1 hour.

Place Italian sausage links in a frying pan and cook until browned. Prick holes in casings to release excess fat. Drain and set aside.

At the end of 1 hour remove baking dish from oven and arrange sausage links among other ingredients, stir gently to distribute. Cover pan and return to oven to bake another 15 minutes. Remove bay leaf before serving.

VEGETABLE NUT LOAF

⅓ cup butter or margarine
½ cup chopped onion
1 cup finely chopped celery
1 cup shredded carrot
¼ cup all-purpose flour
1½ teaspoons salt
¼ teaspoon pepper
½ teaspoon rubbed sage
¼ teaspoon *each:* crushed dillweed and rosemary
1½ cups milk
1 cup grated cheddar cheese
1 cup chopped pecans
¾ cup wheat germ
3 eggs, lightly beaten

Garnish: Serve with Marsala Mushroom Sauce (see Page 172).

Preheat oven to 350°F. Line a 9 x 5 x 3-inch loaf pan with foil. Generously butter foil.

Melt butter in a large saucepan over medium-high heat. Add onion, celery and carrots, cook until soft, about 3 minutes.

Stir in flour, salt, pepper and herbs. Reduce heat and add milk. Cook over medium heat until mixture thickens, stirring constantly.

Remove from heat. Add cheese, stirring until melted. Add nuts, wheat germ and eggs. Combine thoroughly.

Spoon into prepared pan and bake for 50-60 minutes, or until loaf tests firm in the center. Allow Vegetable Nut Loaf to remain in pan for 10 minutes before turning out onto serving platter. Serve hot with Marsala Mushroom Sauce.

Salads & Dressings

These stone walls were once the foundation stones of an old Western Reserve barn. They now enclose the four quadrants of the fragrant garden.

BRANDIED SPINACH SALAD

yield 6 servings

6 cups spinach, washed, dried and torn (about ½ pound)
1½ cups cauliflower florets, bite-size pieces
8 cherry tomatoes, cut in half

DRESSING:

1 tablespoon olive oil
3 green onions, thinly sliced
1 clove garlic, minced
1 tablespoon brown sugar
1 tablespoon vinegar
¼ teaspoon crushed thyme
2 tablespoons brandy

In a large salad bowl, combine prepared vegetables.

In a small frying pan, heat oil and add onions and garlic. Cook until soft. Stir in sugar, vinegar and thyme. Reduce heat and stir in brandy. Simmer until mixture just begins to bubble. Pour over vegetables, toss gently to coat. Serve immediately.

BROCCOLI SALAD

yield 6 servings

1 large bunch broccoli
⅓ cup mayonnaise
2 tablespoons sugar
2 tablespoons freshly grated Parmesan cheese
1 tablespoon red raspberry vinegar
½ cup chopped red onion
⅓ cup golden raisins

Garnish: 8 strips of bacon, cook crisp, drained and crumbled

Cut broccoli florets into bite size pieces. Blanch in boiling water for 1½ minutes. Drain and chill in ice water. Redrain, pat with paper towels to remove excess moisture.

Combine mayonnaise, sugar and cheese in small bowl. Add vinegar and blend thoroughly.

Place broccoli florets, onions and raisins in a large glass bowl. Add dressing, toss gently to coat. Cover and allow to chill for 4 hours. Just before serving, add crumbled bacon.

ROMAINE LIGHT

Salad ingredient proportions for each serving:

1 cup shredded romaine
2 tablespoons grated Parmesan or Gruyere cheese
1 tablespoon toasted pine nuts
1 tablespoon snipped fresh chive, or green onions
1 tablespoon vinaigrette dressing

VINAIGRETTRE DRESSING

¼ cup white wine vinegar
2 teaspoons Dijon-style mustard
2 cloves garlic, pressed
½ cup olive oil
½ cup safflower oil
salt and pepper, to taste

Combine dressing ingredients and beat until well blended. May be prepared ahead and chilled. Bring to room temperature before servng.

To serve, arrange salad proportions in individual bowls.

NUTRITIOUS SALAD   yield 4 servings

Here is a quick and tasty combination of ingredients. A slice of whole wheat toast and fresh fruit would complete the meal.

1 (10-ounce) package frozen mixed chopped vegetables
1 (16-ounce) carton cottage cheese
1 green onion, finely sliced
1 tablespoon minced fresh parsley
¼ teaspoon crushed thyme

Blanch vegetables in boiling water until just tender, 2 to 4 minutes. Drain and cool.

Blend all ingredients and serve on lettuce greens if desired.

CRISPY VEGETABLE SALAD

yield 8 - 10 servings

1 medium head cauliflower
6 green onions, finely sliced
1 large carrot, shredded
3 ribs celery, finely sliced
¼ cup *each:* diced red and green pepper
½ cup raisins
1 cup shredded Chinese cabbage
½ cup chopped walnuts, toasted

DRESSING:

3 tablespoons red wine vinegar
1 teaspoon spicy prepared mustard
6 tablespoons salad oil
2 tablespoons finely chopped chutney (such as Major Grey's)
salt and pepper, to taste

Separate cauliflower into bite-size pieces. Place in large serving bowl. Add onion, carrots, peppers and raisins.

Prepare dressing. In a small bowl whisk vinegar, mustard and oil until blended. Stir in chutney. Add salt and pepper, if desired. Pour dressing over vegetables and toss to coat. Cover and chill. Just before serving, stir in Chinese cabbage and toasted nuts.

TANGY CARROT SHREDS

yield 4 - 6 servings

4 cups shredded carrots, about 1½ pounds
1 teaspoon salt
½ teaspoon ground white pepper
2 tablespoons red wine vinegar
⅓ cup salad oil
3 tablespoons fresh lemon juice

Garnish: minced fresh parsley and sliced black olives

Place shredded carrots in large bowl. Sprinkle with salt and pepper. Toss well to combine. Let stand 5 minutes.

Add vinegar, oil, and lemon juice, toss to coat. Cover and chill. May be refrigerated overnight.

Just before serving, toss lightly. Garnish with minced parsley and sliced black olives. May be served as individual salads on plates of shredded mixed greens.

Two light salads to enjoy when springtime asparagus is at its best.

ASPARAGUS SALAD I

yield 4 servings

1 pound asparagus
1 (8-ounce) can bamboo shoots, drained
1 sweet red pepper, seeded
1 tablespoon capers, drained and chopped
Salad greens for 4 servings

Dressing: Honey Celery Seed Dressing (see Page 198)

Wash asparagus, snap off tough ends, cut into 1-inch lengths. In a small amount of water, cook asparagus until tender-crisp, about 3 minutes. Drain and chill.

Cut bamboo shoots and red pepper into thin strips.

To serve, line salad plates with torn greens, arrange bamboo shoots and red pepper strips over greens, top with asparagus.

Just before serving pour dressing over salad and sprinkle with chopped capers.

ASPARAGUS SALAD II

1 pound asparagus
¼ cup minced chive, or
4 green onions, finely sliced
Romaine or other salad greens for 4 servings

Dressing: Raspberry Vinaigrette (see Page 195)

Wash asparagus, snap off tough ends, cut into 1-inch lengths. In a small amount of water cook asparagus until tender-crisp. Drain and chill.

Shred romaine (or other greens), arrange on 4 serving plates. Top with asparagus, sprinkle with chives or green onions. Just before serving pour dressing over salad.

GRECO GREEN BEAN SALAD

Very young, tender green beans are preferred for this salad.

2 pounds fresh green beans, washed, snap off ends
1 cup finely sliced red onion
½ cup toasted pine nuts
1 cup crumbled Feta cheese

DRESSING:

½ cup (packed) fresh mint leaves, washed and dried
⅓ cup white wine vinegar (or mint vinegar)
½ teaspoon salt
¼ teaspoon black pepper
1 teaspoon sugar
1 small clove garlic, minced
⅔ cup olive oil

Blanch green beans in boiling water for 3 minutes. Drain immediately and chill in ice water. Redrain and pat dry with paper towels. Chill until ready to serve.

Just before serving prepare dressing in food blender. In a serving bowl place green beans, onion slices, pine nuts and cheese. Pour on dressing, toss to coat and serve.

When ready to serve place green beans in serving bowl. Add pine nuts, onion and cheese. Add enough dressing to coat. Toss gently. Serve immediately.

NOTE: Coarsely grated Romano, Parmesan or Gruyere may be substituted for Feta cheese. Fresh basil leaves could be used in place of mint, along with basil vinegar.

E.R.D.

CITRUS MINT AND ONION SALAD   yield 6 - 8 servings

This makes an appealing composed salad which may be prepared early in the day.

2 grapefruits, pink or white
4 navel oranges
2 lemons
2 limes
1 medium red onion
4 tablespoons extra virgin olive oil
¼ cup chopped fresh mint leaves

Garnish: sprigs of fresh mint

Peel, seed, and cut fruit into thin slices. Arrange on glass serving platter.

Slice onion very thin and arrange rings on top of fruit. Sprinkle with chopped mint. Drizzle with olive oil. Cover and refrigerate 8 hours or overnight.

Garnish with fresh mint sprigs just before serving.

NOTE: The orange and grapefruit peel may be saved to candy. See Sweets and Sours section for recipe. Also strips of dried citrus peel are often added to pot-pourris and tea blends.

GINGERED CARROT PEAR SALAD   yield 4 - 6 servings

1 pound carrots, cleaned and shredded
½ teaspoon salt
1 teaspoon sugar
2-4 firm ripe pears (allow ½ pear per serving)
1 head Bibb lettuce, wash and dry
½ cup chopped pecans, toasted

Gingered Mayonnaise Dressing:

1 cup mayonnaise
3 tablespoons minced, candied ginger
2 tablespoons lime juice
⅛ teaspoon ground allspice

Place shredded carrots in glass bowl, sprinkle with salt and sugar. Toss to combine. Set aside.

Combine dressing ingredients in a small bowl. Add ½ cup of the dressing to the carrots. Toss to coat. Cover and chill.

Just before serving, cut pears in half, remove stem and core. Place lettuce cup on each serving plate. Top with pear half and fill with carrot mixture. Add a dollop of remaining dressing and sprinkle with toasted pecans.

FRESH BASIL IN PASTA SALAD

A colorful herb-flavored salad for summer buffets. Proportions may be cut in half for family use. Fresh basil and herb vinegar add special flavor.

1 (16-ounce) package small spiral-shaped pasta, cooked and drained
1 sweet red pepper, seeded, thinly sliced
1 green pepper, seeded, thinly sliced
4 green onions, use part tops, finely sliced
1 (6-ounce) can pitted black olives, drained
16 ounces Mozarella cheese, cut in small chunks
2 tablespoons chopped fresh basil
2 ripe tomatoes, coarsely chopped

HERB VINAIGRETTE

3 tablespoons opal basil vinegar (or red wine vinegar)
2 tablespoons grated Parmesan cheese
8 large basil leaves, chopped
¼ cup chopped chive
⅔ cup olive oil

Combine dressing ingredients in food blender and whirl until basil and chives are finely cut. Set aside.

In a large serving bowl combine pasta with salad ingredients, except tomatoes. At this point the salad may be chilled; however, it has better flavor if served at room temperature.

Just before serving add tomatoes and dressing. Toss to combine.

If available, nasturtium blossoms make an attractive garnish.

MARINATED TOMATOES

Summer-ripe tomatoes and fresh herbs will enhance this easy salad. If dried herbs are used, marinate them in the dressing for several hours.

3 ripe tomatoes, sliced
8 ounces fresh mushrooms, sliced
1 large red onion, thinly sliced
2 cloves garlic, minced
2 tablespoons chopped fresh basil
1 tablespoon chopped fresh tarragon
½ teaspoon chopped fresh oregano

DRESSING:

1 cup olive oil
½ cup opal basil vinegar (or red wine vinegar)
2 teaspoons sugar, optional
salt and pepper, to taste

Layer tomatoes, onions and mushrooms in a 13 x 9 x 2-inch glass serving dish. Sprinkle with fresh herbs. Prepare dressing and pour over ingredients. Marinate for 1 hour before serving.

ROAST BEEF PICNIC SALAD

No extra picnic plates or forks, this salad is served in leaves of romaine.

1 pound roast beef, chill after roasting
12 ounces fresh mushrooms, cleaned and sliced
1 head romaine, separate leaves, wash and dry

DRESSING:

½ cup finely chopped onion
½ cup finely chopped celery
¾ cup mayonnaise
2 tablespoons lemon juice (or red wine vinegar)
2 tablespoons prepared horseradish
1 tablespoon spicy, prepared mustard
¼ cup minced fresh parsley
½ teaspoon finely crushed thyme
½ teaspoon finely crushed marjoram

Combine dressing ingredients in a large bowl.

Cut beef into thin strips and place in dressing. Add mushrooms and toss to combine. Cover and chill.

Separate romaine leaves, wash and dry. Chill until ready to serve.

To serve, place a large spoonful of salad in a romaine leaf, fold over and eat, out of hand.

MOLDED GAZPACHO

A popular cold summer soup becomes a colorful salad.

2 packages unflavored gelatin
3 cups tomato juice
2 tablespoons lemon juice
2 tablespoons red wine vinegar
1 teaspoon salt
4 drops hot pepper sauce
2 small, ripe tomatoes, peeled, seeded, and diced
1 medium cucumber, peeled and diced (or about a 7-inch section of an
    English cucumber, no need to peel)
1 green pepper, seeded and diced
¼ cup chopped onion
¼ cup chopped celery
1 tablespoon chopped chive
1 tablespoon minced parsley
Salad greens for serving

Dressing: Creamy Herb Dressing is suggested (see Page 198).

In a saucepan, sprinkle gelatin over tomato juice to soften. Let stand 5 minutes. Place over medium heat and stir until gelatin is dissolved. Remove from heat. Stir in lemon juice, vinegar, salt and hot pepper sauce. Chill until partially set.

Add vegetables and pour into a 1½-quart ring mold or shallow serving dish. Chill until firm.

To serve, unmold on a bed of salad greens. Serve dressing in a separate bowl.

TAWNY BING CHERRY MOLD

Port wine adds a special flavor to this easy salad.

1 (3-ounce) package black cherry flavored gelatin
1⅓ cups boiling water
⅔ cup Tawny Port Wine
1½ cups pitted Bing cherries, fresh or frozen

DRESSING: mayonnaise is suggested.

In a small bowl, dissolve gelatin in boiling water. Stir in wine. Let cool slightly; then refrigerate until partially set.

Stir in cherries and transfer to 1-quart mold. Chill until firmly set.

NOTE: Create a special treat by stuffing each cherry with half an English walnut before adding to gelatin.

MOLDED CRANBERRY RELISH SALAD   yield 8 - 10 servings

This is a good after-Thanksgiving salad to serve with turkey sandwiches.

2 envelopes unflavored gelatin
2½ cups cranberry juice, divided
½ cup boiling water
1 tablespoon lemon juice
¼ tablespoon ground coriander
1¼ cups cranberry-orange relish (homemade is preferable)
1 cup chopped apple
1 cup chopped celery
½ cup chopped pecans or walnuts, toasted
Salad greens for lining salad plates

Soften gelatin in ½ cup of the cranberry juice. Add boiling water and stir until gelatin is dissolved.

Place remaining 2 cups of cranberry juice in large mixing bowl, add remaining ingredients and stir in gelatin.

Pour into shallow 2-quart glass dish or mold. Chill until firm.

NOTE: A Cranberry-Orange Relish recipe is in the Sweets and Sours section, see Index.

RASPBERRY MOLD WITH FRESH FRUIT

2 cups boiling water
1 (6-ounce) package raspberry-flavored gelatin
1 pint raspberry sherbet

Shredded salad greens for lining serving platter

In a large mixing bowl dissolve gelatin in boiling water. Let cool slightly, then add sherbet and stir until melted. Pour into 4-cup ring mold. Chill until firm. Prepare fruit filling and dressing.

FRUIT FILLING

½ cup *each*: sliced seedless grapes, red or green
strawberries, sliced
cantaloupe balls
honeydew melon balls
1 (13½-ounce) can pineapple chunks, drained
½ cup unsweetened grated coconut (optional)
1 cup dairy sour cream

Combine fruit filling ingredients in a bowl and chill.

VANILLA YOGURT HONEY DRESSING

1 (8-ounce) carton vanilla-flavored yogurt
2 teaspoons honey
1 teaspoon ground poppy seed

Combine dressing ingredients and chill.

To serve, unmold gelatin on serving platter lined with salad greens. Fill center with fruit filling. Serve dressing in separate bowl.

HAM TARRAGON MOUSSE

2 envelopes unflavored gelatin
2 tablespoons lemon juice
½ cup boiling water or chicken broth
1 tablespoon Marsala wine
1½ cups mayonnaise
1 tablespoon prepared horseradish
1 tablespoon Dijon-style mustard
1 tablespoon minced fresh tarragon, or
　½ teaspoon crushed dried tarragon
½ teaspoon salt
¼ teaspoon black pepper
3 cups ground cooked ham, about 1½ pounds
¼ cup coarsely chopped green onions
⅓ cup finely chopped celery
1 cup whipping cream
Salad greens for serving plates

Lightly grease a 9 x 5-inch loaf pan or 2-quart mold.

In a large mixing bowl soften gelatin in lemon juice. Let stand 5 minutes. Add boiling water or broth, stir until gelatin is dissolved.

Let cool then add Marsala wine, mayonnaise, seasonings, ground ham, onions and celery. Stir to combine.

Whip cream until stiff. Fold into ham mixture. Turn into prepared pan. Chill until firm. Prepare dressing.

TARRAGON MAYONNAISE

1 cup mayonnaise
1 tablespoon minced fresh tarragon (or ½ teaspoon dried)
½ teaspoon Dijon-style mustard

In a small bowl combine ingredients. Cover and chill.

To serve, unmold salad, cut into slices and serve on plates lined with salad greens. Add a dollop of dressing to each serving.

CANTALOUPE AND CHICKEN SALAD

½ pound green seedless grapes
¾ cup slivered almonds, toasted
2 cups cooked, coarsely chopped chicken, chilled
1 (5-ounce) can water chestnuts, drained and sliced
⅓ cup mayonnaise
⅓ cup plain yogurt
¼ teaspoon curry powder (or to taste)
¼ teaspoon salt
1 teaspoon soy sauce
1 large ripe cantaloupe, chilled
lettuce cups, 2 to 3 leaves per serving

Garnish: reserve 1 cup of grapes to frost and ¼ cup of toasted almonds

Prepare ahead: Lightly beat 1 egg white in a small bowl. Brush the reserved grapes with egg white. Coat with granulated sugar. Place on plate and chill until ready to use.

Place almonds in a pie plate and toast in a preheated 350°F. oven until lightly browned. Stir several times. Watch closely to prevent overbrowning. Set aside ¼ cup for garnish.

To prepare salad, combine chicken, water chestnuts, grapes and ½ cup of the toasted almonds in a serving bowl.

Combine mayonnaise, yogurt, curry powder, salt and soy sauce. Add to chicken mixture and toss to coat. Cover and chill until ready to serve.

Just before serving, peel and remove seeds from cantaloupe and cut into ½-inch slices. Arrange lettuce cups on serving plates. Top with 3 or 4 slices of cantaloupe. Spoon chicken mixture over cantaloupe. Garnish with frosted grapes and toasted almonds.

TUNA CANNELLINI SALAD

1 (16-ounce) can cannellini (white kidney beans)
3 tablespoons finely chopped onion
2 tablespoons finely chopped fresh parsley
1 garlic clove, finely minced
1 (9¼-ounce) can solid white tuna, chilled
Salad greens for lining serving plates

Garnish: black olives and red onions sliced

VINAIGRETTE:

2 tablespoons red wine vinegar
1 teaspoon Dijon-style mustard
1 teaspoon sugar
6 tablespoons olive oil
salt and pepper, to taste

Combine dressing ingredients and set aside.

Drain beans and place in glass dish. Add onions, parsley and garlic. Pour on dressing and toss to combine. Chill for an hour.

When ready to serve, arrange greens on plates, top with marinated bean mixture. Drain tuna and break into bite-size chunks. Place a portion on each serving. Add garnishes.

NOTE: This vinaigrette is a useful blend for a variety of green salads. Variations may be created with flavored oils and vinegars.

SAVORY SALMON DILL MOLD

yield 6 servings

Capers and fresh dill have been added to this recipe which was printed in our 1960 cookbook, MORE SAVORY SEASONING.

2 envelopes unflavored gelatin
½ cup cold water
1 cup chicken broth
1 cup mayonnaise
1 cup sour cream
2 tablespoons lemon juice
1 teaspoon Worcestershire sauce
¼ cup finely minced onion
1 pound can red sockeye salmon, drained, bones and skin removed
½ cup chopped cucumber
½ cup chopped celery
2 tablespoons fresh snipped dill
2 tablespoons capers, drained and chopped

Garnish: salad greens, black olives, fresh parsley and dill. If desired, additional mayonnaise for dressing.

In a small saucepan soften gelatin in the cold water. Add chicken broth and stir over low heat until gelatin is dissolved. Cool. Add mayonnaise, sour cream and seasonings, including minced onion. Chill until slightly thickened.

Lightly flake the salmon before adding to gelatin mixture. Fold in cucumber, celery, dill and capers. Spoon into lightly oiled 6-cup mold and chill until firm.

To serve, unmold on bed of salad greens and arrange garnishes.

CRABMEAT SALAD

yield 4 servings

1 pound prepared crabmeat
1 cup *fresh* bread crumbs, crusts removed
3 tablespoons lemon juice
¾ cup chopped celery
1 medium onion, chopped
2 cups frozen green peas, thawed
salt and pepper, to taste

Prepare lettuce cups for 4 servings

Garnish: tomato wedges and minced fresh parsley

DRESSING:

yield about 1 cup

4 tablespoons mayonnaise
4 tablespoons sour cream
2 tablespoons chili sauce
2 teaspoons prepared horseradish
3 teaspoons lemon juice

Drain crabmeat to remove excess moisture and pick over to remove any bits of shell.

After peas have thawed, remove any excess moisture from peas. No need to cook.

Combine salad ingredients with enough dressing to moisten. Cover and chill.

To serve, arrange lettuce cups on salad plates. Fill with crabmeat mixture. Garnish each serving with tomato wedges and minced parsley.

ESCABECHE WITH COOKED SEAFOOD

yield 4 - 6 servings

1 pound cleaned, white-fleshed fish fillets
½ pound scallops
½ pound raw shrimp
Juice of 2 large limes, about ½ cup
2 tablespoons olive oil

Poach or microwave fillets and scallops until opaque. Do not overcook. Boil shrimp until it turns pink, about 2 minutes. Drain immediately, shell and devein. Cut seafood into bite-size pieces and place in glass bowl. Combine lime juice with olive oil and pour over seafood. Cover and chill for 2 hours. Prepare dressing and vegetable garnishes.

DRESSING:

2 tablespoons olive oil
¼ cup ketchup
½ teaspoon Worcestershire sauce
1 tablespoon chopped fresh coriander leaves
1 clove garlic, finely minced
½ teaspoon salt
¼ teaspoon hot pepper sauce, or to taste

Combine ingredients and set aside.

VEGETABLE GARNISH:

3 ripe tomatoes, seeded and chopped
½ cup finely sliced red onion
shredded romaine for lining serving plates
½ cup sliced black olives

Just before serving drain lime juice and oil from seafood and add to dressing. To serve, line plates with shredded romaine, add a portion of the seafood, top with tomatoes and onions. Spoon dressing over each serving and garnish with black olives.

THAI BEEF SALAD

yield 4 servings

Fresh peppermint is preferable for use in this recipe.

½ pound deli-style roast beef, thinly sliced

Garnish: 1 cup thinly-sliced zucchini or cucumber and thin strips of red and green bell peppers

Cut roast beef into thin strips. Prepare marinade.

MARINADE:
1 tablespoon olive oil
¼ cup rice wine vinegar
⅓ cup chopped fresh peppermint
1 teaspoon sugar
2 tablespoons slivered green onions or chives
Salt and pepper, to taste

Blend marinade ingredients and place in a glass bowl, add beef strips and chill for several hours or overnight.

To serve, place a portion of beef on each serving plate, surround with zucchini slices, and arrange pepper strips on top.

CHILLED PASTA FRUIT SALAD

yield 4 - 6 servings

A variety of seasonal fruits may be used in this refreshing salad.

1 cup dry small pasta shells, cooked and drained
1 cup seedless grapes (red or green)
1 cup strawberries, sliced
1 large tart apple, peeled and diced
1 (8-ounce) container lemon-flavored yogurt
1 teaspoon minced fresh lemon thyme leaves
1 tablespoon chopped fresh mint leaves

Cool the cooked pasta slightly, then combine in a mixing bowl with the fruits and herbs. Add lemon yogurt and toss to coat. Chill before serving on beds of lettuce.

DRESSINGS

RASPBERRY VINAIGRETTE

yield 1 cup

¼ cup raspberry vinegar
¼ cup maple syrup*
1½ teaspoons Dijon-style mustard
½ teaspoon dried tarragon
½ teaspoon salt
¼ teaspoon ground pepper
¼ cup olive oil
¼ cup vegetable oil

Blend ingredients until emulsified. Refrigerate leftover dressing.

May substitute 2 tablespoons sugar with ½ teaspoon maple extract.

HONEY LIME DRESSING

yield 1½ cups

A favorite dressing from Western Reserve Herb Society's first cookbook, SAVORY SEASONING, published in 1957.

¼ cup honey
1 teaspoon Dijon-style mustard
½ teaspoon salt
1 teaspoon sweet paprika
¼ cup lime juice
2 tablespoons minced onion
1 teaspoon celery seed
1 cup salad oil

In a small saucepan combine honey, mustard, salt, paprika and lime juice. Heat just to boiling, whisking continuously. Remove from heat and cool slightly. Pour into food blender, add onion and celery seed. With machine running, slowly add oil and beat until dressing is emulsified. Store in refrigerator.

MADALENE'S FRENCH DRESSING*

yield 2½ cups

2 eggs (see note)
⅓ cup white wine
⅓ cup white wine vinegar
⅓ cup water
1 teaspoon salt
½ teaspoon ground white pepper
½ teaspoon paprika
1 tablespoon lemon thyme
2 tablespoons parsley
2 tablespoons chives, cut fine
1½ cups salad oil, may use part olive oil

Place all ingredients except oil in blender. Combine thoroughly. Add oil slowly and keep beating until emulsified. Taste to adjust seasonings. Keep chilled until ready to use.

Used with permission of Madalene Hill, former president of The Herb Society of America. This recipe also appears in the book, SOUTHERN HERB GROWING, written by Madalene Hill and Gwen Barclay.

NOTE: If you do not wish to eat uncooked eggs, use the equivalent of a pasturized egg substitute.

GINGER LIME VINAIGRETTE

yield 1 cup

Use with seafood salads or as a marinade for seafood or poultry.

1 teaspoon minced fresh ginger
2 green onions with part tops, finely sliced
¼ to ½ teaspoon hot red pepper flakes
¼ cup fresh lime juice
½ teaspoon Oriental sesame oil
2 tablespoons soy sauce
⅔ cup salad oil

In blender combine all ingredients, except salad oil, and blend thoroughly. With machine running, slowly add oil and beat until emulsified. Store in refrigerator.

MANGO CHUTNEY DRESSING

yield 2 cups

2 cloves garlic, minced
1 tablespoon chopped fresh ginger
1 tablespoon prepared spicy mustard
½ cup mango chutney (such as Major Grey's)
⅓ cup red raspberry vinegar
1 cup salad oil

In a blender combine first 5 ingredients. Blend until smooth. With machine running, slowly add oil and beat until emulsified. Store in refrigerator.

NOTE: Fresh ginger and ground ginger are not interchangeable flavors; however, if ground ginger is preferred, it will add a warm spicy tone that is acceptable for this dressing. Use ½ teaspoon of the ground ginger.

CILANTRO DRESSING

yield 1½ cups

½ cup, lightly packed, *fresh* cilantro leaves
2 tablespoons chopped fresh dillweed (or 2 teaspoons dried)
¾ cup Greek black olives, pitted and chopped
1 tablespoon chopped onion
½ teaspoon dried crushed oregano
¼ teaspoon ground black pepper
2 tablespoons red or white wine vinegar
⅓ cup olive oil

Finely chop the cilantro leaves and place in a small mixing bowl with remaining ingredients. Whisk until well blended. Store in refrigerator.

FRESH TARRAGON HONEY DRESSING

yield 1 cup

⅓ cup tarragon vinegar
1 tablespoon chopped sweet onion
1 teaspoon Dijon-style mustard
½ teaspoon salt
¼ teaspoon ground black pepper
2 teaspoons honey
⅔ cup olive oil (may use part salad oil)
2 tablespoons chopped fresh tarragon leaves (two 6-inch sprigs)

In blender or food processor combine first 6 ingredients. Beat until blended. Taste to adjust seasoning. With machine running, slowly add oil until emulsified; then add chopped tarragon and beat until well mixed. Store in refrigerator.

CREAMY HERB DRESSING

yield 1 cup

½ cup cottage cheese
½ cup buttermilk (shake carton before measuring)
1 tablespoon minced onion
2 tablespoons chopped fresh tarragon
2 tablespoons chopped fresh parsley
2 tablespoons chopped fresh chive
Salt and pepper, to taste

In a blender or food processor, beat the cottage cheese and buttermilk until smooth and creamy. Add onion and herbs, beat until blended. Add salt and pepper, to taste. Store in refrigerator.

NOTE: Fresh herbs are preferable. If only dried herbs are available, substitute one-third the amount of the fresh herb, or approximately 2 teaspoons of a crushed dry herb. Other herb choices may be combined to suit individual taste.

HONEY CELERY SEED DRESSING

yield 1½ cups

This recipe was printed in ANOTHER SAVORY SEASONINGS, Western Reserve Herb Society's 1969 cookbook. The amount of sugar has been reduced from the original recipe. Note that poppy seed may be substituted for celery seed.

¼ cup sugar
1 teaspoon dry mustard
1 teaspoon paprika
½ teaspoon salt
2 tablespoons minced onion
⅓ cup honey
⅓ cup vinegar
2 tablespoons lemon juice
1 cup safflower oil
1 teaspoon celery seed
(or 1 teaspoon poppy seed)

In blender or food processor combine first 8 ingredients. With machine running, slowly add oil until dressing is emulsified. Stir in celery seed. Store in refrigerator.

SCENTED GERANIUM DRESSING

yield ⅔ cup

A special dressing for summer fruit salad.

1 large leaf apple-scented geranium
1 large leaf rose-scented geranium
4 large leaves lemon-scented geranium
1 small leaf mint-scented geranium
3 tablespoons red raspberry vinegar
(or use white wine vinegar)
1 tablespoon granulated sugar
½ cup light fresh olive oil

Wash and dry geranium leaves. Cut out the large center leaf veins. Place all ingredients, except olive oil, in blender. Use high speed to puree. With machine running, slowly add olive oil until emulsified. Let stand 30 minutes before using. Plan to use this dressing the same day as prepared.

MINTED PINEAPPLE-POPPY SEED DRESSING

yield 2¼ cups

No oil is used in this dressing.

1 teaspoon unflavored gelatin
2 cups unsweetened pineapple juice
3 tablespoons honey
1½ tablespoons lemon juice
2 tablespoons chopped fresh mint
1 tablespoon poppy seeds

In a small saucepan soften gelatin in pineapple juice. Then cook over medium heat, and stir until gelatin is dissolved. Remove from heat and blend in remaining ingredients. Store in refrigerator.

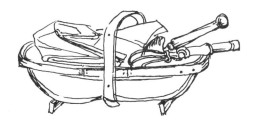

WHITE FRENCH DRESSING

yield about 5 cups

This dressing keeps well in refrigerator for up to 2 weeks.

3 tablespoons cornstarch
¼ cup cold water
¾ cup boiling water
¼ teaspoon paprika
½ cup sugar
2 teaspoons salt
¼ teaspoon ground white pepper
1 teaspoon dry mustard
¼ teaspoon garlic powder (or onion powder)
1 cup vinegar
2¾ cups safflower oil

In a 3-quart stainless steel pan, dissolve cornstarch in cold water. Add boiling water and cook over medium heat until thick and clear, about 5 minutes. Stir continuously.

Add paprika, sugar, salt, pepper, mustard and garlic powder. Stir until ingredients are blended. Taste to adjust seasonings. Remove from heat. Add vinegar. With rotary or hand-held electric mixer, slowly beat in oil until emulsified.

When cool transfer to glass containers with non-corrosive lids. Store in refrigerator.

NOTE: Favorite herbs may be added to vary flavor.

PASTA SALAD DRESSING

yield ⅔ cup

An easy dressing for chilled pasta and vegetable salads.

juice of 1 lemon (about 4 tablespoons)
2 cloves garlic, minced
½ teaspoon crushed marjoram
¼ teaspoon crushed thyme
1½ tablespoons Dijon-style mustard
4 tablespoons opal basil vinegar (or red wine vinegar)
1 tablespoon sugar, or to taste
3 tablespoons mayonnaise
3 tablespoons grated Parmesan or Romano cheese

In a small bowl, combine all ingredients and whisk until well blended. Taste to adjust seasonings. Store in refrigerator.

Soups

The trial and cutting garden is specifically utilitarian in its purpose. This sizeable garden, beautifully planned and planted, yields many blooms for drying and herbs for cooking.

ESCAROLE PLUS SOUP

yield 6 - 8 servings

A fresh head of escarole makes a colorful holder for crudites. A variety of fresh, bite-sized vegetables tuck in nicely among the crinkly leaves, along with an assortment of olives. The escarole may be used for this easy soup the next day.

1 large head escarole, washed and dried
8 cups rich chicken broth
salt and pepper, to taste
½ cup grated Parmesan cheese (Gruyere or Monterey Jack)

Garnishes: Fresh parsley, chervil, chive or green onions are good additions as is a cup of shredded carrot.

Remove root end from escarole. Coarsley chop leaves. In a large saucepan bring broth to a boil, then reduce heat to simmer. Add chopped escarole to the broth. Let simmer for about 5 minutes or until leaves are *just wilted*. Season with salt and pepper.

Serve hot with a sprinkle of grated cheese over each serving. Add garnishes, if desired.

VERY EASY BEET SOUP

yield 6 servings

The main ingredients for this Borsch-style soup can be kept on the pantry shelf. Serve hot or cold.

1 16-ounce can cubed or julienne beets
1 16-ounce can prepared sweet and sour cabbage*
2 cans (10½-ounce each) consomme
1 (13¾-ounce) can beef bouillon
2 tablespoons opal basil vinegar (or red wine vinegar)

Garnishes: 1 whole boiled potato per serving, dairy sour cream, finely sliced green onions, snipped chive or fresh dillweed.

In a 3-quart saucepan combine undrained beets, cabbage, consomme, boullion and vinegar. Bring to a boil then immediately reduce heat to simmer and let cook about 5 minutes or until heated through.

To serve hot: Place a hot boiled potato in each serving bowl, ladle over hot soup. Add other garnishes of choice.

To serve cold: Let soup cool slightly, then cover and chill. Serve with dollops of sour cream, green onion or herbs.

A good rye bread goes well with this soup.

*The sweet and sour cabbage may be omitted and replaced with another can of beets.

GREEN MINESTRONE

yield 6 - 8 servings

These quick versions of Italy's famous soup require only handy vegetables, a large can of chicken broth, and herbs. Green minestrone existed long before Columbus returned with tomatoes from the New World.

1 (46-ounce) can chicken broth
1 (15-ounce) can cannellini (or other white beans)
½ cup dry pasta, such as orzo or tiny shells
1 clove garlic, minced
3 carrots, scraped and diced
1 teaspoon crushed basil (1 tablespoon chopped fresh)
½ teaspoon crushed rosemary (1 teaspoon minced fresh)
salt and pepper, to taste

Garnishes: Fresh chopped parsley, grated Parmesan cheese, pesto sauce.

In a 5-quart Dutch oven or soup pan bring chicken broth to a boil. Add vegetables of choice, along with beans, pasta, carrots, garlic and herbs. Reduce heat to simmer and cook until vegetables are just tender. Taste for seasoning. To serve, ladle into bowls and add garnishes.

VEGETABLE SUGGESTIONS FOR WINTER VERSION:

1 large potato, peeled and diced
1 rib celery with leaves, diced
2 cups finely shredded cabbage
1 turnip, peeled and diced
1 onion, chopped
1 (10½-ounce) package frozen Italian green beans

VEGETABLE SUGGESTIONS FOR SUMMER VERSION:

Omit cabbage and turnip; include
1 cup green peas, fresh or frozen
5 asparagus spears, sliced
6 green onions, thinly sliced
4 small zucchini, cut in slices
2 cups shredded Romaine or escarole
2 cups diced fresh green beans

TOMATO SAUSAGE SOUP

yield 6 - 8 servings

Crusty Italian bread or focaccia will complement this easy, full meal soup.

1 pound bulk Italian sausage, mild or hot
1 tablespoon olive oil
1 medium green pepper, seeded and chopped
1 medium onion, chopped
1 clove garlic, minced
2 (28-ounce) cans crushed or stewed tomatoes, undrained
1 (8-ounce) can tomato sauce
3 cups chicken broth
1 teaspoon crushed basil (1 tablespoon chopped fresh)
½ teaspoon crushed marjoram
1 teaspoon sugar, optional
¾ cup dry small pasta shells
1 cup grated Mozzarella cheese

In a 4-quart Dutch oven fry sausage until nicely browned. Stir to break up pieces. Remove to bowl lined with paper towels, press to remove excess fat. Drain fat from pan and wipe with paper towel.

Heat olive oil in same pan. Add green pepper, onion and garlic. Cook until soft.

Return sausage to pan; then add remaining ingredients, except pasta and cheese. Simmer for about 10 minutes; add pasta. Simmer until pasta is tender, about 10 minutes. To serve, sprinkle grated cheese over each bowl.

NOTE: About 3½ pounds of fresh, ripe tomatoes, peeled and chopped, may be substituted for the canned tomatoes and sauce.

CORNY ZUCCHINI SOUP

yield 4 servings

This soup is pureed so it appears creamy rich, without the cream.

6 small zucchini (about ¾ pound), chopped
1 cup corn kernels, fresh or frozen
1 small onion, quartered
4 tablespoons minced fresh parsley
1 teaspoon rubbed sage
1½ cups chicken broth
salt and pepper, to taste

In a 1½-quart saucepan combine all ingredients except salt and pepper. Bring to a boil; then reduce heat to simmer, cook about 10 minutes. Taste for seasoning, adding salt and pepper, if desired.

Remove from heat. Place one cup of hot mixture at a time in food blender. Puree until smooth. Repeat with remainder of soup mixture. (Use care when pureeing hot mixtures in blender.) Serve warm.

SAVORY BEEF BARLEY SOUP

yield 6 - 8 servings

Summer savory, lovage, parsley and bay leaves impart a rich flavor to this old favorite.

1½ pounds beef shank
4 quarts cold water
½ cup pearl barley
1 large onion, chopped
2 bay leaves
3 medium potatoes, peeled and diced
3 carrots, scraped and diced
8 ounces tomato sauce (or 2 fresh tomatoes, peeled and chopped)
2 teaspoons beef soup base or 2 beef bouillon cubes
1 teaspoon crushed summer savory
1 tablespoon crushed lovage (or substitute ½ cup chopped celery leaves)
2 tablespoons dry parsley flakes (or ¼ cup minced fresh parsley)
salt and pepper, to taste

Remove excess fat from beef shank.

In a large soup pan combine meat, water, barley, onion and bay leaves. Bring to a boil; then reduce heat to simmer and cook until meat is fork-tender, about 2½ hours. Skim off white foam as it forms.

When meat is tender, remove to plate. Cut off meaty portions and return to pan. Add remaining vegetables, soup base or bouillon cubes, and herbs. Simmer until potatoes and carrots are tender.

Taste for seasoning. Add salt and pepper, if desired. Remove bay leaves before serving soup.

MINTED YOGURT WITH CUCUMBER

yield 4 servings

3 sprigs mint (4-6 inches of top tender leaves)
2 cups plain yogurt
¼ cup diced cucumber (peeled if skin is waxed)
salt and pepper, to taste

Garnishes: additional coarsely chopped cucumber, mint leaves and blossoms.*

Wash mint sprigs and pat dry. Strip off leaves and coarse chop.

n food blender or processor, combine yogurt, mint and cucumber. Blend until smooth. Taste for seasoning, add salt and pepper, if desired.

Place in covered container and chill for 2 hours allowing flavors to blend. For a thinner soup add milk.

The sweet nectar hidden in flowers as well as the flavor of the petals produce pleasing tastes. There are a number of books dedicated to the use of edible flowers which are worth exploring.

TOMATO HAPPINESS SOUP

yield 6 servings

An easy chilled soup. Make it rich or lean. Skimmed milk and low-fat cottage cheese may be substituted. This recipe was printed in our 1960 cookbook, MORE SAVORY SEASONING.

1 (10¾-ounce) can condensed tomato soup
2 cups light cream
3-5 drops hot pepper sauce
¼ cup thinly-sliced green onions
½ cup cottage cheese

Garnish: ¼ cup snipped fresh chive.

In a large mixing bowl combine soup, cream and pepper sauce. Beat with rotary beater or whisk until smooth. Stir in cottage cheese and onions until well blended. Taste for seasoning.

Chill for 2 hours. Serve in individual bowls with a sprinkle of snipped chive.

NOTE: Substitute garden-ripe tomatoes. Core and quarter 4 large tomatoes, puree in blender. Then mix with remaining ingredients. Favorite herbs may be added, such as a teaspoon of fresh chopped basil and mint.

CHEESY VEGETABLE SOUP

yield 4 - 6 servings

A tasty way to use up small amounts of fresh or cooked vegetables.

Select a combination of the following vegetables to make about *4 cups* of bite-size pieces — a little more or less will not matter.

Asparagus - 2 or 3 spears
Broccoli - about 1 cup florets and stems
Carrots - 2 or 3
Celery - 2 ribs with some leaves
Green beans - about 1 cup
Onion - 1 medium, chopped
Potato - 1 or 2 medium size, peeled and diced
Turnip - 1 medium-size, peeled and diced
Zucchini - yellow or green, sliced and quartered
4 cups chicken broth, or enough to cover vegetables
¼ teaspoon ground cumin
⅛ teaspoon allspice
½ teaspoon crushed marjoram
½ teaspoon crushed summer savory
2 teaspoons rubbed sage
¼ teaspoon pepper
1 cup light cream
1 cup shredded sharp cheddar cheese, or bits of other cheeses

(Add zucchini and any precooked vegetables during last 5 minutes of cooking time.)

Prepare the vegetables of choice and combine with chicken broth in a large saucepan. Bring to a simmer; then add seasonings. Cook until vegetables are tender.

Taste for seasoning. Stir in cream. Remove from heat; then add cheese and stir until melted. Serve warm.

NOTE: Chili Bread Sticks are good with this soup, see Index.

SPRING HERB SOUP

yield 6 servings

Garden-fresh herbs are preferred for their special flavor.

¼ cup butter
1 cup chopped lovage leaves (or substitute rib of celery, chopped)
¼ cup snipped chive
¼ cup chopped French sorrel leaves (or use
¼ cup finely sliced escarole)
¼ cup chopped chervil leaves
2 tablespoons minced tarragon leaves
2 tablespoons chopped mint leaves
1 tablespoon minced thyme leaves
6 cups chicken broth
salt and pepper, to taste

Garnishes: grated nutmeg, herbed croutons, ½ cup grated cheese such as cheddar, Gruyere or Parmesan.

Melt butter in 3-quart saucepan. Add lovage leaves (or celery) and cook until soft. Add remaining herbs and cook for 3 minutes.

Stir in broth and bring to a boil. Reduce heat to simmer, cover pan and cook for 15 minutes. Add salt and pepper to taste.

Serve hot in bowls with a dusting of nutmeg, some croutons and grated cheese.

ZUCCHINI SAGA BLUE SOUP

yield 4 servings

This soup may be served hot or cold. It also freezes well.

3 slices bacon, diced
1½ pounds zucchini, chopped
1 onion, chopped (about ½ cup)
3¼ cups chicken broth, divided
¼ teaspoon crushed thyme
½ teaspoon crushed summer savory
4 ounces Danish Saga Blue cheese

Garnishes: Chopped parsley or additional crisp bacon bits.

In a large saucepan or Dutch oven, fry bacon until crisp. Spoon off fat. Add chopped zucchini, onion, ¼ cup of chicken broth and herbs. Simmer until zucchini and onions are soft, about 10 minutes.

Add remaining chicken broth and cheese. Puree in food blender in small batches. Return to pan and keep warm over low heat until ready to serve.

Ladle into bowls, garnish and serve.

DOUBLE DELIGHT SQUASH SOUP

yield 6 - 8 servings

⅓ cup butter or margarine
1 medium onion, chopped
1 clove garlic, minced
2 ribs celery, chopped
1 pound zucchini, sliced
1 pound yellow summer squash, sliced
3 cups chicken broth
1 cup grated carrots (reserve ¼ cup for garnish)
½ teaspoon crushed marjoram
½ teaspoon crushed lemon thyme
½ teaspoon crushed rosemary
1 bay leaf
¼ teaspoon black pepper
½ cup grated Colby cheese (Swiss or Gruyere may be used)
½ cup light cream

Garnish: ½ cup dairy sour cream and reserved grated carrot.

In a 4-quart Dutch oven or soup pan melt butter over medium-high heat. Add onion, garlic, and celery. Cook until soft. Add sliced zucchini and summer squash, ¾ cup of grated carrots and herbs. Reduce heat and simmer about 15 minutes. Remove bay leaf.

In food blender or processor, puree soup mixture; return to pan and simmer to reheat.

Remove pan from burner. Add cheese and cream. Stir until cheese is melted.

To serve, add a dollop of sour cream and a sprinkle of grated carrot to each bowl.

GOLDEN AUTUMN SOUP

yield 4 - 6 servings

Crispy, early fall apples and tart cider provide good flavor to this squash soup. It may be prepared ahead and reheated.

1½ pounds buttercup squash (substitute butternut or acorn)
2 tablespoons butter or margarine
1 large onion, chopped
1 rib celery, chopped
3 medium carrots, scraped and diced
2 tart apples, peeled, cored and diced
3 cups chicken broth
¼ teaspoon grated nutmeg
1 teaspoon rubbed sage
¼ teaspoon ground cumin
¼ teaspoon crushed rosemary
2 tablespoons butter or margarine (additional)
2 tablespoons all-purpose flour
1½ cups tart apple cider
¼ teaspoon ground cinnamon

Garnishes: ½ cup grated sharp cheddar cheese, ½ cup toasted chopped walnuts.

Cut squash in half, remove seeds. Place squash in a shallow baking pan and bake in preheated 375°F. oven until tender, about 40 minutes. Remove from oven and set aside.

In 4-quart Dutch oven or soup pan melt butter over medium-high heat. Add onions and celery, cook until soft.

Remove pulp from squash and place in soup pan. Add carrots, apples, broth, and seasonings. Reduce heat and simmer for 30 minutes. (For a smoother texture, soup may be pureed in food blender or processor.)

In small saucepan melt additional butter. Whisk in flour and let cook over medium heat for 3 minutes. Gradually whisk in apple cider, add cinnamon. Cook and stir until smooth and slightly thickened. Stir into soup. Taste for seasoning; salt and pepper may be added. Let simmer about 5 minutes.

To serve, ladle soup into bowls and sprinkle with grated cheese and walnuts.

MUSHROOM DILL SOUP

¼ cup unsalted butter (divided)
2 cups chopped onion
¾ pound fresh mushrooms, thinly sliced
½ cup dry white wine
1 teaspoon crushed dillweed (1 tablespoon fresh)
1 teaspoon sweet paprika
1 tablespoon soy sauce
1 cup medium white sauce (see Page 271)
1½ cups chicken broth
salt and pepper, to taste
½ cup sour cream

Garnishes: ¼ cup chopped fresh dill weed or chive.

In a 2-quart saucepan over medium heat melt butter. Add onions and cook until soft. Stir in mushrooms, wine, dill, paprika and soy sauce. Cover and simmer for 15 minutes. Stir occasionally.

Make white sauce. Add to mushroom mixture; then stir in chicken broth. Taste for seasoning; add salt and pepper, if desired. Remove from heat and stir in sour cream.

Serve warm, garnished with snips of fresh dillweed or chive.

SCANDINAVIAN FRUIT SOUP

yield 10 - 12 servings

Serve piping hot as an appetizer or chilled with a dollop of whipped cream as a dessert.

1 pound mixed dried fruit, such as peaches, apricots and pears
¾ cup golden raisins
¼ cup Zante currants
½ pound pitted prunes
4 large apples, such as Golden Delicious

Snip dried fruit into bite-size pieces. Place all ingredients, except the fresh apples, in a large, non-reactive saucepan. Cover with water and let stand overnight.

To cook, bring liquid to a boil, then reduce heat to simmer. Cover pan and cook until fruit is soft.

Peel and core apples. Coarse chop and add to fruit mixture. Cook about 5 minutes, or until apples are just softened. Do not allow apples to overcook.

May be refrigerated until ready to serve. To serve hot, reheat slowly over low heat.

MELON CITRUS BISQUE

yield 6 - 8 servings

2 small cantaloupe
1 medium-size honeydew melon
2 cups orange juice
zest from 1 lime
juice of 1 lime
1 tablespoon chopped fresh mint leaves
2-3 tablespoons sugar or honey
1 cup ginger ale or white wine

Garnish: whipped cream and fresh mint leaves.

Cut melons in half, remove seeds. Scrape pulp into a bowl. Coarsely chop and measure, should have 6 to 7 cups.

Place half the melon pulp in food blender along with 1 cup of the orange juice; add lime zest, lime juice and mint leaves. Puree until smooth. Transfer to a bowl. Puree remaining melon pulp and orange juice. Add to first batch. Stir to combine and taste for sweetness. Add sugar or honey to taste. Cover and refrigerate until chilled.

Just before serving, stir in ginger ale or wine. Serve in cups or small bowls with dollops of whipped cream and mint leaves.

VARIATIONS: Puree chopped melon with 1 pint lime sherbet. Add fruit juice or wine to create desired consistency. Use other fresh fruits and complementary sherbets for easy and refreshing summer soups.

KOOLER KIWI SOUP

yield 4 servings

9 ripe kiwis (about 3 cups peeled and diced)
1 ripe starfruit (carambola), seeded and diced (save a slice for garnish)
1½ cups apple juice or apple cider
½ cup yogurt, plain or vanilla-flavor
sugar to taste

Garnishes: extra yogurt, sliced strawberries, diced starfruit.

In food blender puree diced kiwi and starfruit. Add juice and yogurt; puree until smooth. Taste for sweetness. Add sugar, if desired. Pour into a container, cover and refrigerate until chilled.

Serve in small cups with a dollop of yogurt and choice of garnish.

PEACH MELBA SOUP

An attractive beginning for a luncheon menu or a light dessert, and especially good when local peaches are juicy-ripe.

2 pounds fresh, ripe peaches, peeled and pitted
1 cup orange juice
¼ cup honey, or to taste
⅛ teaspoon ground mace
1 teaspoon lemon juice
2 (8-ounce) cartons vanilla-flavored yogurt
1 (10-ounce) package frozen raspberries, thawed

Prepare peaches. Cut into small pieces. In a stainless steel 1½ quart saucepan combine peaches, orange juice, honey to taste, and mace. Bring to a boil; then reduce heat to simmer and cook for 10 minutes.

Remove from heat and stir in lemon juice. Let mixture cool slightly; then puree mixture in small batches in food blender. Place in large glass bowl, stir in yogurt. Cover and refrigerate until chilled.

While soup is chilling, press thawed raspberries through a sieve until pulp and juice create a puree and seeds are removed. Cover bowl and chill until ready to serve.

To serve, place peach mixture in individual bowls or wine glasses, adding a swirl of raspberry puree to each serving.

AMERICANO SOUP

Our native corn, peppers and tomatoes go into this quick soup.

1 tablespoon vegetable oil
1 medium onion, chopped
1 small green pepper, seeded and diced
1 small sweet red pepper, seeded and diced
2½ cups chicken broth
¼ teaspoon ground cumin
⅛ teaspoon hot pepper sauce
3 cups sweet corn kernels (fresh or frozen)
2 large ripe tomatoes, peeled and chopped
salt and pepper, to taste
1½ cups light cream or milk

Heat oil in a large saucepan, add chopped onion and peppers. Cook until just tender. Add chicken broth, cumin and hot pepper sauce. Bring to a boil; then reduce heat to simmer. Stir in sweet corn and tomatoes. Cook over low heat about 30 minutes.

Taste for seasoning; add salt and pepper, if desired. Stir in cream and let simmer 3 minutes. Serve hot.

NOTE: A sprinkling of chopped cilantro leaves gives this soup a southwestern flavor, or use fresh chopped parsley. Hot peppers and green chilies also flavor Mexican versions of this soup.

CAWL CENNIN

yield 6 - 8 servings

In Wales leek broth is served often, but especially on St. David's Day. Chicken broth is substituted for the traditional lamb broth.

3 medium-sized potatoes, peeled and thinly sliced
3 medium-sized leeks, thoroughly washed and sliced
6 cups chicken broth
2 tablespoons butter or margarine
1 teaspoon salt
¼ teaspoon white ground pepper

Garnish: ¼ cup chopped fresh parsley

In a large saucepan combine potatoes, leeks and broth. Bring to a boil, reduce heat to simmer; cover and cook until vegetables are tender, about 30 minutes.

With potato masher or wooden spoon mash vegetables in the saucepan. Stir in butter, salt and pepper. Bring soup back to a bubbling simmer for 3 minutes.

Serve hot with a sprinkle of fresh parsley.

NOTE: 1 teaspoon lemon thyme, dried or fresh, imparts good flavor; add while vegetables are cooking.

FISH CHOWDER

1 pound cleaned fillets (cod, haddock or other firm white fish)
4 medium potatoes, pared
1 quart milk (may use part cream)
1 bay leaf
1 teaspoon crushed thyme
¼ teaspoon grated nutmeg
⅛ teaspoon ground allspice
4 slices lean bacon, diced
1 medium onion, chopped
1 carrot, scraped and diced
1 rib celery, chopped
salt and pepper, to taste

Garnishes: chopped parsley, reserved crumbled bacon, paprika.

Rinse fish fillets and pat dry. Set aside.

Microwave or boil potatoes until tender. Cut into small cubes and set aside.

Pour milk into 2-quart saucepan, add bay leaf, thyme and spices. Place over **low** heat to warm.

In a frying pan, fry bacon until crisp. Remove from pan and drain on paper towels. When cool, crumble and reserve for garnish.

Spoon off all but 1 tablespoon of bacon fat. Add onion, carrot and celery. Cook until tender. Add to warm milk along with diced potatoes.

Place fish fillets in frying pan. Cover and lower heat. Cook until flesh is opaque and flakes easily. Dice the fish and add to milk mixture. Taste for seasoning. Add salt and pepper. Let simmer gently for about 15 minutes. Do not allow milk to boil. Remove bay leaf.

Serve hot in bowls with a sprinkle of parsley, crumbled bacon and a dusting of paprika.

WHITE WINE COURT BOUILLON

A flavorful liquid for poaching fish as well as the basis for a meatless vegetable stock.

8 cups water
4 cups dry white wine
2 onions, chopped
2 celery ribs with leaves, chopped
2 carrots, scraped and diced
¼ cup fresh parsley, chopped
1 teaspoon crushed thyme (2 long sprigs fresh)
2 bay leaves
1 clove garlic
1 teaspoon peppercorns, cracked
2 teaspoons salt
1 lemon, seeded, then sliced

Combine all ingredients in stock pot. Bring to a boil. Reduce heat and simmer for about 1 hour. let cool, then strain through sieve into large bowl. Press the vegetables with a spoon to extract juices into broth. Makes about 2 quarts.

USE TO POACH FISH: Save stock after poaching fish. Add fish trimmings. Do not use fish skin with scales and remove gills from fish heads. Simmer over low heat for about 45 minutes. Strain and freeze in small containers. Use this fish stock, or fumet, in recipes calling for bottled clam juice.

VEGETABLE STOCK: Court Bouillon becomes a rich vegetable stock by adding potatoes, lettuce leaves, turnips, a small amount of shredded cabbage (about 1 cup), asparagus trimmings, and broccoli stems. Add herbs of choice, such as basil, mint, thyme or bay leaves. Simmer for about an hour. Allow to cool slightly before straining. Freeze in small containers. May be used in place of chicken or beef stocks.

LENTIL AND BROWN RICE SOUP

yield 6 servings

2 tablespoons butter or olive oil
1 large clove garlic, minced
1 onion, chopped
3 medium carrots, scraped and diced
1 rib celery with leaves, chopped
½ cup lentils (red or brown), pick over and rinse
½ cup brown rice
4 cups rich chicken stock or broth
1 cup diced cooked ham (or 1 meaty ham bone)
¼ teaspoon ground cumin
½ teaspoon *each:* crushed marjoram and thyme
1 tablespoon red wine vinegar
salt and pepper, to taste

Melt butter in large soup pan over medium-high heat. Add garlic, onion, carrots and celery. Cook until tender. Add lentils and brown rice. Cover with stock and bring to a boil; then reduce heat to simmer. Add ham (or ham bone), cumin, and herbs. Simmer until lentils and rice are tender, about 1 hour.

If using a ham bone, remove from soup after simmering, cut off meaty portions and return to pan.

Just before serving, stir in vinegar. Taste for seasoning, adding salt and pepper if desired.

This becomes a thick soup which may be thinned with stock or water.

Sweets & Sours

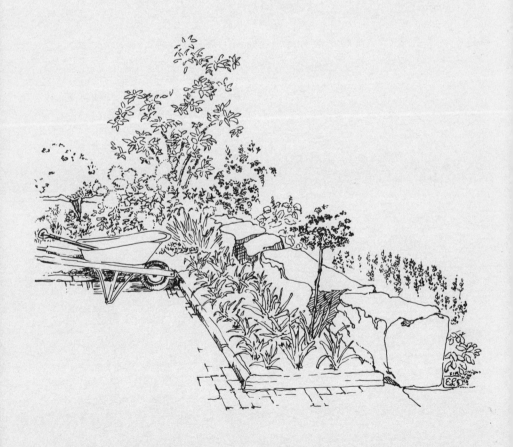

Here in one of the four quadrants of the fragrant garden hyacinths perfume the spring air. Later summer fragrances will come from scented geraniums, heliotrope and fairy roses.

BUCKEYES

1 cup butter or margarine
1 cup smooth or crunchy peanut butter
1½ cups graham cracker crumbs, finely ground
1 pound sifted confectioners' sugar
1 cup finely chopped flake coconut (optional)
12 ounces dark coating chocolate, or 12-ounce package semisweet
    chocolate chips

Place butter and peanut butter in a large saucepan. Melt over low heat, stirring constantly. Remove from heat. Add graham cracker crumbs, confectioners' sugar (and coconut, if using). Mix and blend *thoroughly.*

Shape into 1-inch balls, pressing firmly with palms of hands. The balls must be very firm. Insert a toothpick into each ball and place on a waxed paper-lined baking tray. Freeze balls for at least 2 hours.

When ready to assemble, melt chocolate in top of double boiler over hot water. Remove balls from freezer. Partially dip each one in melted chocolate, leaving an area around toothpick uncoated to resemble a buckeye.

Place balls on waxed paper-lined trays and return to freezer for 2 hours. When firm, remove toothpicks. Place in freezer containers between layers of waxed paper. Return to freezer.

When ready to serve, remove from freezer and let stand at room temperature for 10 minutes.

NOTE: Coating chocolate is available from candy making and cake decorating shops.

EASY NUT TOFFEE

1 cup butter (2 sticks)
1 cup granulated sugar
1 to 1½ cups finely chopped nuts (pecans, almonds or walnuts)
¼ pound semisweet chocolate, melted

Topping: ½ cup finely chopped nuts (additional)

Generously butter a jelly roll pan and set aside.

In a heavy saucepan melt butter with sugar, stirring until sugar is dissolved. Boil until mixture reaches hard-crack stage, or 300°F. on candy thermometer.

Quickly turn out onto buttered pan. Spread about ¼ to ⅜-inch thick. Let cool 15 minutes. Spread with melted chocolate. Sprinkle with ½ cup chopped nuts.

Let cool in pan. Then place in refrigerator to chill before breaking into pieces. Store in airtight tins.

SWEETLY SPICED PECANS

yield 2 cups

It would be wise to make double or triple batches of these popular nibbles.

2 egg whites
2 cups pecan halves (or walnut halves)
½ cup granulated sugar
2 teaspoons ground cinnamon
1 teaspoon grated nutmeg
¼ teaspoon ground ginger
pinch of ground cloves

Preheat oven to 350°F. Lightly grease a cookie sheet.

In a mixing bowl whisk egg whites until foamy. Add pecans, stir gently to coat thoroughly.

Combine sugar and spices in a mixing bowl. Gently toss pecans until well coated. Arrange in a single layer on cookie sheet. Bake about 10 minutes or until crispy. Do not overbake.

Cool completely before storing in airtight tins.

CHOCOLATE PEANUT CLUSTERS

yield about 4½ pounds

A cold day and an enclosed porch make a convenient combination for chilling these chocolate-nut treats. Wrap the clusters in festive little packages for gifts.

2 ½-pound bars dark, mildly sweet chocolate
2 ½-pound bars milk chocolate
1 12-ounce package semisweet chocolate bits
1-ounce square unsweetened baking chocolate
2 pounds roasted Spanish peanuts

Line cookie sheets and pans with waxed paper and set aside.

Break up chocolate bars. Place all chocolate in a heavy 4-quart saucepan or Dutch oven. Melt chocolate over *low* heat, stirring until smooth. (Be careful to maintain an even low heat during melting step.) Remove from heat. Let cool 5 minutes, stirring occasionally to maintain smoothness. Stir in nuts.

Drop by tablespoonfuls onto prepared pans. *Cool until chocolate becomes firm before storing.*

Clusters may be wrapped individually in plastic or store between layers of waxed paper in airtight tins. Keep refrigerated until ready to serve.

SESAME SEED BRITTLE

yield about 1 pound

This crunchy-good confection recipe was printed in our 1969 cookbook, ANOTHER SAVORY SEASONING.

2 cups granulated sugar
1 cup light corn syrup
½ cup water
⅛ teaspoon salt
½ cup untoasted sesame seed
3 tablespoons butter
¼ teaspoon baking soda

Generously butter 2 large cookie sheets. Set aside.

Combine first 4 ingredients in a heavy 3-quart saucepan over medium heat. Stir until sugar is dissolved.

Maintain a gently rolling boil until candy thermometer registers 250°F. Stir in sesame seeds and butter until blended.

Continue to boil until 300°F. registers on thermometer. Immediately remove pan from burner; stir in baking soda until mixture is very foamy. Spread mixture onto prepared cookie sheets. Cool completely before breaking into pieces. Store in airtight tins.

TIGER BUTTER

yield about 1½ pounds

This is an easy candy to make for holiday treats and gifts.

1 pound white chocolate (good quality)
½ cup crunchy peanut butter
8 ounces semisweet chocolate chips

Line cookie sheet with foil. Preheat oven to 200°F.; then turn off. Place white chocolate in shallow Pyrex casserole and place in oven to melt.

When softened remove from oven and add peanut butter. Swirl to incorporate.

Use a spatula to help pour mixture onto prepared cookie sheet. Spread to ¼-inch thickness. Set aside to cool.

Melt chocolate chips in double boiler over simmering hot water. Spread in marbleized pattern over white chocolate.

Place cookie sheet in refrigerator and chill until candy is firm. Remove from foil and break into pieces. Store in airtight containers lined with waxed paper.

CREAMY TRUFFLES

yield 35 to 40 pieces

10½ ounces bittersweet chocolate (good quality)
1 cup heavy cream (not ultra-pasturized)

Coating mixture: In a small dish mix 1 tablespoon confectioners' sugar with 3 tablespoons unsweetened cocoa. In another small dish place ½ cup finely chopped pecans or walnuts.

Line an 8-inch square pan with foil, which should extend above rim.

Finely chop the chocolate and place in work bowl of food processor.

Place cream in a small saucepan and heat to a low boil, or until bubbles begin to form around edge of pan. With processor running, slowly pour hot cream through feed tube and process until chocolate is melted.

Pour chocolate mixture into prepared pan; spread evenly. Chill for 3 hours or until chocolate is firm; then remove from pan by lifting the foil. Invert on a cookie sheet. Peel off foil. Cut chocolate into little squares of desired size. Form into balls. (Coat fingers with cocoa powder to prevent chocolate from sticking.

Roll each ball in cocoa mixture and then in chopped nuts. Place on a plate lined with waxed paper. These truffles are perishable and must be stored in refrigerator. May also be placed in a container and frozen up to 1 month.

MARZIPAN

Only 3 ingredients, plus various food colors, are required to create these molded confections. Molding tiny flowers, fruits and vegetables is somewhat like working with pliable clay. A great many small confections may be made from the following basic proportions.

1 8-ounce package almond paste
1 pound (approximately) confectioners' sugar (sifted)
1 unbeaten egg white

1. Collect almond paste into a ball, add 1 teaspoon egg white, knead with hands

2. Add 2 to 3 tablespoons of the sugar and knead into the paste.

Repeat these 2 steps until the paste is no longer sticky, though still quite pliable.

Divide dough into 8 portions. Using small amounts of vegetable food coloring, knead it into a portion of the dough until it is evenly colored.

Fruits and vegetables are shaped with the fingers, not a mold. They should be very small, not over an inch long. The attractiveness depends on the delicate coloring, small size and good shaping.

Store marzipan in tightly-covered tins.

CANDIED GINGER

yield about 1¼ pounds

Crystallized ginger is easy to make but takes a little patience. "Stem ginger" is preferable and may be found in Oriental specialty stores in July. Mature ginger rhizomes may also be used in any season. Select firm, smooth, satiny-skinned roots. Mature ginger will be hotter than tender young "stem ginger," but the fiery pungency is reduced by repeated blanchings.

1 pound fresh ginger
3 cups granulated sugar
2 tablespoons light corn syrup
3 cups water

Coating: about ¾ cup granulated sugar

With a sharp knife scrape off skin. Cut off bruised ends and trim leaf stem nodes. Cut ginger into ¼-inch slices.

Place in a non-reactive saucepan and cover with water. Bring to a boil, reduce heat to simmer and cook for 30 minutes. If necessary, add more hot water to keep ginger covered.

Drain ginger in colander. Return to pan and cover with fresh water. Repeat this blanching and draining process twice more. Taste a small piece. If the flavor is too strong and fiery to suit, repeat blanching process again. When ginger is tender and pleasantly pungent, drain and set aside.

Prepare sugar syrup. Place sugar, corn syrup and water in saucepan. Bring to a boil, stirring to dissolve sugar. Boil for 3 minutes. Add ginger slices. Return syrup to a boil and cook for 5 minutes. Remove from heat and let cool. May stand overnight.

Bring to a boil once more; reduce heat to simmer and cook until syrup is almost completely reduced. Watch carefully during this final cooking step to prevent scorching.

With tongs place ginger slices on wire rack. Let dry for about 2 hours or until slices are slightly tacky.

Place ¾ cup sugar in mixing bowl. Add ginger slices and gently toss to coat. Return sugar-coated slices to wire rack to dry for an hour. Store in airtight containers.

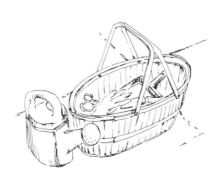

CANDIED VIOLETS

These must be made in May when common wood violets are in bloom. Avoid using blossoms that have been touched with pesticides or other garden sprays. Violets are at their best for only a short period of time so plan ahead for this project.

Equipment needed:

Large airtight tins for storage.

Very small camel hair artist brush

Deep violet *powdered* food color, available from cake decorating supply stores. (Violet blossoms lose color during storage. The food coloring added to the sugar keeps blossoms an attractive violet color.)

Superfine grade of sugar

A supply of flat toothpicks

Large cookie sheets

Method:

1. Pick violets just as the blossoms open full. Leave 2-inch stem attached. Work with only a dozen blossoms at a time to prevent wilting.
2. Wash gently; pat dry with soft cloth.
3. In a small shallow glass bowl combine ⅔ cup granulated sugar with ⅓ cup Superfine sugar. Stir in a *tiny* amount of violet food coloring. Only a small amount is needed to create an attractive violet color.
4. In another small glass bowl (a Pyrex custard cup is handy) blend 1 egg white with 1 teaspoon water. Stir until just slightly frothy.
5. Cover cookie sheet with waxed paper.
6. Hold violet by stem; dip flower gently into egg white to cover entire blossom. Remove excess egg white with paintbrush or toothpick.
7. Place blossom face down in sugar. Use a spoon to sprinkle sugar over back of blossom. The entire flower must be well covered with sugar.
8. Place flower face down on waxed paper. Use a clean toothpick to straighten petals.
9. Allow to air dry for at least 24 hours. Snip off stems and carefully turn blossoms over. Continue to dry for another 24 hours. Sugar must be completely dry, or crystallized, before storing.
10. Store between layers of waxed paper in a large airtight tin. Keep tin in a cool dry cupboard. Candied violets will keep for at least a year, if properly dried and stored.

NOTE: Candied violets make attractive garnish for petit fours, tea sandwiches, special cakes and tarts. Rose petals, violas, leaves of mint and lemon verbena may also be candied and stored in the same manner as violets.

CANDIED ORANGE PEEL

yield about 5 cups

The thick peel from navel oranges is preferable. Candied orange peel may be chopped for use in cakes, cookies or muffins, or just nibbled for a sweet treat.

3 large navel oranges (about 2½ pounds)
¾ cup water
2 tablespoons light corn syrup
2 cups granulated sugar

Coating: ¾ cup granulated sugar (additional)

Wash and dry oranges. Cut peel into quarters on each orange. Remove each section and slice peel into narrow strips, about ¼-inch wide. There should be approximately 4 cups.

Place strips in a non-reactive saucepan. Cover with water. Bring to a boil and cook for 15 minutes. Drain strips in a colander. Set aside.

Rinse out saucepan. Place ¾ cup water, corn syrup and 2 cups sugar in pan. Bring to a boil, stirring to dissolve sugar. Add drained orange peel. Reduce heat to simmer and cook for 30 to 35 minutes or until peel is tender and appears translucent.

Place large wire rack over waxed paper-lined cookie sheet. Remove peels from syrup with tongs or slotted spoon and place on rack to drain. When cool to touch, separate pieces. Let stand for about 1 hour. Peel should feel slightly tacky for sugar coating to cling.

Place remaining ¾ cup sugar in a large bowl. Add peel in batches and toss with fork until evenly coated.

Place sugar-coated peel on rack to air-dry, about 2½ to 3 hours, in a warm place.

Store in airtight containers for a month. May be refrigerated or frozen for longer storage.

CARAMEL POPCORN

yield about 1½ quarts

A candy thermometer is necessary to cook syrup to proper temperature.

½ cup popcorn kernels
1 cup blanched slivered almonds
1 cup slivered pecan halves
1 cup granulated sugar
½ cup packed brown sugar
3 tablespoons light corn syrup
¼ pound (1 stick) butter or margarine
½ cup water
1 teaspoon salt

Preheat oven to 275°F. Butter a *large* ovenproof mixing bowl. Butter a 9 x 13-inch baking pan. You will need 2 pie pans for the nuts.

Pop the corn *without* using oil. Place popped corn in buttered bowl. *Remove every unpopped kernel.* Place bowl in oven to keep corn warm.

Place nuts in separate pie pans and place in oven to warm.

In a 3-quart saucepan combine remaining ingredients. Stir over medium heat until sugars dissolve. Cook mixture until temperature registers 240°F.

Stir continuously until thermometer registers 275°F. Remove almonds from oven and stir into syrup. Continue to stir until thermometer registers 295°F. Remove pecans from oven and stir into syrup. Remove from heat immediately.

Remove bowl of corn from oven. Slowly pour syrup mixture over corn. Mix with buttered wooden spoon until corn is well coated. Turn out into shallow pan and spread out as evenly as possible. Allow to cool. Break into pieces. Store in airtight tin.

APRICOT GINGER SAUCE

yield about 3 cups

Serve chilled over ice cream or warmed as a condiment with roast pork or baked ham.

¼ cup granulated sugar
2½ cups water
8 ounces dried apricots, chopped
1 tablespoon chopped candied ginger
2 tablespoons apricot brandy

Place sugar and water in saucepan. Bring to a boil, stirring to dissolve sugar. Add chopped apricots and ginger. Reduce heat to simmer. Cook for 15 minutes or until apricots are tender. Stir in apricot brandy and simmer for 2 minutes. Remove from heat.

If a smooth texture is preferred, let sauce cool; then puree in small batches in food blender. Store in refrigerator.

HOT FUDGE SAUCE

1 (3-ounce) bar dark semisweet chocolate
2 (1 ounce) squares unsweetened chocolate
1⅓ *sticks* unsalted butter
½ cup Dutch-style unsweetened cocoa powder
½ cup granulated sugar
½ cup packed brown sugar
⅔ cup cream
2 tablespoons chocolate-mint liqueur
2 tablespoons coffee-flavored liqueur

In heavy saucepan melt chocolate with butter over **low** heat. Stir until smooth.

In a small bowl combine cocoa powder with sugars and stir until combined. Slowly stir into chocolate mixture until sugars are dissolved. Stir in cream and liqueurs.

Cook just until bubbles begin to form. Remove immediately from heat. Let cool to room temperature before storing in covered jar in refigerator. To reheat place sauce in double boiler over hot water.

BUTTERSCOTCH SAUCE

yield about 2½ cups

1¼ cups packed brown sugar
1 cup corn syrup (light or dark)
¼ cup butter
½ cup heavy cream (or use undiluted evaporated milk)
1 teaspoon vanilla extract

In a 1-quart saucepan combine butter with sugar and corn syrup. Stirring constantly cook over low heat until butter is melted and brown sugar is dissolved. Do not allow to boil. Remove from heat and cool to room temperature. Add cream and vanilla, stir until well blended.

Store in covered jar in refrigerator.

SUGAR SYRUP

Amounts may be doubled. Keeps well in refrigerator to use in iced beverages.

⅔ cup water
⅓ cup granulated sugar

In a small saucepan combine water and sugar. Bring to a boil, stirring to dissolve sugar. Reduce heat and simmer for 5 minutes. Remove from heat and allow to cool. Store in refrigerator in covered container.

PEPPERMINT SUGAR

¼ cup dried, crushed peppermint leaves
1½ cups granulated sugar

Pulverize peppermint leaves in food processor. Add sugar and process into a fine mixture. Store in tightly capped container.

PRUNE COMPOTE SYRUP   yield about 1½ cups

Serve this with baked ham or as a topping for French toast or waffles.

1 cup pitted prunes
½ cup apple juice
4 teaspoons fresh lime juice
cinnamon stick, 1-inch piece

Place ingredients in a small saucepan and simmer for about 8 minutes, or until prunes are plump and liquid has thickened slightly. Remove cinnamon stick before serving.

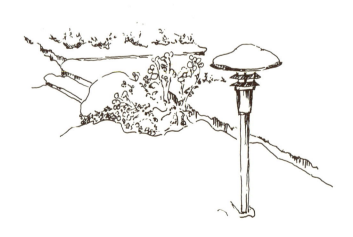

VEGETABLE RELISH
yield about 2 pints

An easy relish to make any time. It will keep for a month in refrigerator. Tastes great with hamburgers.

¼ cup vinegar*
1 tablespoon cornstarch
¾ cup granulated sugar
½ teaspoon celery seed
¼ teaspoon *each:* ground cinnamon, cloves, cumin, ginger and allspice
salt and pepper, to taste
⅛ teaspoon cayenne pepper or 2-3 drops hot pepper sauce (optional)
2 cups chopped cucumber (or substitute zucchini)
1 clove garlic, minced
1 cup chopped onion
1 cup *each:* chopped green and red bell pepper
1 rib celery, chopped

(Minted Herbs and Spice Vinegar would enhance this relish. See Index.)

In a 3-quart saucepan combine vinegar and cornstarch, stirring until smoothly blended. Add sugar and seasonings. Bring to a boil for 3 minutes. Taste to adjust seasoning.

Add vegetables. Reduce heat to a simmer and cook until mixture thickens, about 15 minutes. (Relish will become thicker as it cools.)

Ladle into clean *hot* jars. Seal with lids. Cool to room temperature. Store in refrigerator.

EASY REFRIGERATOR PICKLES
yield about 2 quarts

For pickle fans, this is an economical recipe which can be made year-round. Small tender zucchini may be used in place of cucumbers.

2 cups sugar
1 tablespoon salt
1 cup vinegar
1 tablespoon celery seed
6 cups thinly-sliced cucumbers
2 large onions, thinly sliced in quarters

NOTE: Lovage Vinegar will complement this recipe. See Index.

In a mixing bowl dissolve sugar and salt in vinegar. Stir in celery seed.

Place cucumber and onion slices in large glass container. Pour vinegar mixture over to cover. Stir gently.

Store in refrigerator for 24 hours before using. Will keep in refrigerator for 2 to 3 weeks.

Wide-mouth canning jars are convenient to use for storing pickles.

CRANBERRY-ORANGE RELISH

yield about 3 cups

1 (12-ounce) package fresh cranberries
1 large navel orange
1 lemon
¼ teaspoon ground cloves
1 cup granulated sugar
½ cup water
1 large apple
½ cup brandy (optional)

Rinse and pick over cranberries. Cut orange in quarters (remove white pith from center) and chop to fine dice. Cut lemon in quarters (remove seeds) and chop to fine dice.

In a large non-reactive saucepan combine all ingredients except apple and brandy. Bring to a boil, stir to dissolve sugar. Reduce heat to simmer and cook until fruits are tender.

Peel and core apple. Chop to fine dice. Add diced apple and brandy to cranberry mixture and cook until apple is soft, about 3 minutes. Remove from heat.

When cool, place in glass container, cover, and refrigerate for 24 hours before serving.

TOMATO OLIVE RELISH

yield about ¾ cup

Combine dried tomatoes with fresh for an easy relish to serve with veal or chicken.

2 tablespoons extra-virgin olive oil
¼ cup chopped black olives
¼ cup chopped oil-packed dried tomatoes
2 fresh Italian tomatoes, diced
1 tablespoon minced onion
1 small clove garlic, minced
½ teaspoon crushed dried oregano
salt and pepper, to taste

Combine all ingredients in a small saucepan over medium heat. Stir to combine and cook *until oil absorbs the flavor,* about 8 minutes. The fresh tomatoes should not become overcooked.

Serve warm or at room temperature over sautéed veal or chicken.

PLUM CHUTNEY

yield 6 pints

8 ounces fresh ginger root
5 pounds Damson or tart, red plums
1 pound tart apples (such as Granny Smith)
2 large onions, chopped
2 large cloves garlic, minced
1½ cups golden raisins
2 cups packed brown sugar
1 cup granulated sugar
2 cups cider vinegar
1 tablespoon salt
1 tablespoon hot pepper sauce (or flakes)
2 teaspoons mustard seed

Scrape skin off ginger root, cut off nodes and bruised ends. Chop into fine dice. Place in small saucepan. Cover with water and simmer for 30 minutes.

Wash plums, cut into small pieces. Discard seeds. Peel and core apples. Cut into quarters.

In a large non-reactive pan (5-quart size), place plums, apples, onions, garlic, raisins, and cooked, *undrained* ginger. Stir in remaining ingredients. Bring to a boil, then reduce heat to simmer. Cook gently over low heat for about 2 hours, stirring frequently to prevent ingredients from sticking to bottom of pan. When ready, the mixture should be quite thick.

Prepare canning jars. Sterilize jars and lids in a kettle of boiling water.

Ladle chutney into scalding, hot jars to within ¼-inch from tops. Seal at once. Cool and label jars. Store in cool, dark cupboard. Let mellow for 6 weeks before serving.

PAPAYA CHUTNEY

yield about 1½ cups

An easy sauce to enhance broiled lamb or chicken.

¼ cup granulated sugar
⅓ cup cider vinegar
¼ cup minced onion
½ cup golden raisins
1 teaspoon *each:* ground cinnamon and ginger
1 large, firm-ripe papaya

NOTE: Lemon Vinegar may be substituted for cider vinegar. See Index.

In a small saucepan place all ingredients except papaya. Over low heat stir to dissolve sugar. Simmer for 5 minutes.

Cut papaya lengthwise, peel and remove seeds. Cut into thin slices and stir into sugar-vinegar mixture. Simmer for 3 more minutes; then remove from heat. Serve warm as a sauce. Store leftover chutney in refrigerator.

APRICOT CHUTNEY
yield about 8 cups

This sweet-pungent condiment may be made any time from readily available ingredients. Your food processor will make quick work of the chopping.

1 large lemon
8-ounces fresh ginger root
3 medium-size tart apples
1 cup chopped onion
1 clove garlic, minced
1-pound jar apricot preserves
1½ cups packed brown sugar
1½ teaspoons salt
½ teaspoon cayenne pepper
2 cups cider vinegar
2 cups golden raisins

Scrape skin from ginger root and trim off bruised ends. Cut into 1-inch pieces. Cut lemon into quarters and remove seeds. Peel and core apples, cut into quarters.

Coarsely chop ginger, lemon, and apples by hand or in food processor to a uniform size.

Place all ingredients in a heavy non-reactive large Dutch oven or wide pan. Bring to a boil, reduce heat to simmer and cook until mixture thickens, about 30 minutes. Stir frequently to keep mixture from sticking to bottom of pan.

Let cool to room temperature. Store in glass containers in refrigerator.

NOTE: Chutneys and other preserves will thicken more readily in a *wide, low-sided pan*. When a deep saucepan is used the steam falls back into the pan, preventing the mixture from thickening in the allotted cooking time.

WINTER CHILI SAUCE
yield 1 quart

2 (1 pound, 13-ounce) cans tomatoes
½ cup chopped onion
⅓ cup cider vinegar
¾ cup packed brown sugar
½ teaspoon *each:* salt, ground allspice, cloves, cinnamon and ginger
⅛ teaspoon cayenne pepper

In a large non-reactive saucepan with heavy bottom, combine all ingredients. Bring to a boil. Reduce heat to simmer and cook until sauce is thick, about 2 hours. Taste to adjust seasoning.

Cool to room temperature. Store in glass container in refrigerator.

SWEET TOMATO CHUTNEY

yield about 3 cups

From India comes this sweet and pungent recipe.

1 *whole* garlic bulb
2-inch piece fresh ginger root (1 inch thick)
1½ cups red wine vinegar (divided)
1 (1-pound, 12-ounce) can whole tomatoes or 2 pounds fresh tomatoes, peeled
1½ cups granulated sugar
1½ teaspoons salt
⅛ to ½ teaspoon cayenne pepper
2 tablespoons golden raisins
2 tablespoons blanched slivered almonds

Separate garlic bulb into cloves, peel and coarsely chop. Peel ginger root. In food blender place chopped garlic, ginger and ½ cup of the vinegar. Blend at high speed until smooth.

NOTE: The fumes of the chopped ginger can be irritating to the eyes. Be careful when removing lid of blender.

Place undrained canned tomatoes in a non-reactive, 4-quart saucepan. Add remaining vinegar, sugar, salt and cayenne pepper. Bring to a boil. Add puree mixture from blender. Lower heat and simmer gently, uncovered, for about 1½ hours or until chutney thickens. Consistency should be like thick honey.

Add raisins and almonds. Simmer and stir for another 5 minutes. Allow to cool. Store in glass jars in refrigerator.

APRiCOT GLAZE

yield 1½ cups

Use with baked ham, roast pork or poultry.

1 (17-ounce) can apricot halves, drained
½ cup light corn syrup
1 teaspoon Dijon mustard
½ teaspoon ground ginger
¼ teaspoon ground cloves
¼ teaspoon ground allspice

Place all ingredients in blender or food processor and puree. Store glaze in covered container in refrigerator.

To use as a glaze, brush on meats or poultry during last 30 minutes of baking or grilling. Or serve as a warm sauce over meats and poultry.

SWEET RED PEPPER SAUCE

yield about 1 cup

4 tablespoons butter
4 red bell peppers, seeded and chopped
¼ cup chopped onion
1 small clove garlic, minced
¼ teaspoon crushed oregano
¼ teaspoon ground cumin
1 teaspoon sugar
3-4 drops hot red pepper sauce
salt and pepper, to taste

Melt butter in large frying pan over medium low heat. Add peppers, onion and garlic. Cook slowly until vegetables are soft, about 20 minutes. Stir occasionally.

Spoon mixture into food blender. Add oregano, cumin, sugar and hot pepper sauce. Puree until smooth.

Transfer to small saucepan and keep warm over low heat. Add salt and pepper to taste.

Serve over hot, cooked pasta, grilled pork, poultry or fish.

FRUIT AND WINE SAUCE

yield about 1 cup

We offer two versions which complement a variety of foods. The Sherry-Orange combination goes well with salmon steaks.

1 cup orange juice
1 tablespoon cornstarch
¼ cup packed brown sugar
2 teaspoons Dijon mustard
¼ teaspoon ground allspice
2 tablespoons sherry wine

Variation: Substitute cranberry juice and Tawny Port wine for the orange juice and sherry. This version goes well with poultry and ham.

In a small saucepan dissolve cornstarch in juice. Add brown sugar, mustard and allspice. Over medium heat cook and stir until clear and thickened. Stir in wine and cook for 2 minutes. Remove from heat. May be made ahead and reheated.

NEARLY HOLLANDAISE
yield about 1½ cups

Serve this sauce warm or cold with vegetables, fish or with Eggs Benedict.

½ cup mayonnaise (not salad dressing)
2 tablespoons Dijon mustard
2 tablespoons all-purpose flour
1 cup milk
·1 tablespoon lemon juice

In a small saucepan blend mayonnaise, mustard and flour. Gradually stir in milk and whisk until smooth.

Cook over low heat until thickened, about 8 minutes. Stir constantly. Stir in lemon juice and remove from heat.

NOTE: Favorite herbs may be added during cooking time.

ORANGE SAUCE
yield about 1¾ cups

Serve this sauce warm over broiled or baked fish.

1 recipe Nearly Hollandaise (lemon juice may be omitted)
4 tablespoons melted butter
2 tablespoons grated orange peel (remove peel before juicing orange)
¼ cup fresh orange juice
salt and pepper, to taste

Add butter, orange juice and grated peel to Nearly Hollandaise after mixture has thickened slightly.

LIME TAMARI MARINADE AND SAUCE

yield about ⅓ cup

Adds good flavor to salmon steaks, poultry or pork.

juice of 1 lime
2 tablespoons Tamari sauce
2 tablespoons olive oil
¼ teaspoon garlic powder
¼ teaspoon ground ginger
⅛ teaspoon ground allspice
2 teaspoons sugar

Combine ingredients in a glass measuring cup. Whisk until blended and sugar is dissolved.

Use a shallow *glass* casserole or pie plate for marinating foods.

SAUCE FROM MARINADES

Most marinades can be turned into easy sauces to enhance the food after grilling. If not used immediately, store marinades in glass jar and refrigerate.

1 tablespoon butter or margarine
1 tablespoon flour
2 tablespoons wine (Marsala, Madeira or sherry)
leftover marinade, about ⅓ cup
water or broth to make 1 cup liquid

Melt butter in small saucepan until bubbly. Whisk in flour. Cook and stir for 2 minutes. Stir in wine, leftover marinade and water or broth. Simmer and stir until slightly thickened, about 5 minutes.

Serve hot over grilled food.

ENGLISH PUB MUSTARD

yield about 1 cup

This nippy mustard is similar to the pub mustards served with Plowman's Lunches in England. It also complements sausages and cold roast beef.

1 cup dry mustard
½ cup packed brown sugar
1 teaspoon salt
½ teaspoon ground coriander
5 ounces flat beer or ale (do not use a "light" beer or ale)

Place ingredients in food blender and whirl until creamy and smooth. Scrape sides of blender with spatula several times. Place in glass jar (with non-reactive lid) and let stand uncovered for an hour before capping. Store in refrigerator.

RASPBERRY HONEY MUSTARD

yield about ¾ cup

Fruit-flavored mustards to make from prepared ingredients. Use for sandwich spreads, in sauces for meats and poultry, and salad dressings.

½ cup Dijon-style mustard
4 tablespoons red raspberry jam or preserves
1 teaspoon honey

In a small bowl combine ingredients. Stir until well blended. Place in a glass jar with a non-reactive lid. Store in refrigerator.

VARIATIONS: Substitute other fruit jams or preserves such as apricot, cherry, or plum.

FRESH RED SALSA

yield about 3 cups

2 cups diced ripe tomatoes
6 green onions, finely sliced
1 large green bell pepper, seeded and diced
2 tablespoons minced fresh cilantro leaves or fresh parsley
1 teaspoon minced fresh marjoram
1 tablespoon minced fresh basil
2 teaspoons lime or lemon juice
¼ teaspoon hot pepper sauce
1 tablespoon olive oil
salt and pepper, to taste

Combine ingredients. Served chilled or at room temperature.

SALSA VERDE

yield about 3 cups

1 tablespoon olive oil
1 medium onion, chopped
1 pound small green tomatoes, cored and chopped
½ cup chicken broth
2 tablespoons chopped fresh cilantro leaves
2 tablespoons chopped green chilies, canned or fresh
1 teaspoon minced fresh oregano
¼ teaspoon ground cumin
salt and pepper, to taste

Heat oil in saucepan. Add onions and chopped tomatoes. Cook until soft, about 5 minutes. Stir in remaining ingredients. Simmer until tomatoes can be mashed with fork, about 30 minutes. Taste for seasoning.

Refrigerate overnight for flavors to mellow.

236

CAPONATINA
yield about 1½ quarts

This tangy Italian relish goes well with grilled meats or served with crusty Italian bread and an antipasto selection of cold cuts and cheeses.

1 cup diced celery
⅓ cup olive oil
2 pounds eggplant, peeled and diced (about 6 cups)
2 cups chopped fresh tomatoes, peeled and drained
1 cup green olives, chopped
1 cup Greek or Nicoise olives, pitted and chopped*
1 large onion, finely chopped
2 cloves garlic, minced
1 tablespoon chopped fresh parsley
1 teaspoon crushed oregano
⅓ cup red wine vinegar
1 teaspoon crushed hot red pepper flakes (or more to taste)
salt and pepper, to taste

*The pits will be easier to remove if the olive is pressed until the skin cracks. Use a ceramic mortar and pestle or press with back of a spoon in a small dish.

In a large saucepan heat olive oil. Add chopped celery and saute for 5 minutes. Add remaining ingredients, cover pan, and simmer on low heat for 20 minutes, or until vegetables are soft.

Remove cover and simmer until consistency of thick relish. Let cool to room temperature. Store in refrigerator in glass containers for 24 hours for flavors to blend.

Caponatina may be frozen or spooned into pint-size canning jars and processed in a hot water bath for 15 minutes.

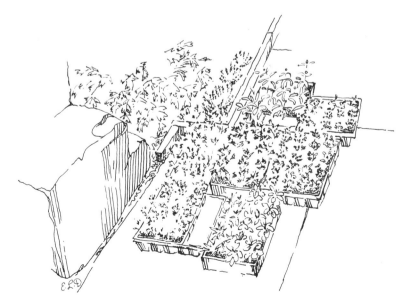

INTRODUCTION TO VINEGARS

Flavored vinegars are a cook's secret treasures for adding special flavors to many dishes.

1. Fresh fruit and herbal vinegars may be interchanged with regular vinegars in salad dressings.
2. Add a spoonful of fruit vinegar to stewed fruits or a splash of herbal vinegar to cooked vegetables in place of lemon juice.
3. Deglaze sauté pans with a flavored vinegar. Stir in a bit of butter for an easy sauce.
4. A touch of herbal vinegar improves the flavor of many soups and stews.

GENERAL INSTRUCTIONS FOR MAKING VINEGARS

1. Use quality 5% acidity, white, cider or wine vinegars.
2. If recipe requires heating vinegar, use a non-reactive saucepan.
3. Steep vinegars in clean jars, with non-corroding caps.
4. Sprigs and leaves of fresh herbs, as well as fresh fruits, should be carefully washed and patted dry before steeping in vinegar.
5. For herbal vinegars, fill clean glass jars about ¾ full with herbs. Add vinegar to cover. Infuse for 3 to 4 weeks in cool, dark cupboard. Shake occasionally.
6. When flavor has developed, strain through coffee filters until clear. Pour into clean glass bottles and cap. Decorative bottles (with corks or non-corroding caps) filled with flavored vinegars make thoughtful gifts.

MIXED HERB VINEGAR   yield 1½ quarts

¼ cup thyme, cut sprigs into small pieces
¼ cup basil leaves
¼ cup tarragon leaves
¼ cup oregano, cut sprigs into small pieces
1 quart cider vinegar (5% acidity)

Wash herbs; pat dry. Place in 2-quart glass container. Press herbs to crush slightly. Stir in vinegar. Cap and place in dark cupboard for 4 weeks. Strain and rebottle.

LEMON VINEGAR

yield 1½ quarts

2 large lemons
1 quart white vinegar (5% acidity)
6 sprigs lemon verbena (6 to 8 inches long)
10 sprigs lemon thyme (4 to 5 inches long)
2 to 3 drops pure lemon extract

Wash and dry lemons. Remove peel with sharp knife or zester. Cut lemon into small chunks, remove seeds.

Wash lemon verbena and lemon thyme. Pat dry.

Place lemon and herbs in 2-quart glass jar. Stir in vinegar. Cap and place in dark cupboard for 4 weeks. Strain, add lemon extract, and rebottle.

LOVAGE VINEGAR

yield 1 quart

2 cups lovage leaves
1 quart vinegar (5% acidity)

Wash lovage leaves; pat dry. Tear and slightly crush the leaves. Place in 2-quart glass container. Stir in vinegar. Cap and place in dark cupboard for 4 weeks. Strain and rebottle.

CRANBERRY VINEGAR

yield 1½ quarts

¼ cup sugar
1½ cups fresh cranberries, washed and picked over
2 cups cider vinegar (5% acidity)
1 cup dry red wine
Stick cinnamon (about 6 inches long)

In non-reactive saucepan combine sugar, cranberries and vinegar. Bring to a boil and cook until cranberry skins split open. Remove from heat. Add wine and cinnamon stick.

Let cool to room temperature; then place in glass container. Cap and let stand in a dark cupboard for 4 weeks. Strain and rebottle.

BLUEBERRY VINEGAR

yield 1½ quarts

1 cup blueberries, washed and dried
1 quart white vinegar (5% acidity)
¼ cup granulated sugar
10 whole cloves

Place the blueberries and 2 cups of vinegar in food blender or processor. Coarsely chop the berries, but *do not puree.*

In a 2-quart glass container place remaining vinegar, cloves, and chopped blueberry mixture. Stir to combine. Cap and store in a dark cupboard for 4 weeks. Strain and rebottle.

MINTED HERBS AND SPICE VINEGAR

yield 1 quart

1 cup fresh mint leaves
4 sprigs rosemary (5 inches long)
4 sprigs lemon thyme (4 inches long)
2 sprigs tarragon (5 inches long)
6 tender sage leaves
1 dried bay leaf
1 teaspoon mustard seed
½ teaspoon *each:* ground cinnamon, cloves, allspice, and black pepper
1 quart vinegar (5% acidity)

Wash fresh herbs, pat dry. Place in 2-quart glass container. Press herbs slightly to crush.

In non-reactive pan place bay leaf, mustard seed and spices. Add vinegar and heat *just until* bubbles begin to form around edge of pan.

Remove from heat. Let stand 5 minutes, then pour over herbs. Stir to combine. Cap and place in dark cupboard for 4 weeks. Gently shake the bottle occasionally to keep spices distributed.

Strain and rebottle.

Vegetables

The terrace with its stone benches is a peaceful area, surrounded by a patchwork of low-growing green and gray-green plants.

ASPARAGUS WITH
LEMON PARMESAN CRUMBS

yield 2 - 4 servings

¾ pound asparagus

Wash spears and snap off the tough bottom part. Cook in a small amount of boiling water until just tender-crisp, about 3 minutes. Drain immediately and place in serving dish. Sprinkle generously with this tasty crumb topping.

LEMON PARMESAN CRUMBS

3 tablespoons butter, melted
½ cup dry white bread crumbs
2 tablespoons grated Parmesan cheese
¾ teaspoon crushed marjoram
½ teaspoon grated lemon rind

Place ingredients in a small bowl. Stir with fork until well blended.

SEASONED ARTICHOKE HEARTS

yield 2 - 4 servings

This mild-flavored vegetable is an asset to party menus. This easy recipe may be doubled.

1 (9-ounce) package frozen artichoke hearts, cook according to package directions

SEASONED CRUMBS

1 tablespoon olive oil
½ cup dry white bread crumbs
¼ cup grated Parmesan cheese
2 teaspoons crushed oregano
1 teaspoon crushed rosemary

Place ingredients in a small bowl. Stir with fork to blend.

Drain cooked artichoke hearts. Arrange in buttered 1-quart casserole. Sprinkle with salt and pepper. Top with seasoned crumbs. Place under preheated broiler unit until crumbs are lightly browned. Serve immediately.

NOTE: Dry seasoned bread crumbs (without oil or butter) may be stored in the refrigerator for handy use. Add oil or butter just before using.

MARINATED BRUSSELS SPROUTS

1 package (10-ounce) frozen Brussels sprouts (or 1 pint fresh)
2 tablespoons chopped green onion

Garnish: 1 tablespoons snipped fresh dillweed (optional).

MARINADE:

⅓ cup white wine vinegar
1 clove garlic, minced
2 teaspoons crushed dillweed (or 1 tablespoon fresh)
½ teaspoon crushed rosemary
½ teaspoon crushed summer savory
½ teaspoon celery seed
⅔ cup olive oil

Combine ingredients in a small bowl and whisk until blended. Set aside.

Cook frozen Brussels sprouts according to package directions. If using fresh sprouts, parboil until just tender. Drain and place in 1-quart glass dish. Add chopped green onion and marinade; toss to coat. Cover and chill overnight.,

Before serving, drain marinade from sprouts. Garnish with fresh dillweed if desired.

BRUSSELS SPROUTS WITH CARAWAY

The little touch of beef broth adds a good flavor.

1 pint fresh Brussels sprouts
½ cup beef bouillon
1 small onion, sliced
1½ teaspoons caraway seeds, slightly crushed
1 tablespoon butter
½ teaspoon lemon juice

Rinse Brussels sprouts, cut off stems and remove tough outer leaves.

In a small saucepan bring bouillon to a rapid boil. Add sprouts, onion, and caraway seeds. Reduce heat to a simmer and cook until sprouts are just tender. Test with fork after 3 minutes of cooking.

Remove from heat and drain. Stir in butter and lemon juice. Serve immediately.

DANISH RED CABBAGE

1½ pounds red cabbage (about 2 quarts shredded)
2 tablespoons butter or margarine
1 tablespoon vinegar
¼ cup water
3 tablespoons vinegar (additional)
1 tablespoon brown sugar
¼ cup applesauce
2 teaspoons caraway seed (optional)
2 tablespoons red currant jelly

Remove tough outer leaves from cabbage head. Cut in quarters (remove core), and shred coarsely.

In a large stainless-steel frying pan or 4-quart Dutch oven melt butter over medium high heat. Add cabbage and 1 tablespoon vinegar. Cook and stir until cabbage is tender-crisp.

In a small bowl combine water, additional vinegar, brown sugar, applesauce, and carraway seed. Stir mixture into the cabbage and simmer for 5 minutes. Stir in currant jelly and cook for 5 more minutes. Serve warm.

SWEET AND SOUR CARROTS

A wide-mouth canning jar is convenient to use for storing these tasty carrots.

1 cup cider vinegar
½ cup sugar
¼ to ½ teaspoon hot pepper sauce
1 3-inch cinnamon stick
1 bay leaf
3 whole cloves
3 whole allspice
1¼ pounds carrots, cut julienne style (8 to 9 medium-size carrots)
1 cup orange juice

Place vinegar, sugar and seasonings in 3-quart saucepan. Bring to a boil and cook for 5 minutes. Stir to dissolve sugar. Add carrot sticks and orange juice. Reduce heat to simmer and cook until carrots are just tender crisp. Test after 5 minutes of cooking. Do not overcook.

Ladle carrots and liquid into clean *hot* glass jars.

Cover and chill for 24 hours before serving. Cinnamon stick may be removed. Will keep for 2 to 3 weeks in refrigerator.

MARJORY CARROTS WITH PINEAPPLE
yield 3 - 4 servings

1 pound carrots, washed and scraped
½ cup water
1 tablespoon butter
1 (8-ounce) can pineapple tidbits
½ teaspoon sugar
¾ teaspoon crushed sweet marjoram
1 teaspoon lemon juice
salt and pepper, to taste

Cut carrots into ½-inch slices. Bring water to a boil in a small saucepan, add carrots, reduce heat to simmer, and cook carrots until tender, about 8 minutes. Add remaining ingredients.

Simmer, uncovered, until liquid is reduced by half, but do not overcook the carrots. Serve hot.

CAULIFLOWER IN SHRIMP SAUCE
yield 4 - 6 servings

Adapted from a recipe in our 1960 cookbook, MORE SAVORY SEASONINGS.

1 head cauliflower, about 1½ pounds
1 (10¾-ounce) can cream of shrimp soup
½ cup milk
2 tablespoons butter
1 (8-ounce) package cream cheese, softened
½ teaspoon crushed summer savory
½ pound cooked, peeled shrimp (optional)
1 cup croutons, plain or seasoned

Wash cauliflower and break into small florets. Parboil until tender-crisp and drain immediately.

Preheat oven to 350°F. Butter a 2-quart casserole.

In a small sauce pan combine soup, milk, butter, cream cheese, and savory. Stir over low heat until smoothly blended.

Place cauliflower in prepared casserole. If using shrimp, arrange over top of cauliflower; add shrimp sauce and bake in oven until bubbly, about 20 minutes. Top with croutons during last 5 minutes of baking time.

VARIATION: Substitute 1 bunch of broccoli florets for cauliflower, or use a combination of both vegetables. Parboil broccoli for 2 minutes, drain immediately; then proceed with recipe instructions.

SIMMERED CELERY WITH DILL

yield 4 servings

4 cups sliced celery
½ cup chicken broth
2 tablespoons butter
1 tablespoon fresh, minced dillweed (or ½ teaspoon dried)
Black pepper, to taste

Place celery and broth in a large frying pan. Cover and bring broth to a simmer over medium-low heat. Cook until celery is just tender-crisp, about 5 minutes. Stir in butter, dill, and pepper. Simmer, uncovered, for 5 more minutes. Serve hot.

CORN IN GREEN PEPPERS

yield 4 servings

2 large green peppers
2 cups fresh (or frozen), whole kernel corn
6 ounces grated sharp cheddar cheese (about 1½ cups)
1 (2-ounce) jar pimientos, drained and chopped
1 medium onion, chopped
1 teaspoon celery seed
1 teaspoon crushed marjoram
salt and pepper, to taste

Garnish: additional grated cheddar or buttered crumbs for topping

Preheat oven to 350°F. Lightly butter a shallow baking dish.

Wash and cut green peppers in half lengthwise. Remove stems, white center ribs, and seeds.

In a small bowl combine remaining ingredients. Stuff peppers with corn mixture and place in prepared baking dish. Add topping of grated cheese or buttered crumbs. Bake for about 1 hour, or until peppers and corn are just tender. Serve warm.

CRISPY EGGPLANT SLICES

yield 4 - 6 servings

1½ pound eggplant
1 egg, slightly beaten (or use a ½ cup buttermilk)
1 envelope extra-crispy fried chicken coating mix
½ teaspoon Italian herb blend (see Index)

Preheat oven to 350°F. Lightly oil cookie sheet.

Slice off each end of eggplant and discard. Cut ½-inch thick slices and dip in beaten egg (or buttermilk).

Place coating mix in shallow pan and coat both sides of eggplant slices. Place in single layer on prepared cookie sheet. Sprinkle each slice with Italian herb blend. Bake until coating is crispy and golden brown, about 20 minutes. Serve hot.

VARIATION: After eggplant slices are almost golden brown, remove from oven and cover each portion with a slice of mozzarella cheese; sprinkle with grated Parmesan cheese and return to oven to bake 5 more minutes or until cheese is slightly melted. Serve with favorite spaghetti sauce.

DOUBLE FRESH GREEN BEANS
AND TOMATOES

yield 2 - 4 servings

¾ pound tender green beans, washed and snapped
2 or 3 ripe tomatoes, peeled and chopped
¼ cup chopped onion
2 large sweet basil leaves, minced
4 or 5 mint leaves, minced
salt and pepper, to taste

In a small amount of water cook green beans until tender-crisp. Remove from heat and set aside.

Place chopped tomatoes in a large frying pan and simmer until cooked down. Add onions, herbs, and green beans. Simmer uncovered about 5 more minutes to reduce part of the tomato juices. Serve hot in individual dishes.

A bit of leftover cooked rice may be added to absorb the juices.

BELGIAN ENDIVE IN
LEMON CHERVIL BUTTER

yield 4 - 6 servings

This recipe is adapted from our 1969 cookbook, ANOTHER SAVORY SEASONING.

1 pound Belgian endive (or 1 or 2 per serving, depending on size)
3 tablespoons butter
2 tablespoons lemon juice
2 tablespoons finely minced *fresh* chervil*
salt and pepper, to taste

Garnish: additional chopped fresh chervil.

Remove any damaged leaves from endive. Rinse quickly and pat dry. Avoid soaking in water which will induce bitterness. With small sharp knife, hollow out a small core (the cone) in the center of each stem base, which is where the bitterness is most concentrated.

Place a steamer basket, spread flat, in a large frying pan with lid. Add about ¾-inch of water and bring to a boil. Place endive in basket, cover, and steam until just tender, about 5 minutes.

Remove steamer basket with endive from pan. Drain off water. Melt butter in same pan. Add lemon juice, salt and pepper. Lay the endive in the butter and gently simmer for a few minutes. Stir in fresh chervil and let it wilt for *30 seconds.* Serve immediately, garnished with additional fresh chopped chervil.

*Herb note: If fresh chervil is not available, substitute ½ teaspoon crushed fennel seed. Add to pan while butter is melting. Parsley may be used for garnish.

SAUTÉED MUSHROOMS AND HERBS

yield 6 - 8 servings

2 tablespoons butter
1 pound fresh white mushrooms, cleaned and sliced
¼ cup chopped fresh parsley
2 tablespoons snipped fresh chive
1 tablespoon minced fresh tarragon
1 teaspoon minced lemon thyme
1 teaspoon lemon juice
⅛ teaspoon ground ginger
salt and pepper, to taste

In a large frying pan melt butter over medium-high heat. Add mushrooms and saute until browned on both sides.

Reduce heat and stir in parsley, chive, tarragon, lemon thyme, lemon juice, and ground ginger. Cook for 2 minutes. Taste to adjust seasoning; add salt and pepper to taste.

BAKED MUSHROOMS PARMESAN

yield 6 - 8 servings

1½ pounds whole fresh mushrooms
2 tablespoons butter
½ cup chopped onion
1 clove garlic, minced
¾ cup fresh bread crumbs
¼ cup chopped fresh parsley
1 teaspoon crushed marjoram
½ teaspoon crushed summer savory
¼ teaspoon crushed thyme
¼ teaspoon pepper
4 tablespoons grated Parmesan cheese
¼ to ½ cup beef broth (or chicken broth)
3 tablespoons grated Parmesan cheese (additional)

Preheat oven to 350°F. Lightly butter a 1½ quart casserole.

Wipe mushrooms clean with damp cloth and trim stems. Place mushrooms in prepared casserole. Set aside.

Melt butter in a frying pan. Cook onions and garlic until soft. Stir in bread crumbs, herbs, pepper and cheese. Remove from heat and combine with mushrooms. Pour beef broth over top. Cover casserole and bake for 20 minutes.

Halfway through baking time check for dryness. The mushrooms should be evenly moist. It may be necessary to add a little more broth. Just before serving sprinkle with additional Parmesan cheese.

SAUTÉED SNOW PEAS

yield 4 servings

½ pound snow peas
1 tablespoon olive oil
1 small garlic clove, finely minced
1 teaspoon Tamari sauce
salt and pepper, to taste

Cut off tip ends of pods and pull off side strings.

Heat oil in large frying pan. Add minced garlic and cook until soft.

Add snow peas and use stir-fry method to cook until just tender-crisp, 2 to 4 minutes depending on size of pods. Stir in Tamari sauce and serve immediately.

VARIATION: Add ¼ cup diced red sweet pepper to cook along with garlic. Add ½ cup drained and sliced water chestnuts to cook along with snow peas.

MAQUECHOU

The interesting name given to this stewed corn and tomato dish comes from the area around the bayous of Louisiana.

6 bacon slices
4 cups fresh sweet corn kernels (about 6 ears)
3 tablespoons butter
1 onion, chopped
1 red sweet pepper, seeded and diced
2 large ripe tomatoes, peeled and chopped
2 teaspoons sugar
1 tablespoon minced fresh basil (or 1 teaspoon dried)
½ teaspoon crushed summer savory
2 to 3 drops hot pepper sauce, or to taste
½ cup water
½ cup light cream
salt and pepper, to taste

Garnish: ¼ cup chopped chive (or finely-sliced green onion), and crisp crumbled bacon.

In a large frying pan cook bacon until crisp. Drain on paper towels. Crumble and set aside.

Pour fat from pan, reserving 1 tablespoon for flavor, if desired. Add butter to pan and melt over medium heat. Stir in corn, onion, and red pepper. Cook for 5 minutes.

Stir in chopped tomato, sugar, herbs, hot sauce, and water. Simmer until tomatoes are cooked down and corn is tender, about 20 minutes.

Stir in cream and half of the crumbled bacon. Simmer for 10 more minutes. Serve hot, garnished with chive and reserved crumbled bacon.

BAKED SWEET ONIONS

yield 1 onion per serving

This method works best with large Bermuda or Spanish onions. It is even better with Vidalias and other super-sweet onions when available.

1 large onion, per serving
1 teaspoon melted butter per onion
½ teaspoon beef bouillon granules per onion
½ teaspoon crushed summer savory

Preheat oven to 350°F. Use 10-inch squares of foil or a deep, covered casserole.

Peel onions. Scoop out a ½-inch oval in top of each onion. Cut a thin slice off root end so onion remains level while baking.

Drizzle melted butter in center of each onion. Add ½ teaspoon beef bouillon granules and a pinch of summer savory. With a nutpick or sharp knife make 1 or 2 holes in center of onion to allow butter and seasoning to seep into onion while baking.

Wrap each onion in the square of foil; bring corners up high (to allow steaming room) and twist tightly. Put the foil-wrapped onions in a shallow pan and bake in 350°F. oven for 1 hour.

NOTE: The broth which develops in the foil packets is very tasty poured over a split baked potato.

VARIATION: Give a sweet-sour taste to the onions by adding ½ teaspoon of sugar plus ½ teaspoon of red wine or balsamic vinegar to each onion along with the listed ingredients.

HERB POTATO "FRIES"

yield 4 - 6 servings

4 firm white potatoes
¼ cup vegetable oil (approximately)
Italian herb blend (see Index)

Garnish: (Optional) grated Parmesan cheese and paprika.

Preheat oven to 400°F. Line cookie sheet with foil.

Wash and pare potatoes. Cut into ½-inch wedges or French-fry style. Spread potatoes in a single layer on prepared cookie sheet and lightly brush oil on each piece. Sprinkle with herb blend.

Bake for 20 minutes, or until tender and crispy. Turn over once half way through baking time.

If desired, sprinkle with grated Parmesan cheese and paprika after removing from oven.

VARIATION: Pared sweet potatoes or yams may also be baked in this manner. Try a Cajun-style spice blend on sweet potatoes for a flavor contrast.

ORANGE YAM CASSEROLE

yield 6 - 8 servings

6 large yams, scrubbed
4 tablespoons butter, softened
½ teaspoon ground cinnamon
¼ teaspoon ground ginger
½ teaspoon vanilla extract
1 (6-ounce) can frozen orange juice concentrate
salt and pepper, to taste
½ cup pecan halves

Preheat oven to 350°F. Butter a 1½-quart casserole.

Cook yams until tender (boil or microwave); cool and peel.

In a large mixing bowl combine yams with remaining ingredients (except pecans), and mash until smooth and fluffy.

Transfer to prepared casserole; arrange pecans on top of yam mixture, pressing in slightly. Bake for 15 to 20 minutes or until heated through. May also be reheated in microwave oven.

MOUSSAKA STIR-FRY

yield 4 servings

1 small eggplant, cut in cubes
2 cloves garlic, minced
1 rib celery, sliced
1 small zucchini, diced
1 medium onion, chopped
1 green pepper, seeded and diced
1 large ripe tomato, peeled and chopped
1 tablespoon butter or margarine
1 tablespoon olive oil
½ teaspoon crushed oregano
2 or 3 large fresh basil leaves, minced (or ½ teaspoon dry)

Garnish: ½ cup grated Parmesan cheese

Prepare vegetables and set aside.

In large frying pan melt butter with olive oil over medium-high heat. Add eggplant and garlic. Stir-fry for about 5 minutes. Add celery, zucchini, onion, and peppers and continue to stir-fry until vegetables are tender-crisp.

Add chopped tomato and herbs. Reduce heat and stir until tomato cooks down, about 5 minutes. Serve warm with plenty of grated cheese.

VARIATION: Omit eggplant and basil. Use 1½ cups fresh corn kernels. Along with oregano, add a dash of cayenne pepper or Cajun seasoning. Garnish with shredded Monterey Jack cheese instead of Parmesan.

ONLY SUMMER TOMATOES

yield 2 - 4 servings

2 or 3 red-ripe tomatoes
¼ cup freshly-grated Parmesan cheese
salt and pepper, to taste
1 tablespoon *each:* chopped fresh basil and chives
¼ cup white wine vinegar
¼ cup olive oil
1 teaspoon sugar, or to taste

Peel tomatoes and cut into slices. Place in a single layer in a shallow glass dish. Sprinkle with grated cheese, salt, pepper, and herbs. Let stand for 30 minutes at room temperature.

In a small bowl place vinegar, oil, and sugar and whisk until blended. Drizzle over tomatoes just before serving.

NOTE: This easy combination is also a summer party favorite when our tomatoes are plentiful. Include slices of yellow tomatoes for an extra pretty arrangement on a clear glass dish. Tuck in sprigs of fresh herbs.

PEA TIMBALES WITH CREAMED
CARROT SAUCE

yield 4 - 5 servings

2 packages (10-ounce) frozen green peas, thawed
2 eggs, slightly beaten
1 tablespoon minced onion
2 tablespoons milk
1 tablespoon melted butter
½ teaspoon salt
¼ teaspoon white ground pepper
¼ teaspoon crushed thyme
⅛ teaspoon grated nutmeg

SAUCE:

2 cups medium white sauce, (see Index)
½ cup cooked carrots, finely diced
⅛ teaspoon ground ginger

Preheat oven to 350°F. Butter 4 or 5 timbales or custard cups.

Place peas in a saucepan over low heat to warm.

In food blender puree peas with remaining ingredients (except sauce) until very smooth. There should be about 1¼ cups puree. Taste to adjust seasoning.

Distribute mixture among prepared timbales and place in pan filled with 1 inch of water. Bake until firm, about 30 minutes.

Prepare white sauce. When smooth and slightly thickened, add cooked carrots and ground ginger. Keep warm over low heat.

To serve, unmold timbales onto serving plates and ladle sauce over each one.

NOTE: This dish may be assembled ahead of time to bake just before serving. Pea Timbales make an attractive addition to a dinner plate.

FRESH TOMATO PIE

yield 6 servings

A special treat for lunch or supper when tomatoes are garden-fresh.

1 9-inch unbaked pie shell
1 cup dry bread crumbs
3 medium-size, ripe tomatoes, peeled, sliced ½-inch thick
3 fresh basil leaves, minced (1 teaspoon dried)
¼ cup snipped chive
salt and pepper, to taste
2 cups grated sharp cheddar cheese
⅓ cup mayonnaise (not salad dressing)

Preheat oven to 425°F.

Spread bread crumbs in unbaked pie shell. Bake for 5 minutes. Remove from oven and set aside. Reduce oven heat to 400°F.

If tomatoes are extra juicy, drain slightly; then arrange slices on top of bread crumbs. Sprinkle with basil, chive, salt and pepper.

In a small bowl combine cheese and mayonnaise. Spread over tomato slices and to edge of pie shell. Bake until cheese topping is golden brown, 25 to 30 minutes. Let stand 15 minutes before cutting.

DILLED POTATO AND TURNIP GRATINS

yield 4 servings

4 tablespoons butter or margarine
3 small turnips, peeled and diced
2 large potatoes, peeled and diced
2 tablespoons minced fresh dill (or 1 teaspoon dried)
¼ teaspoon grated nutmeg
salt and pepper, to taste
½ cup light cream
½ cup chicken broth
½ cup dried, white bread crumbs
½ cup grated Gruyere or Swiss cheese

Preheat oven to 425°F. Butter 4 individual gratins, 1¼ cup size; or use a shallow 2-quart casserole.

In a large frying pan over medium-high heat melt butter. When hot add diced turnips and potatoes and cook until tender. Stir in dill, nutmeg, salt, and pepper. Distribute mixture in prepared baking dishes.

In a small bowl combine cream and chicken broth. Pour ¼ cup over each gratin; sprinkle with bread crumbs and top with cheese. Bake for 20 minutes. Serve hot.

FRESH FRIED RIPE TOMATOES

yield 4 servings

4 firm-ripe tomatoes (cut in ¾-inch slices)
½ cup all-purpose flour
5 tablespoons bacon fat

Put flour in shallow dish. Generously coat both sides of tomato slices. Place on waxed paper or large plate. Let stand for 5 minutes.

In a large 12-inch frying pan heat bacon fat to sizzling. Carefully place floured tomato slices in hot fat. Fry about 1 minute per side or until lightly browned and crusty. Remove to platter and keep warm while frying remaining slices and making the sauce.

SAUCE:

1 whole tomato (additional) peeled and chopped
1 cup milk
1 tablespoon flour
1 tablespoon minced fresh basil (or 1 teaspoon dried)
1 cup shredded sharp cheddar cheese

Using the same frying pan over medium-high heat add chopped tomato and begin stirring to create a sauce consistency. Sprinkle the flour over the sauce and stir until smooth. Gradually stir in milk. When sauce is smooth add basil and continue stirring until sauce begins to bubble. Remove from heat and add 4 tablespoons of the cheese; stir until melted.

To serve, place warm tomato slices on plates, spoon sauce over each serving, and sprinkle generously with shredded cheese. Serve immediately.

ZUCCHINI, CORN AND HERBS

yield 2 - 4 servings

2 small zucchini, 4 to 5-inches long
1 tablespoon olive oil
1 small sweet onion, thinly sliced
1 cup fresh corn kernels
1 tablespoon purple basil vinegar (or red wine vinegar)
1 teaspoon sugar
1 tablespoon chopped fresh mint leaves
1 tablespoon chopped fresh basil leaves
1 teaspoon minced summer savory leaves

Cut zucchini julienne-style in 2-inch strips

Heat oil in large frying pan over medium-high heat. Add vegetables and stir-fry until just tender. Stir in vinegar, sugar, and herbs. Reduce heat to simmer and cook for 2 minutes.

SPICY WINTER SQUASH AND APPLE CASSEROLE

yield 4 - 6 servings

The hard, protective skins of winter squashes repel most kitchen knives. Steam, boil, bake, or microwave these vegetables until a fork can pierce the skin. One pound of winter squash will yield about 1 cup of cooked, mashed pulp.

3 pounds winter squash
2 tablespoons melted butter or margarine
1 tablespoon brown sugar
2 tablespoons Madeira wine (may use orange juice or apple cider)
¼ teaspoon *each:* ground cinnamon, nutmeg, ginger, and cloves
2 tart apples, peeled, cored, and chopped
½ cup chopped pecans (divided)

Cook the squash until tender using any of the methods noted above. Cut in half, remove and discard seeds, and any stringy fiber portion.

Preheat oven to 350°F. Butter a 1-quart casserole.

Scoop out tender pulp into a mixing bowl (or food processor.) Add melted butter, sugar, wine, and spices. Mash until texture is smooth. Stir in chopped apple and ¼ cup of the pecans.

Transfer to prepared casserole. Sprinkle with remaining chopped pecans. Bake for 20 minutes. (Or follow instructions for microwaving.)

EASY ZUCCHINI CIRCLES

yield 1 - 2 servings

1 small zucchini
olive oil
½ teaspoon crushed dillweed (or 1 tablespoon fresh)
2 tablespoons finely grated Parmesan cheese

Preheat oven broiler unit. Lightly oil a 9-inch pie plate or broiler-proof pan.

Cut zucchini in ¼-inch slices; arrange in single layer on baking pan and lightly brush with olive oil.

Broil 4 inches from heat until just tender, about 2-3 minutes. Sprinkle with dill and grated Parmesan cheese; return to oven and broil until cheese is golden and bubbly.

Herb Scents

An old stone Shaker lawn roller, turned on end, helps support the armillary sphere, a curious timepiece of ancient origin. The rings are intended to tell the time by representing the great circles of the heavens.

This section contains herb and spice blends, flavored butters and other mixes which may be created from ingredients found in supermarkets or specialty stores. The last part of this section contains information about the most popular herbs grown in the garden.

The herb blends are made from dried herbs in whole leaf form. The leaves are coarsely crushed then measured.

A small electric coffee mill (or spice grinder) is useful for pulverizing herb leaves and whole spices to the desired texture.

Herbs and spices retain flavor longer if kept in glass jars with tight lids. Label and date each container; then store away from heat, light, and moisture. Good flavor is also preserved by storing herbs and spices in the refrigerator or freezer.

As a general rule, use ¼ teaspoon of an herb or spice blend for every 4 servings.

FINES HERBES BLEND

¼ **cup parsley flakes**
¼ **cup chervil**
¼ **cup freeze-dried chive**
1 **tablespoon tarragon**

Use in omelets and other egg dishes, butter sauces for fish, poultry, and vegetables.

PARSLEY DILL BLEND

3 **tablespoons parsley flakes**
3 **tablespoons dillweed**
½ **teaspoon garlic powder**
½ **teaspoon onion powder**
¼ **teaspoon salt**
¼ **teaspoon ground white pepper**

Use in herb butter, sauces, salad dressings, cottage cheese, and dips.

BOUQUET GARNI

Herb bouquets are used to impart subtle flavor to soups and stews. Bouquet garni is added at the beginning of cooking time then removed when desired flavor has developed.

1 tablespoon parsley flakes
1 teaspoon summer savory
½ teaspoon marjoram
½ teaspoon thyme
1 bay leaf
2 whole cloves
4 peppercorns

Cut a 4-inch square of soft muslin, place ingredients in the middle, gather up the corners and tie securely with string. A triple-layer of cheese cloth may also be used. Several bouquet garnis may be prepared at one time and stored in an airtight container for handy use.

HERBES DE PROVENCE

2 tablespoons thyme
2 teaspoons basil
2 teaspoons summer savory
2 teaspoons rosemary
1 teaspoon marjoram
1 teaspoon dried lavender buds

Use in salad dressings, marinades, butter sauces for poultry, and fish.

ITALIAN HERB BLEND

3 tablespoons oregano (or marjoram)
3 tablespoons summer savory
3 tablespoons basil
1 tablespoon thyme
1 tablespoon sage
2 teaspoons crushed fennel seed

Use in tomato sauce, meatballs, eggplant dishes, salad dressings, and dishes with chicken or veal.

GREEK SEASONING

4 tablespoons oregano (or marjoram)
2 tablespoons parsley flakes
1 teaspoon minced dried lemon peel
1 teaspoon onion powder
¼ teaspoon black pepper
¼ teaspoon garlic powder

Use in salad dressings, butter sauces, eggplant and rice dishes, lamb or chicken stews.

POULTRY SEASONING

4 tablespoons parsley flakes
4 tablespoons sage
2 tablespoons lovage (or celery leaves)
2 teaspoons summer savory
1 teaspoon marjoram
1 teaspoon rosemary
½ teaspoon thyme

Use to season flour for coating poultry; for bread stuffing use 2-3 tablespoons for each 2 quarts of bread cubes. Mix a tablespoon with ½ cup oil for basting roast chicken.

ONION SOUP BLEND

¼ cup dried minced onion
2 tablespoons instant beef bouillon granules
1 teaspoon crushed parsley flakes
1 teaspoon onion powder
1 teaspoon cornstarch
¼ teaspoon celery salt
¼ teaspoon black pepper

Use in sour cream dips, beef stews, vegetable soups, and rice dishes.

BLENDS WITH SPICES

SPICY PEPPER

¼ cup black peppercorns
¼ cup white peppercorns
2 tablespoons whole allspice

Combine ingredients and place a portion in a peppermill to grind over meats, poultry, salads, and vegetables.

A WORD OF CAUTION: Do not be tempted to include red or pink "peppercorns" in a spice blend or for any culinary use. These red berries are related to poison ivy, hence, may produce severe internal reactions. In some individuals the reaction may be latent and, thus, not associated with food. The berries are picked from the Brazilian pepper tree *(Schinus terebinthifolius)* and do not have a history of culinary use.

CAJUN STYLE SEASONING

1 teaspoon celery salt
1 teaspoon onion powder
1 teaspoon paprika
½ teaspoon garlic powder
½ teaspoon finely crushed oregano
¼ teaspoon *each:* white pepper, cayenne pepper, ground cumin, curry powder, ground mace and ground cardamom
¼ teaspoon granulated sugar

Use to season fish and seafoods, chicken, pork, and rice dishes. Add to homemade barbecue sauce.

CHILI SEASONING

4 tablespoons paprika
2 tablespoons ground coriander
2 tablespoons minced dried onion
2 teaspoons ground cumin
2 teaspoons salt (optional)
1 teaspoon crushed oregano
½ teaspoon garlic powder
½ teaspoon black pepper
¼ teaspoon cayenne pepper

Use 1 or 2 teaspoons for each quart of chili, adjust to taste; add to bean or rice dishes, and corn bread.

TACO STYLE SEASONING

1 tablespoon chili powder
1 tablespoon minced dried onion
2 teaspoons cornstarch
1 teaspoon paprika
1 teaspoon crushed oregano
½ teaspoon *each:* garlic powder and ground cumin
½ teaspoon salt (optional)
¼ teaspoon ground allspice
¼ teaspoon cayenne pepper, or to baste

Use to season sauces for Southwestern-style dishes; add to bean or rice dishes, and sour cream dips.

CHINESE FIVE SPICE POWDER

8 star anise
6 whole cloves
stick cinnamon, a ½-inch piece
1 tablespoon Szechuan peppercorns
1 tablespoon fennel seed

In an electric coffee grinder or spice mill grind each ingredient separately to a fine powder and then combine.

Use in Oriental stir-fry dishes, egg rolls, and with roast pork or duck.

QUATRE EPICES

6 tablespoons ground white pepper
2 teaspoons ground cloves
2 teaspoons ground ginger
1 teaspoon ground nutmeg

Use in patés, beef casseroles, meat loaves, soups, and barbecue sauces. This 4-spice blend is often used in Pfeffernusse cookies.

PUMPKIN PIE SPICE

2 tablespoons ground cinnamon
1 tablespoon ground nutmeg
1 tablespoon ground allspice
1 teaspoon ground ginger
1 teaspoon ground cloves

Use in desserts, muffins, breads, cookies, and sweet sauces.

APPLE PIE SPICE

3 tablespoons ground cinnamon
1½ tablespoons ground nutmeg
1 teaspoon ground cardamom (optional)

Use in desserts, rice puddings, applesauce, spice cakes, and breads.

PICKLING SPICE BLEND

2 tablespoons mustard seed
1 tablespoon whole allspice
2 teaspoons black peppercorns
2 teaspoons whole cloves
1 teaspoon ground ginger
1 teaspoon hot red pepper flakes (optional)
1 bay leaf, cut in pieces
cinnamon stick, 2-inch length, cracked in small pieces

Use in recipes calling for a pickling spice. Stir ingredients before measuring.

SPICY HERB SALT

⅓ cup salt
1 teaspoon garlic powder
1 teaspoon paprika
1 teaspoon chili powder
1 teaspoon rubbed sage
1 teaspoon ground white pepper
1 teaspoon crushed thyme
½ teaspoon crushed rosemary
½ teaspoon *each:* dry mustard, ground ginger, onion powder
½ teaspoon crushed celery seed
½ teaspoon crushed dillseed

Use in recipes calling for seasoned salt.

GARAM MASALA STYLE SEASONING

1 teaspoon ground cumin
1 teaspoon ground cardamom
1 teaspoon black pepper
¾ teaspoon ground cloves
½ teaspoon ground cinnamon
½ teaspoon ground mace
¼ teaspoon ground ginger
¼ teaspoon ground nutmeg
⅛ teaspoon cayenne pepper, or to taste
1 teaspoon finely crushed dried rose petals (optional)

India's "mixed spices" may be substituted for curry powder. Use in rice or bean dishes, with chicken, lamb or shrimp, vegetarian dishes, and chutneys.

MADRAS CURRY POWDER

This recipe is adapted from a blend made by the Western Reserve Herb Society in 1970. Commercial preparations of Madras Curry may contain as many as 17 ingredients which produces an aromatic, complex flavor. British colonials began using the world "curry" to describe the various blends of herbs and spices used by Indian cooks.

4 tablespoons ground turmeric
3 tablespoons ground coriander
2 tablespoons ground cumin
1 tablespoon ground cardamom
1½ teaspoon ground allspice
1 teaspoon ground cinnamon
1 teaspoon ground ginger
1 teaspoon black pepper
½ teaspoon ground cloves
½ teaspoon ground mace
½ teaspoon ground fennel seed
½ teaspoon ground fenugreek*
¼ teaspoon cayenne pepper

Use in veal, lamb, poultry, seafood, lentil, bean or rice dishes, also with vegetables, stewed fruits, and in white sauces.

*FENUGREEK, (Trigonella foenum-graecum), has a bitter taste reminiscent of burnt sugar. It is an ingredient in commercial chutneys and curry powders. Fenugreek extract is the principal flavoring in imitation maple syrup. Ancient Egyptians cultivated fenugreek to use as food and medicine. A member of the bean family, fenugreek is rich in protein, vitamins, and minerals.

FLAVORED BUTTERS

Measurements are given for dried herbs unless otherwise indicated. Margarine may be substituted for butter. Flavored butters keep well in the refrigerator for up to 2 weeks in covered containers and may be frozen up to 3 months.

METHOD FOR MIXING:

1. In a small mixing bowl combine softened butter and lemon juice. Cream until fluffy.
2. Add finely crushed or powdered herbs along with other seasonings. Mix well.
3. Store in covered container in refrigerator. Chill overnight or for 24 hours for flavors to blend.

SAVORY HERB BUTTER

½ pound butter
1 tablespoon lemon juice
½ teaspoon marjoram
½ teaspoon summer savory
½ teaspoon lemon thyme
¼ teaspoon garlic powder (optional)

Use with cooked vegetables, grilled meats, and in sauces.

ONION DILL BUTTER

½ pound butter
1 tablespoon lemon juice
2½ teaspoons minced dried onion
2 teaspoons dillweed
1 teaspoon parsley flakes
¼ teaspoon garlic powder

Use as spread for breads, add to cooked vegetables, grilled meats, and fish.

HORSERADISH BUTTER

½ pound butter
1 tablespoon lemon juice
3 tablespoons prepared horseradish, drained

Use as a topping for grilled steaks or hamburgers and in sauces for seafood. Spread on bread for roast beef sandwiches.

ROSEMARY BUTTER

½ pound butter
1 teaspoon lemon juice
1 tablespoon finely crushed rosemary
⅛ teaspoon ground white pepper

Use with cooked vegetables or in sauces for poultry and seafood.

TACO BUTTER

½ pound butter
1 tablespoon lemon (or lime) juice
1 teaspoon chili powder
½ teaspoon crushed oregano
½ teaspoon crushed hot red pepper flakes (optional)
¼ teaspoon ground cumin
⅛ teaspoon cayenne pepper (optional)

Use in sauces for Southwestern-style meat and vegetable dishes, with rice or beans; melt to baste grilled chicken.

PIZZA BUTTER

½ pound butter
1 teaspoon lemon juice
2 tablespoons finely-grated Parmesan cheese
1 tablespoon sweet paprika
1 teaspoon crushed oregano
½ teaspoon garlic powder
⅛ teaspoon cayenne pepper (optional)

Use as a spread for toasted English muffins; add to sauces for pastas.

The following butters contain fresh herbs. The mixing method is the same as for butters with dried herbs.

BARBECUE BUTTER

½ pound butter
2 tablespoons barbecue sauce
1 tablespoon minced fresh onion
1 clove garlic, minced

Use to baste grilled meats and poultry; spread on breads or rolls and heat until butter melts.

MAITRE D'HOTEL BUTTER

½ pound butter
1 tablespoon lemon juice
4 tablespoons minced fresh parsley

Use as a sauce for cooked vegetables, meats, poultry, and seafood.

FINES HERBES BUTTER

½ pound butter
1 tablespoon lemon juice
¼ cup chopped fresh chervil
2 tablespoons chopped fresh parsley
2 tablespoons minced fresh chive
1 teaspoon minced fresh tarragon (optional)

Use in sauces for fish, seafood and cooked vegetables, omelets, and egg dishes; brush on grilled meats and poultry.

TARRAGON BUTTER

½ cup butter
1 tablespoon lemon juice
1 tablespoon minced fresh tarragon
⅛ teaspoon white ground pepper

Use in sauces for vegetables, fish, meats, and poultry.

NOTE: Substitute chive, dill, parsley, marjoram or oregano to create butters using one herb.

The sweet butters will complement hot muffins, breads, biscuits and may be used as spreads for tea sandwiches. The mixing method is the same as for herb butters.

HONEY CINNAMON BUTTER

½ pound butter
¼ cup honey
1½ teaspoons ground cinnamon
¼ teaspoon vanilla extract

ORANGE BUTTER

½ pound butter
2 tablespoons confectioners' sugar
grated rind of 1 orange
grated rind of 1 lemon
¼ cup orange juice

STRAWBERRY BUTTER

½ pound butter
½ cup mashed strawberries
2 tablespoons confectioners' sugar
¼ teaspoon vanilla (or almond) extract

FRUIT AND NUT BUTTER

½ pound butter
¼ cup orange marmalade
½ cup finely chopped prunes
¼ cup chopped pecans, toasted

(May substitute chopped dried apricots and apricot jam for the prunes and marmalade.)

HONEY GINGER BUTTER

½ pound butter
¼ cup honey
2 tablespoons finely minced candied ginger
⅛ teaspoon ground cardamom

PARTLY BUTTER

1 cup butter, softened
1 cup polyunsaturated oil, such as canola

Combine the equal parts of butter and oil in food blender or processor. Puree to achieve a smooth, thick liquid. Place in covered containers and refrigerate. When chilled the mixture solidifies to a firm, but easily spreadable consistency. This blend may be used with good results in almost any recipe.

HERB SCENTS BOURSIN

1 (8-ounce) package cream cheese, softened
¼ cup butter or margarine, softened
4 tablespoons minced fresh parsley
1 small clove garlic, minced
1 teaspoon minced dried onion
½ teaspoon *each:* crushed dillweed, oregano, and summer savory
¼ teaspoon crushed rosemary

Combine ingredients in mixing bowl and blend thoroughly. Place in covered container and refrigerate for 24 hours to allow flavors to blend. Use as a spread for crackers or add to sauces for cooked pastas.

APRICOT CHEESE SPREAD

¼ cup toasted pecans or slivered almonds
¾ cup dried apricots (about ¼ pound)
1 (8-ounce) package cream cheese, softened
¼ cup butter, softened
2 tablespoons apricot jam
2 teaspoons finely grated orange rind (optional)

Place nuts and apricots in food processor; pulse on/off until mixture forms a coarse paste. Add remaining ingredients and process until blended, scraping sides of work bowl several times. Store in covered container and keep refrigerated. Before using, bring to room temperature.

Use to spread on muffins, crackers, and to stuff dates or prunes.

GARLIC BREAD SPREAD

¼ cup mayonnaise (not salad dressing)
¼ cup finely-grated Parmesan cheese
1 teaspoon finely-crushed oregano
¼ teaspoon garlic powder
⅛ teaspoon ground white pepper

Combine ingredients until well blended. Spread on slices of Italian bread and place under broiler until bubbly. Keep unused portion in covered container in refrigerator.

SOUR CREAM SUBSTITUTE

2 cups low-fat cottage cheese
½ cup buttermilk (shake container before measuring)
1 teaspoon lemon juice

Place ingredients in electric blender and beat until smooth. Store in covered container in refrigerator.

Use as a base for dips and spreads.

MAKE-AHEAD ROUX (WHITE SAUCE BASE)

This is a time saver for busy cooks. A well-cooked roux (flour and butter mix) is the secret of a smooth, tasty sauce or gravy. Professional chefs save time by preparing the roux in large amounts. The roux is then proportioned and stored in refrigerator or freezer for direct use in sauces and gravies, or whenever a thickening agent is necessary.

Suggested formula for home use:

1 cup butter (or use ½ butter and ½ oil)
1 cup all-purpose flour (16 tablespoons)

Melt butter in saucepan over medium heat. Stir in flour and mix until smooth. Reduce heat; stir and cook for 3 to 5 minutes, or until flour taste disappears. Do not allow roux to brown unless using for brown gravy.

Place mixture in a square pan (8 x 8-inch), spread evenly; then refrigerate until firm. Mark and cut into 8 equal cubes. Wrap each cube in plastic wrap or waxed paper. Place in a covered container and refrigerate or freeze for future use.

Use the following proportions to make a sauce:

Thin sauce   1 cup liquid + ½ cube roux
Medium sauce   1 cup liquid + 1 cube roux
Thick sauce   1 cup liquid + 1½ cubes roux

(If you are making white sauce in the traditional manner, ½ cube roux = 1 tablespoon butter + 1 tablespoon flour for a thin sauce.)

To prepare sauce:

In a small saucepan place roux cube and liquid (milk, broth or water). Over low heat allow cube to melt; stir until smooth and thickened.

(For traditional white sauce, the butter and flour must first be thoroughly cooked together and the liquid is then slowly incorporated.)

Herbs, spices, grated cheese, wine, lemon juice, salt and pepper are among the ingredients added to give desired flavors.

HERBS IN OUR GARDEN

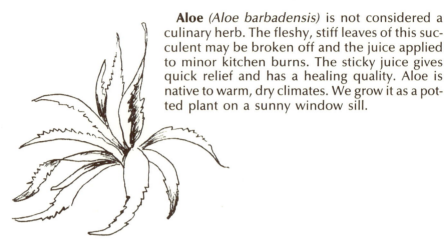

Aloe *(Aloe barbadensis)* is not considered a culinary herb. The fleshy, stiff leaves of this succulent may be broken off and the juice applied to minor kitchen burns. The sticky juice gives quick relief and has a healing quality. Aloe is native to warm, dry climates. We grow it as a potted plant on a sunny window sill.

Anise *(Pimpinella anisum)* is an annual requiring a warm, sunny growing season of at least 120 days to produce the familiar licorice-flavored seeds. Anise is often grown in the culinary garden for its attractive feathery, green foliage and clusters of small white flowers. The leaves also have a licorice flavor and may be used in salads and for garnish. The seeds are used to flavor cookies, cakes, breads, applesauce, and fruit desserts. Anise extract and oil of anise are products manufactured from the seeds.

Anise is not related to the true licorice, *Glycyrrhiza glabra,* a perennial European plant whose roots are used for their sweet licorice flavor.

Star anise *(Illicium verum),* a favorite spice in Oriental cooking, is also licorice flavored. It comes from an evergreen tree native to China.

Sweet basil *(Ocimum basilicum)* is a tender annual. The seeds germinate quickly in soil temperature of 72°. Once established, the plants grow rapidly and produce an abundance of aromatic leaves. The flower heads are pinched out to extend the harvest. There are many varieties of basil. Several are found in the trial and cutting bed, including purple basil, which provides leaves for a flavorful and attractive vinegar.

The peppery, clove-like flavor of basil adds a special taste to soups, green salads, vegetables (especially tomatoes), pasta sauces, chicken and fish. Fresh basil leaves are used to make pesto sauce.

Bay leaves *(Laurus nobilis)* are among the world's oldest sources of flavoring. Bay (also known as sweet bay or laurel) is the only laurel used in cooking. In northern climates bay is a tender perennial. It is grown in deep pots and brought indoors during winter months. Spicy, pungent bay leaves flavor sauces, soups (especially bean soup), bouillon, meats, and fish-poaching water. Remove bay leaves from the food before serving.

In the Western Reserve Herb Garden the bay plants are placed in the culinary garden during the summer.

Borage *(Borago officinalis)* is among the herbs grown in the culinary garden. Cultivation is easy from seed, which will often self-sow. The tender leaves give a cucumber-like flavor to salads. The mature leaves are coarse and hairy; bright blue, five-petaled flowers nod above. Fresh borage flowers make an appealing garnish. The star-like flowers may also be frozen in ice cubes to enhance summer beverages.

Burnet *(Poterium sanguisorba)*, commonly known as salad burnet, is a pleasing addition to perennial borders. Its evergreen leaves form charming rosettes on the ground. The round heads of the thimble-shaped blossoms are tipped with rosy stigmas and bearded with yellow or white filaments. The young, fresh leaves are used for the cucumber taste they give to salads, herb butters, and vinegars. This hardy perennial may be viewed in the culinary garden.

Caraway *(Carum carvi)* is a hardy biennial. The umbels of tiny white flowers resemble Queen-Anne's-lace. The feathery leaves resemble the foiliage of carrots. Both leaves and roots have culinary uses. The seeds have long been used in rye bread, sauerkraut, and other cabbage dishes. The distinct, sweet flavor of caraway enhances tomato soup, baked apples, cheese, and roast pork.

Chervil *(Anthriscus cerefolium)* is one of the few herbs that prefers partial shade. During the growing season, seed may be planted at two-week intervals to maintain a fresh supply. The dainty white flowers should be kept clipped to promote leaf growth. The fresh leaves have a delicate anise flavor to accent omelets, soups, sauces, salads, herb butters, and vinegars. Chervil is added to hot foods at the end of cooking time. Extended cooking destroys its flavor. Chervil also loses flavor when dried. In the culinary garden chervil is located under the *Prunus americanus.*

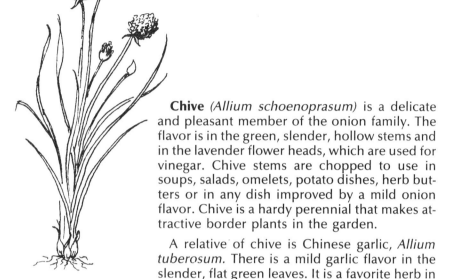

Chive *(Allium schoenoprasum)* is a delicate and pleasant member of the onion family. The flavor is in the green, slender, hollow stems and in the lavender flower heads, which are used for vinegar. Chive stems are chopped to use in soups, salads, omelets, potato dishes, herb butters or in any dish improved by a mild onion flavor. Chive is a hardy perennial that makes attractive border plants in the garden.

A relative of chive is Chinese garlic, *Allium tuberosum.* There is a mild garlic flavor in the slender, flat green leaves. It is a favorite herb in Oriental cooking.

Coriander *(Coriandrum sativum)* is an ancient seasoning and a plant of contrasting flavors. The seeds have a spicy taste resembling orange peel and sage. The parsleylike leaves are known as cilantro or Chinese parsley. Coriander seeds are used in curries, chutneys, pickling spices, sausages, and stews. Ground coriander flavors breads, apple dishes, cookies, and spice cakes. Coriander seed oil is used commercially in perfumes, liqueurs, and as a masking agent for unpleasant tasting medicines.

Spaniards brought coriandro to their Southwestern settlements. The fresh green leaves lend a pungent flavor to salsas, chili, salads, and bean dishes.

Dill *(Anethum graveolens)* is easily grown from seed in its permanent place as the tap root resists transplanting. This sturdy annual should not be planted near fennel as the two will cross-pollinate with mediocre results. Fresh dill leaves are used in salad dressings, potato or cabbage dishes, herb butters, tomato soup, in poaching water for fish and seafood, and in cream sauces for vegetables. Dried dillseed is used in pickling spice blends. Crushed seeds add savor to breads and rolls. Dill is grown in the culinary garden near the historic roses.

Epizote *(Chenopodium ambrosioides)* is a native herb of Mexico. In the United States it is commonly called goosefoot, Mexican tea or wormseed. Epizote leaves have a pungent taste and the odor resembles eucalyptus. In Mexican cookery this assertive flavor is used to season hearty stews and bean dishes. Epizote is now being grown in the Western Reserve Herb Garden and members are experimenting with its use.

Fennel *(Foeniculum vulgare)* is a tall perennial with finely divided green leaves, and yellow flower umbels which develop aromatic seeds. The fresh leaves are added to sauces and marinades for fish, or to impart a delicate anise flavor to fruit salad dressings. The seeds are used in breads, pastries, sauces, and soups. Fennel oil is used in perfumes, soaps, liqueurs, and licorice candy.

Another attractive fennel has bronze or coppery foliage. It is used the same way as the green fennel.

Florence fennel *(Foeniculum vulgare* var. *azoricum)* is cultivated as a vegetable. The enlarged base resembles anise-flavored celery and is used raw or cooked.

Garlic *(Allium sativum)* is a pungent vegetable which we treat as an herb. The bulb is covered with a thin papery skin. Inside are many closely-packed "cloves," which are used for flavoring or in the cultivation of new plants. Garlic is available in many forms: fresh, dehydrated, powdered, minced, blended with salt, and many other seasonings. Fresh garlic is preferable for sauces, marinades, salad dressings, herb butters, and to cook with meats, poultry, seafood, and vegetables. Long, slow cooking softens the pungent flavor. Fresh garlic bulbs keep well if stored in little paper sacks in the refrigerator.

Garlic has long been given medicinal attributes with claims for many old cures. It contains disulphides along with several vitamins.

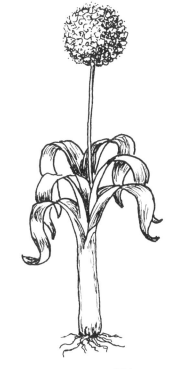

Leek *(Allium ampeloprasum)* is another hardy member of the onion family. The most popular use is in soups such as Welsh leek soup, vichyssoise, and cock-a-leekie. Leek seeds aᴿ slow to germinate. Although the tiny seedlings are quite fragile, once established, leeks will thrive in home gardens. Soil is built up around each plant to blanch the thick stalks.

Lemon balm (*Melissa officinalis*) is an aromatic herb of the mint family. It is a hardy perennial which freely self-sows and spreads. The refreshing lemon fragrance of the leaves is a pleasing addition to hot or cold tea, lemonade, stewed fruits, dressings, mayonnaise, and in sauces for fish. Dried lemon balm is used in tea blends and to lend fragrance to potpourris.

Lovage (*Levisticum officinale*) is a vigorous perennial that grows up to six feet tall. The whole plant is edible: leaves, hollow stems and roots. Each part has the flavor of a pungent celery with a hint of curry. The fresh leaves flavor soups, stews, and salads. Lovage leaves retain good flavor when dried and are used in many herb blends. The umbels of yellow flowers are followed by brown seeds which may be gathered to use for their celerylike flavor. If the seeds are to be used for propagation, they must be planted as soon as ripe for the seed does not remain viable.

Mint *(Mentha species)* has a cool herbal flavor which complements meats, beverages, vegetables, salads, sauces, candies, and desserts. Constant cutting gives a supply of fresh leaves during the growing season. There are many species of garden mints. Spearmint, *M. spicata,* is most commonly grown. For a stronger menthol taste, peppermint, *M.* x *piperita,* is selected. Dried peppermint is often used in tea blends and to scent potpourris. Mints are hardy perennials with free spirits. Their nomadic roots challenge efforts to contain them. Mints hybridize so readily that propogation should be done by root divisions or cuttings.

Sweet marjoram *(Origanum majorana)* has a warm, savory-sweet flavor which complements lamb, veal, and poultry. It is used in herb jellies, herb breads and croutons, and is often substituted for oregano in tomato sauces. When using fresh marjoram leaves in green salads, prevent their wilting by coating the delicate leaves with a teaspoon of salad oil. The soft, grey-green leaves retain good flavor after drying. Marjoram is a tender perennial and treated as an annual in northern gardens. Along the stems the tiny white flowers form terminal clusters which resemble knots; hence, it is often called knotted marjoram.

Greek oregano *(Origanum heracleoticum)* is a perennial which prefers a well-drained, sunny location in the garden. It dies back after the first hard frost and rejuvenates in the spring. Oregano gained popularity in this country after World War II when it soon became known as the pizza herb. Oregano blends with sweet basil for use in tomato sauces, minestrone soup, or lamb stew. Many traditional dishes of the Southwest are also accented with oregano. In this region some native plants have an oreganolike flavor.

Curly parsley *(Petroselinum crispum)* is a popular garnish but it is also valued for its delicate peppery flavor that complements many foods. The flat-leafed Italian parsley, *P.* var. *neapolitanum,* has a more assertive flavor that is preferred for drying to use in herb blends. Both varieties offer nutritional value to foods. Parsley is a biennial that gardeners treat as an annual. The seeds are slow to germinate and are often soaked in tepid water before planting to speed germination. Once established the fresh leaves are available throughout the growing season. Mature stems are snipped off at the base of the plant; new shoots will soon appear. Parsley's fresh greenness makes it an attractive border plant in the culinary garden.

Rose geranium *(Pelargonium graveolens)* is the best known of the scented geraniums. The fresh leaves give a subtle rose flavor to cakes, biscuits, custards, jellies, jams, and fresh fruit compotes. Dried rose geranium leaves are included in potpourris and in herbal tea blends. Rose geranium oil is frequently substituted for rose oil in the cosmetic and perfume industry. Scented geraniums are grown as tender perennials in northern gardens. Cuttings are made in August to provide fragrant house plants during the winter. The four beds of the fragrant garden are filled each summer with many scented species such as nutmeg, lemon, ginger, lime, and mint.

Rosemary *(Rosmarinus officinalis)* is connected with many legends and superstitions. This shrubby evergreen plant has long been treasured for its fragrance and flavor. It complements lamb, poultry, beef, and veal dishes, soups and stews, herb butters, and seasoning blends. The sweet, piny scent of the dried leaves are useful in potpourris and linen closet sachets. Oil of rosemary is used in lotions, soaps, and perfumes. Rosemary is a perennial but not hardy where winters are harsh. So it is potted up in early fall and brought indoors to a sunny window sill where its fresh scent and flavor may be enjoyed.

Saffron *(Crocus sativus)* is our luxury seasoning. Fortunately, only a tiny amount is required
to impart its distinctive, slightly bitter flavor. The
orange-red stigmas are threadlike when dried.
One or two stigmas soaked in a teaspoon of
water will flavor rice dishes, breads, bouilla-
baisse, paellas, and many other soups. The finest
quality of saffron is now imported from Spain.
In the eighteenth century the town of Saffron
Walden in Essex, England, enjoyed a lively
business of growing and exporting saffron. Saffron crocus were grown in Pennsylvania by early Amish settlers. The fragile stigmas, only three
per flower, must be hand-picked during a brief
flowering period which accounts for its scarcity
and high cost. Bargain-priced saffron should be
avoided for it will often contain adulterants.

Garden sage *(Salvia officinalis)* is the best known of over 700 species which grow worldwide. This hardy perennial with the velvety grey-green leaves has an interesting herbal history. Sage has been valued for its medicinal properties since ancient times. Oil of sage is still used today in pharmaceuticals. The natural preservatives in sage are useful in the meat-packing industry.

If properly stored, dried sage leaves have a long shelf-life. The leaves are finely crushed before adding to soups, stews, breads and biscuits, or to season poultry, and meat dressings. There is a dwarf sage which may be grown as a house plant for a supply of fresh leaves in winter. The cultivar, Holt's Mammoth, and the dwarf sage are grown in the culinary garden.

Summer savory *(Satureja hortensis)* is a slender annual which requires regular clipping to extend the harvest; otherwise, it will quickly form flowers and go to seed. Winter savory, *S. montana,* is a perennial evergreen which makes an attractive border plant. Both species have a spicy, peppery flavor which is more pronounced in winter savory. Summer savory is easily propagated from seed and will self-sow. Winter savory is increased by cuttings. Savory complements many soups, especially bean, lentil, and split pea soups. It is used in herb breads and butters; it is added to vegetables, meats, and poultry. Dried savory is used in many herb blends.

Smallage *(Apium graveolens)* is also known as wild celery. A tall-growing biennial, smallage produces an abundance of tiny seeds. As soon as the seed heads turn brown they are snipped from the stems and placed in paper sacks. After cleaning and sorting, the seeds are used as celery seed in dressings and salads. The more seed gathered the better for it readily self-sows. When the tiny shoots appear in the spring they resemble a multitude of parsley plants. These fresh new leaves may be added to soups and stews to give a good celery flavor.

French sorrel *(Rumex scutatus)* is a perennial herb. Its bright green leaves have a mildly acidic, lemony taste. The sharp tangy flavor adds zest to cream soups, sauces for fish, and many vegetables. The tender new leaves are included in green salads. The plant's sour-tasting flavor is due to both its vitamin C and its oxalic acid constituents. As a culinary herb, sorrel should be used with discretion.

Tarragon *(Artemisia dracunculus* var. *sativa)* is a corruption of the French "estragon," or little dragon. In early days it was thought to be a cure for dragon wounds. Today the leaves are used fresh or dried to flavor bearnaise sauce, herb butters, poultry, fish, and meats. Tarragon vinegar is made in early summer from the fresh leaves. French tarragon does not set viable seed. It has become a clone which must be propagated by root division or cuttings. Seed packages labeled tarragon contain seeds of Russian tarragon which is quite flavorless.

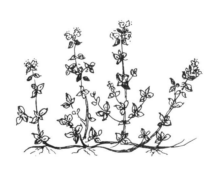

Thyme (*Thymus* species*)* has a long history of usefulness. Oil of thyme (thymol) has antiseptic properties used by pharmaceutical companies. Thyme's crisp herbal flavor suits many foods including fish, poultry, vegetables, sauces, soups, and chowders. Of the many species, French, English and lemon thymes are preferable for culinary use. These three resemble tiny shrubs which can be clipped to form neat borders. Thyme blossoms, which attract honey bees, are cut and dried for use in potpourris.

Watercress *(Nasturtium officinale),* an aquatic perennial, is always used fresh. The leaf stems are gathered before flower buds form. Commercial crops are grown in a controlled aquatic environment; thus, watercress is available in our markets year around. If sprigs of watercress are placed in a glass of water, roots will form which may then be planted in a suitable place. Watercress is used in salads, sandwiches, and mixed in mayonnaise where its mild peppery flavor is enjoyed.

Sweet woodruff *(Galium odoratum)* is a perennial woodland plant. It readily adapts to home
landscaping as a ground cover where partial
shade exists. It creates a leafy mat of whorled
green leaves. In the spring dainty, white flowers
appear. Sweet woodruff was once combined
with rosemary and thyme as strewing herbs to
freshen medieval homes. Fresh sprigs of
woodruff are used to flavor Rhine wine for the
traditional May wine bowl. It is also used in herb
teas, fruit drinks, and for garnish. Dried woodruff
has a sweet hay scent with a hint of lemon, which
makes it a useful ingredient in potpourris.

GARDEN NOTES

GARDEN NOTES

GARDEN NOTES

INDEX

COOKING WITH HERB SCENTS

Please send _____ copies of COOKING WITH HERB SCENTS @ $16.95 each (plus $2.00 shipping and handling per book).

Enclosed is a check for $_____, payable to Western Reserve Herb Society.

Name_____ Street_____

City _____ State _____ Zip _____

Send to: Western Reserve Herb Society
11030 East Boulevard
Cleveland, Ohio 44106

Proceeds from the sale of this cookbook will benefit the Herb Garden and scholarship funds of the Western Reserve Herb Society.

COOKING WITH HERB SCENTS

Please send _____ copies of COOKING WITH HERB SCENTS @ $16.95 each (plus $2.00 shipping and handling per book).

Enclosed is a check for $_____, payable to Western Reserve Herb Society.

Name_____ Street_____

City _____ State _____ Zip _____

Send to: Western Reserve Herb Society
11030 East Boulevard
Cleveland, Ohio 44106

Proceeds from the sale of this cookbook will benefit the Herb Garden and scholarship funds of the Western Reserve Herb Society.

COOKING WITH HERB SCENTS

Please send _____ copies of COOKING WITH HERB SCENTS @ $16.95 each (plus $2.00 shipping and handling per book).

Enclosed is a check for $_____, payable to Western Reserve Herb Society.

Name_____ Street_____

City _____ State _____ Zip _____

Send to: Western Reserve Herb Society
11030 East Boulevard
Cleveland, Ohio 44106

Proceeds from the sale of this cookbook will benefit the Herb Garden and scholarship funds of the Western Reserve Herb Society.